America
without the
Death Penalty

America without the Death Penalty

States Leading the Way

John F. Galliher

Larry W. Koch

David Patrick Keys

Teresa J. Guess

Northeastern University Press
Boston

Northeastern University Press
Copyright 2002 by John F. Galliher

Library of Congress Cataloging-in-Publication Data has been requested.

Designed by Janis Owens

Composed in Janson and Rotis Semi Sans by Graphic Composition in
Athens, Georgia. Printed and bound by The Maple Press Company in York,
Pennsylvania. The paper is Sebago, an acid-free sheet.

MANUFACTURED IN THE UNITED STATES OF AMERICA
06 05 04 03   5 4 3 2

To Hugo Adam Bedau

Contents

Acknowledgments

The authors are grateful for financial support from Amnesty International; the Episcopal Diocese of Missouri; the University of Missouri–Columbia, Peace Studies Program; and the University of Michigan–Flint for financial support for this research. Samuel Jordan compiled the materials for the discussion of Washington, D.C., in Chapter 11, Kate McGonigal wrote part of Chapter 9 on Iowa, and Krista Myer wrote some of Chapter 5 on Minnesota. We also acknowledge the advice and encouragement of Hugo Adam Bedau, Samuel Jordan, Michael Radelet, Patricia Morrow, Susanne Carter, Herbert Haines, Eugene Wanger, John Bessler, James McCartney, Greg Casey, Edwin Vaughan, Steven Weinberg, and the participants in the 1998 Missouri University Peace Studies Death Penalty Abolition Conference.

America
without the
Death Penalty

Introduction

In recent years, two of America's most prominent politicians learned the peril of actively opposing the death penalty. During the 1988 presidential election, Massachusetts Governor Michael Dukakis stumbled in the polls after stating that he would oppose executing first-degree murderers, even, in the hypothetical case, where an offender was convicted of killing Dukakis's wife.[1] New York Governor Mario Cuomo's 1994 reelection loss to a political newcomer was at least partially due to his annual vetoes of death penalty bills passed by the New York State legislature.[2] The current strength of the nationwide death penalty movement is more clearly demonstrated by the dramatic increase in the number of federal provisions that allow capital punishment, the perception of overwhelming support for capital punishment voiced by respondents to public opinion polls, and an upsurge in the number of executions that took place during the 1990s.

The Anti–Drug Abuse Act of 1988[3] allows the execution of drug kingpins, persons who operate "continuing criminal enterprises" that kill, or recruit others to kill, in furtherance of their illegal enterprise. The federal Violent Crime Control and Law Enforcement Act of 1994[4] expanded the punishment of death to cover sixty offenses, three of which do not involve murder: espionage, treason, and large-scale drug trafficking. United States Supreme Court rulings since *Furman v. Georgia*[5] have forbidden executions for non-homicidal crimes.[6] Nevertheless, with President George W. Bush's nomination in 2001 of former Missouri Senator John Ashcroft, a longtime death penalty advocate, to the post of U.S. attorney general, it is probable that federal prosecutors will energetically seek to enforce all capital punishment statutes. It remains to be seen how today's federal courts will react.

According to Gallup Poll data, support for capital punishment among U.S. residents increased continuously through the 1970s and 1980s. By 1994, fully 80 percent of Americans surveyed favored executing convicted murderers. Since that time, however, popular support for capital punishment has eroded. By year-end 2000, 66 percent of Americans voiced support for capital punishment for convicted murderers. Moreover, that proportion declined to 50 percent when the alternative of "life without parole" was offered to respondents.[7] Nevertheless, active support for capital punishment remains more attractive to the electorate than does active opposition to capital punishment. Dukakis and Cuomo were, in part, defeated because they openly opposed the death penalty, while George W. Bush, who, as governor of Texas, presided over more than 150 executions between 1995 and 2000, was elected president of the United States. George W. Bush's well-known death penalty history never became an issue during the 2000 presidential campaign.

Finally, throughout the 1980s, 117 persons were legally killed in the United States. During the 1990s, 763 death row inmates were executed, an increase of nearly 650 percent. Moreover, recent federal reforms suggest that the volume of executions could increase during the first decade of the twenty-first century. The Anti-Terrorism and Effective Death Penalty Act of 1996,[8] which affects both state and federal prisoners, speeds up and reduces the cost of executions.[9] The act dictates tighter filing deadlines, limits the opportunity for evidentiary hearings, and allows only a single habeas corpus filing in federal court for death row inmates.[10]

The continued use of capital punishment distinguishes the United States from all other Western, industrialized nations. That disparity, however, has a relatively brief history. As recently as 1820, English Common Law provided for hanging or drawing and quartering for a vast array of offenses. Between 1765 and 1820, the number of crimes punishable by death in England had risen to about 220.[11] In an 1819 petition presented to Parliament, the Corporation of London noted that "upwards of 200 crimes, very different in their degrees of enormity, are equally subject to the punishment of death, which is enacted not only for the most atrocious offenses, for burglary, for rape, for murder, and for treason, but for many offenses unattended with any

. . . .

cruelty or violence, for various minor crimes, and even for stealing privately to the amount of five shillings in a shop."[12] Circumstances were similar in the rest of Western Europe. For Europeans living in the seventeenth and eighteenth centuries, executions were "a sight with which most people would be familiar."[13] Executions during these years could be swift or protracted. Methods bringing relatively quick death included the following: "hanging, which was typically the most infamous form of death; garroting, which was often the fate of female offenders; and beheading, which was the usual end of homicides [murderers] and offenders who had some claim to social rank." Prolonged executions included such punishments as "breaking on the wheel, burning, and drowning."[14] The mutilation of dead bodies and the exposure of corpses were also commonly practiced to demonstrate the existence and power of law.[15]

By the beginning of the nineteenth century, the ancillary violence that often accompanied executions had disappeared. With the exception of France, Western Europe had abolished public executions by 1870.[16] The Netherlands, Norway, and Denmark conducted their last execution, outside of war, before the end of the nineteenth century. By the end of the twentieth century, all Western European countries had abolished capital punishment for crimes outside of war.[17] In 1981, under President François Mitterrand, France became the last Western European country to reject the death penalty.[18] In 1983, the twenty-one members of the Council of Europe solidified European aversion toward capital punishment by adding a protocol to the European Convention for Protection of Human Rights and Fundamental Freedoms. That protocol formally condemned the use of capital sentences and executions. The protocol, however, grants states the right to preserve capital punishment for acts committed "in time of war or imminent threat of war."[19]

During the latter part of the twentieth century, it appeared for a time that capital punishment was headed toward a similar end in the United States. During the 1930s, the United States averaged 167 executions each year, nearly 2,000 for the decade. Through the entire decade of the 1940s, 1,289 persons were executed. During the 1950s, the number of executions declined to 715. Between 1960 and year-end 1967, 191 persons were executed by state authorities in the United

States. In 1966, popular support for capital punishment among Americans was down to 42 percent, an all-time low. No executions took place in the United States between year-end 1967 and year-end 1976.[20] The downward trend in both executions and the public support for capital punishment concluded with the 1972 United States Supreme Court ruling in *Furman v. Georgia*[21] that Georgia's death statute was unconstitutional, and by extension this applied to all state and federal death penalty statutes existing at that time.

Many Americans believed that the demise of capital punishment was at hand. Nothing was further from the truth. In *Gregg v. Georgia*,[22] the United States Supreme Court upheld the revised death statute of the state of Georgia. Since then, thirty-eight states have remodeled their death statutes along the lines that the Court upheld in the *Gregg* case, and thirty-two of those states have carried out at least one execution. Yet the forces in opposition continue to grow. Recently, over thirty major religious organizations released strong statements of opposition to the death penalty.[23] In 1999, the United Nations Commission on Human Rights supported a worldwide moratorium on executions in nations that maintain capital punishment. Moreover, the commission requested that other nations refuse extradition to retentionist states unless the latter guarantee that capital punishment would not be carried out.[24] Amnesty International noted that for the year 2000, "88 percent of all known executions took place in China, Iran, Saudi Arabia and the USA."[25] Thus, on the world stage the United States is in the company of what many describe as terrorist states.

As the numbers suggest, the movement back to capital punishment in the United States was not absolute. As of January 2001, twelve U.S. states did not have active death penalty statutes. Here we are interested primarily in the abolitionist histories of nine states: Michigan, Wisconsin, Maine, Minnesota, North Dakota, Hawaii, Alaska, Iowa, and West Virginia. Capital punishment in those states was abolished by legislative action before 1972 when the United States Supreme Court ruled existing death statutes unconstitutional. Legislators in three of those states, Michigan, Wisconsin, and Maine, abolished their death statutes during the nineteenth century. The purpose of this book is to identify and explain the historical circumstances in those states that motivated their legislators to abolish capital punishment and to maintain death penalty abolition in the midst of ongoing demands for harsher criminal sanctions. Bedau has noted that while most U.S. states have the death penalty, Americans have something valuable to learn from "being told the full story of how crime and punishment, social vindictiveness, and fear of violence are managed without recourse to the threat of executions."[26] We hope this book will provide practical information to those interested in furthering death penalty abolition in the United States and throughout the world, as well as shed some light on the origins and maintenance of abolitionist law.

The District of Columbia also has a distinguished history of death penalty abolition. The courageous struggles waged by Washington, D.C., residents against concerted efforts by the United States Congress to reestablish capital punishment in the District is discussed in Chapter 11, Summary and Conclusions. This struggle in the nation's capital reflects many of the dynamics found in the nine abolition states. Massachusetts, Rhode Island, and Vermont are recognized as important death penalty abolition states; however, death penalty abolition in these states was not accomplished through legislative action but by court decisions that found capital punishment to be unconstitutional. Massachusetts is a state with a special legacy of emphasizing human rights and justice. The homogeneity of the populations of Rhode Island and Vermont has been especially conducive to the abolition of the death penalty in those states. A discussion of these three states is found in the Epilogue.

Theory

A rigorously tested, formal theory of law formation does not currently exist. In the area of criminal law, the lack of empirically grounded propositions or explanations of the existence or absence of capital punishment statutes is particularly striking. As a consequence, the research discussed here has placed "emphasis upon discovery" rather than on formal hypothesis testing. According to Sjoberg and Nett, "Discovery has been the basis for the development not only of isolated hypotheses but of theoretical systems. Thus one may uncover a set of findings and order these into some classificatory scheme or retroduce a deductive theory to account for them."[27] We began this study with the understanding that much could be learned about the abolition and the retention of capital punishment in the United States by examining the unique abolitionist histories of Michigan, Wisconsin, Maine, Minnesota, North Dakota, Hawaii, Alaska, Iowa, and West Virginia. Merton supports this assertion. He points out that studying deviant cases (here abolitionist states) "provokes curiosity; it stimulates the investigator to make sense of the datum," which can often lead to new theoretical insights.[28]

Since "discovery research" necessarily lacks the direction that formal theory lends to traditional sociological research, we decided to organize this book around six empirical questions concerning state-sanctioned killing. Following is a list of those questions along with the research findings that lend support to their inclusion in our research.

1. What is the relationship between murder rates, the history of executions, and death penalty abolition? Zimring and Hawkins argue that declines in the "rate of violence" will not necessarily lead to nationwide death penalty abolition.[29] Zimring and Hawkins also argue that a history of frequent executions makes executions more acceptable, and therefore more likely to continue: "[A] history of frequent executions . . . [s]erve[s] as a kind of precedent, reassuring political actors that their own participation is neither inhumane nor immoral . . . [o]n grounds that, historically, executions do not violate local community morality."[30] Thus, in states with little tradition of executions one could expect the easiest success with abolitionist efforts.

2. Is economic crisis related to death penalty abolition? Rusche and Kirchheimer argue that lethal punishment is more likely in situations where the economy is depressed and labor is expendable.[31]

3. What is the relationship between public sentiment and death penalty abolition? Fox et al. found that support for capital punishment decreases dramatically when respondents are provided the alternative of life in prison without the possibility of parole. In fact, a majority express opposition to the death penalty if they are assured that parole is not possible.[32]

4. What role do political, social, and economic elites tend to play in abolition debates? Bohm found that people in the highest income bracket are more likely to support capital punishment than those in the bottom income bracket.[33]

5. What is the relationship between mass media and death penalty abolition? Evidence suggests that mass media strongly influence legislative outcomes. Hagan found in his study of legislative initiatives concerning a wide range of substantive issues, that backing from the press was crucial to the success of an initiative.[34] In their study of legislative processes in California, Berk et al. found that the best predictor of a bill's success or failure was the editorial position of the *Los Angeles Times*.[35]

6. Is population diversity associated with death penalty abolition? Civil rights organizations and the academic community routinely claim that the death penalty discriminates against economic and racial minorities.[36] In addition, Yang and Lister found that the geographical mobility of a state's population was a good predictor of death penalty abolition. Less heterogeneous and less mobile populations are more likely to abolish capital punishment.[37]

By pursuing answers to these questions we gained an appreciation for the unique combination of historical (or structural) foundations and cultural dispositions that have facilitated death penalty abolition in the states studied here.

Research Method

This book utilizes "case study" methodology. Being able to generalize findings across time and between cases is the most obvious problem associated with this form of inquiry. Succinctly stated, it is difficult to demonstrate that findings evolving out of a case study are universal traits of a category of events. While this problem is inherent in the method, a number of social scientists contend that increasing the sample size can minimize the problem. Orum et al. suggest that the theoretical value of a case study can be reinforced by additional case studies.[38] Several case studies centering on the same issue enable a comparative framework. Hamel et al. likewise contend that "the case study is . . . only microscopic for want of 'a sufficient number' of cases. . . . The problem . . . is to determine exactly how many cases are needed."[39] To ensure the theoretical integrity of our findings, the history of the death penalty was studied in every state whose legislature abolished capital punishment and maintained abolition. Nine case studies were carried out. Findings associated with each state are presented separately in Chapters 2 through 10. Chapter 11 integrates those findings.

Data Collection

Berg has observed that "what people do, how they behave and structure their daily lives, and even how humans are affected by certain ideological stances can be observed in *traces* people intentionally or inadvertently leave behind."[40] In the writing of this book, newspaper articles and editorials, government documents, and personal interviews (for recollections of legislative action) were treated as the "traces" people left behind. The amount of data reviewed for each case study varied, but in all cases an effort was made to read death penalty articles and editorials published by local newspapers. An effort was made in each case study to locate, retrieve, and read all relevant government documents. Snowball sampling, in which those who are interviewed nominate additional contacts, was used to determine who and how many persons should be interviewed. In most cases, efforts were made to conduct interviews with those involved on both sides of the abolitionist debate. People interviewed tended to be legislators, civil servants, local journalists, and death penalty activists. In some cases, information concerning the specific data-gathering technique applied in each state is located in the Appendix. We believe that in using these data we have created a historically accurate picture of death penalty abolition in Michigan, Wisconsin, Maine, Minnesota, North Dakota, Hawaii, Alaska, Iowa, and West Virginia.

. . . .

CHAPTER
2

Michigan's Continuing Abolition of the Death Penalty and the Conceptual Components of Symbolic Legislation

Hugo Adam Bedau, the dean of death penalty researchers, has noted that

> Michigan . . . became the first English-speaking jurisdiction in the world to abolish the death penalty. . . . One naturally wonders what has been the experience in those few jurisdictions [such as] Michigan . . . that have long relied on imprisonment rather than death as the penalty for even the gravest crimes. . . . Historians seem to have ignored their experience.[1]

We begin our attempt to rectify this reality by examining the state that first outlawed executions.

The History of Death Penalty Prohibition

What is unique about Michigan's early history is that so few executions took place. There exist records of eight executions in Michigan during the 1700s by the French and British colonial governments.[2] Under the U.S. territorial authority, only three additional executions took place—two Native Americans, Ketaukah and Kewabishkim in 1821, and Stephen Simmons in 1830. These data suggest that opposition to the death penalty was in place well before statehood. Michigan's early settlers had Puritan Yankee backgrounds and hailed from upstate New York and New England. They typically brought with them support of both the anti-gallows and anti-slavery movements.[3] Consequently, the death penalty was abolished, except for treason, in 1847. This sole provision for execution was never used.

Nonetheless, those few executed in Michigan reflect the same racial proportions as the massive number executed in Southern states. "Simmons," noted the *Detroit Free Press*,[4] "is the *only* non-Indian ever executed by Michigan under American rule." The Simmons execution is important because the religious revival atmosphere surrounding the execution created such revulsion toward capital punishment that it remains a part of Michigan's current capital punishment debate.[5] As recently as 1977, a Michigan paper mused: "One thing is certain, all through the coming months of debate, Stephen Simmons will be living again along with each morbid detail of his fatal plunge through the gallows' trap door."[6] A law professor in Michigan referred to this execution and noted in an interview that "the real action against capital punishment took place after a white male who had killed his wife in a drunken condition was executed in Detroit." The execution of Stephen Simmons generated considerably more outrage in Michigan than did the execution of the two Native Americans who preceded him to the gallows. The 1837 execution of convicted murderer Patrick Fitzpatrick, even though he was actually put to death in nearby Canada, is also remembered in Michigan because shortly after Fitzpatrick was executed, another person confessed to the murder. The last person executed in Michigan was Anthony Chebatoris, put to death in 1938 by federal authorities. His execution was described as "distasteful"[7] and was carried out over the objection of the Michigan governor.[8] Despite high levels of violence, population diversity, and public support for capital punishment, abolition in Michigan is maintained.

Violence, Racial Immigration, and the Death Penalty

From 1945 to 1954, Michigan's mean murder rate of 4.4 per 100,000 ranked twenty-sixth among all U.S. states, but rose steadily to ninth by 1983.[9] Among abolitionist states, Michigan's murder rates from the 1960s to the 1980s trail only Alaska's.[10] Approximately 50 percent of all executions between 1945 and 1964 were in the ten states with the highest mean murder rates,[11] while these states totaled only 25 percent of the national population.[12] Clearly, Michigan and Alaska are exceptions to the positive relationship between levels of violence and the death penalty.

Michigan's racial and ethnic characteristics also militated against continued abolition. This can be seen in the immigration patterns in Michigan. Blue-collar employment in a booming auto industry continued to increase until the late 1920s and brought with it large numbers of blacks and poor whites from the South. Michigan ranked fourth in the Union in the growth of its black population between 1900 and 1970, and, by 1970,[13] ranked sixteenth in the Union in the percentage of blacks—the only continuously abolitionist state of the top twenty with the highest percentage of blacks. In 1910, the black community in Detroit numbered approximately five thousand. But between 1919 and 1940, the percentage of blacks in the city increased from 1.2 to 9.2 percent. According to Capeci, "[w]hites had dominated the influx during the 1920s . . . but blacks accounted for over 52 percent of the . . . increase in the following decade."[14] Lee and Humphrey noted that Detroit had only 10,000 black citizens in 1916, but approximately 220,000 by 1943. In just three years, from 1940 to 1943, 440,000 whites moved into the city, many from the South.[15] Lee and Humphrey quoted a Michigan social worker who explained that these Southern whites "are ignorant and hold traditional southern attitudes towards Negroes. Socially, they are classed with the 'foreign' elements in Detroit. They are in great need for compensation—to look down on other groups. The Negroes make a convenient target."[16] According to Widick, "[b]y 1948, almost half a million [white] inhabitants of Detroit were Southerners who brought their prejudices, customs, and language with them. A black man was a 'nigger.'"[17] History suggests that the presence of these Southern whites—among whom support for capital punishment has been traditional—and the growing black population should have generated a death penalty.[18]

The usual relationship between capital punishment and race was not negated by positive race relations. As early as the 1920s, the Ku Klux Klan was an important political power in Michigan. In the 1925 Detroit mayoral election, the KKK's candidate was defeated only by the technical invalidation of seventeen thousand votes.[19] The population shifts mentioned above help explain a heated controversy in 1942 between blacks and whites regarding the possible racial integration of a new federally funded housing project.[20] Moreover, Detroit set the high-water mark for interracial violence during the riots of 1943 and 1967.[21]

Michigan Public Opinion

As might be predicted given increasing crime rates and a volatile immigration mix, there has been growing support for the death penalty in Michigan for quite some time. Reflecting these changes, a 1952 prison riot in Jackson that involved guards having been taken hostage triggered a bill calling for the execution of any prisoner convicted of murdering a guard.[22] A death penalty statute might well have been triggered in 1950 when a Michigan murderer "told police he had gone out in the middle of the night to 'get me a woman.' He shot [a] father of four when [the victim] fought to protect his wife against the attack. 'I knew the most I would get was life in prison,' the killer boasted after his capture."[23] A Detroit newspaper responded by providing coupons to its readers. By mailing the coupons to the speaker of the Michigan House of Representatives, readers could demonstrate support for a referendum on the death penalty. Two days later, 2,500 had been received.[24] This response suggested that many, perhaps a majority of Michigan citizens, supported the death penalty. By 1974, no such speculation was needed. A survey found that 58 percent of Michigan residents favored capital punishment for the crime of murder.[25] As of 1976, 64 percent were in favor, and by 1977, 72 percent agreed.[26] A 1978 survey in the Detroit area also found 72 percent favored executions of convicted murderers.[27] In 1982, a 73 percent majority favored reinstitution of the death penalty in Michigan.[28] By 1985, 77 percent of those surveyed supported capital punishment for the crime of murder.[29] All these figures parallel the growth in national support for capital punishment.

Surveys in Michigan in 1982 and 1985 also showed that approximately two thirds of Protestants and Catholics supported reestablishing capital punishment.[30] Correspondingly, in 1980, about two thirds of whites in Michigan supported repeal of the state's constitutional prohibition of capital punishment. Forty-four percent of Michigan's blacks agreed.[31] Surveys from 1974 to 1977[32] demonstrated that approximately half of Michigan's black population supported the death penalty for the crime of murder. Thus, recent surveys have shown that between two thirds and three quarters of whites and between 45 and 50 percent of blacks support a death penalty law for Michigan. Nonetheless, Michigan, which in 1847 abolished the death penalty except for treason,[33] and which, at its 1962 constitutional convention passed a proposal authored by Eugene "Gil" Wanger that abolished death for all crimes by a lopsided 108 to 3 vote,[34] has yet to pass a death penalty statute. Zimring and Hawkins recognized a similar relationship between public opinion and capital punishment: "The inevitable progress of the abolition movement is all the more remarkable when the role of public opinion is examined. Successful and sustained abolition has never been a result of great popular demand."[35] Thus, we are left with the puzzle that in some U.S. states public opinion is reflected in local death penalty legislation and in others it is not.

Arguments Against Capital Punishment

Michigan's record of opposition to capital punishment is long and easy to verify. In 1844, seven years after Michigan became a state, a house select committee issued a majority report calling for the repeal of the death penalty. The report identified four objections to capital punishment: First, "no man hath a power to destroy life but by commission from God, the author of it."[36] Not only did the report claim the death penalty had no basis in the Bible, but also that it slowed the trial process, could lead to the execution of innocent persons, and finally, that it was a mistake that could not later be reversed.

In 1865, the Senate Judiciary Committee released a report on the death penalty that challenged its effectiveness as a deterrent and concluded that capital punishment was not necessary, considering the condition of the populace at the time:

> The soldiers of our own revolution, although discharged and sent home half paid, and poorly clad, at a time when the country was embarrassed, the treasury exhausted, paper money depreciated, and the cost of living

enormously high, like their great commander, quietly betook themselves to the pursuits of life, and it was remarked of them "that the instances were rare where a veteran had returned to his home to disgrace it."[37]

This historical fact was used to argue against the death penalty at the end of the Civil War.[38]

Michigan's capital punishment debate changed little during the twentieth century. In 1929, arguments against a bill to reinstate capital punishment, which passed both state houses, asserted that there was no proof executions deterred crime, that capital punishment represented a step backward for civilization, that the punishment was usually reserved for the poor, and that only a small proportion of murderers actually were executed.[39] One house member reasoned: "I am not in favor of any law which involves the taking of human life . . . [which is] un-Christian . . . uncalled for and ungodly[,] . . . a step backward in the onward and forward march of civilization."[40] During the capital punishment debate of the 1950s, a University of Michigan professor argued that the death penalty reduced the certainty of punishment and therefore did not have the effect of lowering serious crime rates.[41] Approximately twenty years later, a Michigan State University criminology professor was quoted as saying that executions do not stop homicides.[42] In testimony before legislative hearings in 1973, a founder of the Michigan Committee against Capital Punishment argued that the death penalty increased rather than decreased violence.[43] This long-term Republican opponent of the death penalty also stated in 1976 that "[f]orty years of studies in America have shown that society is no safer with a death penalty."[44]

The director of the Michigan Department of Corrections argued against the death penalty in 1980, citing the lack of evidence as a deterrent and the increased difficulty in getting convictions.[45] The head of the Michigan ACLU agreed,[46] as did the lieutenant governor.[47] The United Auto Workers' Union has been a powerful force in Michigan politics, and its opposition to the death penalty has been unwavering since the 1930s. Its opposition is reflected in a 1977 position statement: "There is no evidence to suggest that Michigan's prohibition against capital punishment—in effect since the state was admitted to the Union 140 years ago—has contributed to the recent increase in

. . . .

the rate of homicide."[48] A newspaper column criticized a Florida execution and said that if the death penalty were truly a deterrent, then it should be carried out in a shopping mall or on television where people would "be able to judge the effectiveness of what is supposed to be the ultimate deterrent against murder."[49]

Delegates to the 1962 constitutional convention endorsed familiar reasons for rejecting the death penalty, among them that: executions are not a deterrent because serious offenses are a consequence of mental disturbance; the death penalty results in judicial delays and is biased against the poor and ignorant; the state sets a bad example for its citizens when it takes a human life; conviction of the innocent is possible; and the death penalty is irrevocable.[50] This reasoning was obviously persuasive, for no arguments were presented against the provision for a constitutional ban on executions. Racism and racial discrimination inherent in the application of capital punishment are also frequently mentioned by Michigan's death penalty opponents. Thus, for over one hundred years, Michigan opponents of the death penalty have routinely buttressed their moral position with empirical fact. As convincing as these arguments may seem, they have been used frequently in non-abolition states as well. The strategic use of scientific data does not explain abolition in Michigan.

Michigan's Leaders and Capital Punishment

Michigan is unique in that most of the state's political, economic, and religious leaders generally oppose the death penalty. Former governors, most judges, and even Henry Ford opposed it.[51] The Michigan Federation of Labor called a 1931 death penalty bill a "law of the rich and relic of the past."[52] In vetoing a 1929 death penalty, the state's governor said: "We put rich men in prison but when it comes to electrocuting them it simply would not be done. . . . Juries would be very slow to render a verdict that meant a mandatory sentence of electrocution."[53] In 1931, there was a different Michigan governor, but one with the same opinions as his predecessor. The new governor called that year's death penalty bill "warfare on the individual."[54]

In 1946, the director of the Michigan Department of Corrections

. . . .

opposed reinstating the death penalty,[55] as did the corrections director in a 1985 interview. The latter cited racism as inherent in support for the death penalty. The Michigan Bar has been opposed to the death penalty, stating in 1985 that the state "should not become a brutalizing agent."[56] As early as 1945, a newspaper observed that a majority of the house "has had enough 'legalized murder' legislation."[57] Later another newspaper warned:

> When emotion and not logic rules the administration of justice, we are well on the way to losing sight of justice and of our own claim to civilization. The people of Michigan recognised that dark pit nearly a century and a half ago, and wisely stepped back from the brink. We urge them to exercise the same wisdom.[58]

In 1984, a state representative who favored the death penalty limited his legislative proposal to those convicted of killing police officers. He argued: "I know what the feeling of the people is, and the leaders of the state, and its taboos on the death penalty. I'm trying to establish a beachhead. Maybe this might have a chance."[59]

In an interview for this research a former director of the Michigan Department of Corrections noted that prior to the Civil War, Michigan was an underground railway terminal for escaping slaves on their way to Canada.[60] Paralleling the nineteenth-century opposition to slavery that was linked to forces arrayed against capital punishment, racism associated with the South has for over a century been opposed by Michigan's cultural practices. The editor of the *Detroit Free Press* noted that both black and white Southerners have a history of violence and "if you create a system where life is cheap, the people will see life as cheap." In an interview a cochair of the Michigan Coalition Against the Death Penalty noted there was little immigration to Michigan from the South until World War II and the "[S]outh favors the killing ethos. Earlier Michigan was spared these people who were for capital punishment." As a case in point, the *Detroit Free Press* noted that the first-term senate sponsor of a 1985 Michigan death penalty bill was a graduate of the fundamentalist Bob Jones University in South Carolina. The senator was quoted as saying, "Government has a responsibility to use its authority to punish the wrongdoer. When it [the Bible] talks about the power of the sword, it shows it certainly has the authority and obligation to use the death penalty, as a government."[61]

An amendment proposed for a 1929 death penalty bill called for $25,000 to be paid by the state to the heirs of any person executed and later found to be innocent, emphasizing the degree of concern about such accidents.[62] This proposal was tried again in 1931 with the stipulated payment reduced to $5,000.[63] In 1953, a derisive amendment to a death penalty bill called for execution by stoning on the steps of the capitol building.[64] More recently, a senator who opposed the death penalty was quoted as sarcastically suggesting that if the citizens of the state reinstated the death penalty, they should be required to provide the executioners, who would be selected by lot from the general population.[65]

In 1871, a petition on behalf of eighty-seven ministers, deacons, and elders of the True Dutch Reform church, asking for a return of the death penalty, was delivered to the Michigan house.[66] During the twentieth century, however, the Michigan Council of Churches, along with other major organized religious groups, has generally opposed capital punishment. Roman Catholic clergy through the 1940s and 1950s at times publicly supported executions.[67] Later, however, this changed. Perhaps spurred on by the 1973 *Roe v. Wade* United States Supreme Court decision increasing access to legal abortions, the Catholic church rethought its position on capital punishment. A 1985 policy noted the following:

> For more than a decade, the Michigan Catholic Conference, the voice of the Catholic Church in Michigan in matters of public policy, has opposed efforts to institute the death penalty in our state. This position has always been one linked to the Church's respect for human life in its diversity of circumstances—born and unborn.[68]

The Roman Catholic church's pro-life position was described by a member of the clergy as a "seamless garment." Accordingly, the taking of a human life is never acceptable.[69]

Thus, in Michigan the death penalty has been characterized as barbaric and racist, an attack on the poor and the innocent, linked to abortion, and contrary to Christian dictates. Therefore, those who demand this detestable practice should be compelled to implement it, should be financially accountable for errors in its application, and should be forced to observe it in its most brutal form. All of these claims make a clear and forceful case for the moral superiority of abolition. Also, through the decades, it has been observed repeatedly that the death penalty cannot be reversed in the case of judicial error. The idea that the death penalty may be a deterrent has been rejected by Michigan elites for at least 150 years, long before any reliable statistical evidence was available, a position taken by Michigan governors, lieutenant governors, several directors of the Michigan Department of Corrections, U.S. senators and representatives, state senators and representatives, judges, the Michigan Bar, the Michigan Council of Churches, and the Michigan Catholic Conference.

Characterization of Death Penalty Supporters in the Press

Consistent with the early association of the death penalty with slavery, the Michigan press associates race, racism, and the Deep South with supporters of capital punishment.[70] A columnist pleaded: "Put away those varnished electric chairs, human gas chambers and cyanide pellets, rifles aimed at hearts, and the latest device—the intravenous 'humane' poisoning equipment which looks like it belongs in a Nazi death camp."[71] In 1981, the *Detroit Free Press* published statistics compiled by the NAACP which showed most death row prisoners were in the South—150 in Florida, 137 in Texas, and 97 in Georgia.[72] The *Detroit News* reported in 1983 that there were 1,050 prisoners on death rows throughout the United States, the largest number in history. More than two thirds of this population were in Southern states, and blacks accounted for 40 percent of death row inmates.[73]

Supporters of the death penalty were often presented as crude and unfeeling. In 1979, the father of a murder victim started a petition drive to place the issue of reinstatement on the general election ballot, saying that executions did not eliminate "human" life because those condemned are "subhuman."[74] A senator argued that the death penalty was required to strike back at "mad dogs."[75] The wife of a slain Michigan state highway patrol officer who helped lead a 1982 petition campaign was pictured in both the *Detroit News* and the *Detroit Free Press*[76] wearing a "Fry 'em in Michigan" T-shirt while collecting petition signatures. She expressed regret later, however: "It's a funny shirt if you're wearing it around friends, but I wish I had never put it on. People won't understand."[77]

A sponsor of a house death penalty resolution noted defensively that "[i]t was said in committee that this is a racist proposal, that it's aimed at black people. But I'd like to point out that it's not."[78] In making this point she observed that the killers of both President Kennedy and the Reverend Martin Luther King, Jr., were white. The primary Michigan advocate of capital punishment during the 1970s was a state senator described in the *Lansing State Journal* as "A hard-line conservative . . . who in 1972 switched from Democrat to Republican on the basis of the school busing issue."[79] His reaction to capital punishment statistics showing a bias against blacks was as follows: "It does seem minorities kill more than others. That does not excuse them at all."[80] Thus, in the senator's view the death penalty was not racist; blacks simply behaved worse than whites and should pay the price. The senator was also quoted in the *Detroit Free Press*[81] as saying: "We're talking about putting away an animal." He also indicated that he could execute a first-degree murderer. According to the senator, capital punishment was similar to hunting, or killing with a purpose.[82]

During the 1980s, this senator was succeeded by the Oakland County prosecutor as the primary moving force in the quest to reestablish capital punishment in Michigan. Like the senator, the prosecutor was allegedly elected on the strength of his association with opposition to school busing to achieve racial balance.[83] On the death penalty he was quoted as saying: "I've buried three police officers. I'm tired of it. I'm telling the punk murderers, if you take a life we may damn well take yours."[84] A newspaper article responded to such anger by quoting a death penalty opponent as follows:

> During the debate over busing, the code word was that busing was "impractical." But let's face it—what people really meant was they just didn't want racial mixing. Capital punishment used to be the same way. People could hide their real feelings by saying, "it's a deterrent, it's good for society." Now there's less reluctance to say, "Fry the bastard, he deserves it."[85]

. . . .

A cartoon appearing in the *Detroit News* depicted the prosecutor being lifted into the air by balloons while seated in an electric chair, suggesting that he was a demagogue, using the death penalty for personal gain. The caption read, "Capital Punishment—It's a Real Crowd Pleaser."[86] In an interview the acting director of the Michigan Department of Corrections indicated that the prosecutor was "looking for something to ride into office." In 1984, the *Detroit Free Press* also cast a cynical eye on the career of this prosecutor in an article titled "Capital Punishment and Capital Ambitions." The newspaper's editor observed that "[i]f Michigan has a demagogue—he would be it."[87]

A *Lansing State Journal* article reviewed Southern executions through the critical eyes of a Texas editor who had witnessed the incredible total of 189 executions.[88] The *Detroit News* noted that in Florida demonstrators against a 1981 execution were mocked by a group that displayed a model electric chair, nicknamed Sparky, chanting "go Sparky go."[89] In testimony before the Michigan Senate Judiciary Committee, a local attorney and member of the Michigan Coalition Against the Death Penalty recalled another execution in Florida:

> They were in the process [of an execution and] . . . the Jacksonville police were out en masse at the prison. They were lined up, all wearing T-shirts with an electric chair on them, saying, "kill, kill, kill." After the execution, and the hearse went by, they cheered. It was chilling.[90]

In Alabama the attorney general was elected after promising to "'fry' convicted murderers until smoke comes out of their ears."[91] Virginia was derided in a cartoon depicting an execution there involving an electric chair and a large hooded executioner with "Virginia is for Lovers" emblazoned on his chest.[92] Later, Michigan Representative John Conyers petitioned Virginia's governor to block the scheduled execution of a retarded prisoner in that state. The governor refused.[93] Lester Maddox, the lieutenant governor of Georgia, described the United States Supreme Court *Furman v. Georgia* decision, which halted all executions in 1972, as "a license for anarchy, rape and murder."[94] In short, press coverage of death penalty advocates tends to portray them as being—at the very best—extremely crude.

Isolation of Officials Supporting Capital Punishment

Because of these negative connotations, very few Michigan legislators actively support capital punishment bills. For example, during House Judiciary Committee hearings in 1951, only the bill's sponsor and two others spoke on behalf of reinstating capital punishment.[95] None spoke at the 1962 constitutional convention against the revision abolishing the death penalty.[96] After some initial confusion in 1976 concerning support for a referendum on the death penalty, the Michigan Chamber of Commerce claimed not to be officially in favor of the death penalty.[97] In 1978, even the Fraternal Order of the Police did not formally endorse a referendum to reinstate capital punishment. They limited their support to putting the issue on the ballot.[98] As a long-time leading senate death penalty supporter observed in an interview: "It is easy to get people to speak against capital punishment, but hard to find people to speak in favor of it." He said people would not sign a referendum petition in 1974 because signing their names was somehow different from stating personal opinions.

Echoing the senator's experience, the Oakland County prosecutor who assumed leadership in the efforts to restore the death penalty was nearly alone in his crusade to gather enough signatures to put capital punishment on the state ballot. He felt it necessary to make three to four speaking engagements per week on behalf of the referendum issue.[99] Failure to secure the necessary number of signatures in his initial attempt moved the prosecutor to promise that he would launch a new petition drive for the 1984 ballot only if elected state attorney general.[100] This condition was abandoned after he was defeated, for he nevertheless revived his death penalty crusade. A Michigan State University professor observed that the failure of a 1982 petition reflected the fact that no political organization supported it: "The petition had no circulation and it died." Even though capital punishment was endorsed by the 1985 state Republican convention, individual Republican candidates were not forced to endorse capital punishment, and the Oakland County prosecutor was the sole person to speak in favor of the death penalty at the convention.[101] Political leaders and the press vilified and isolated those bold enough to announce their support for capital punishment. The political marginalization of death penalty ad-

. . . .

vocates has made election in statewide races impossible. Thus, only already marginalized politicians are willing to publicly support death penalty initiatives.

Efforts to Reinstate the Death Penalty in Michigan

During consideration of a 1985 death penalty bill, testimony before the Senate Judiciary Committee noted that from 1930 to 1985, 49 percent of those executed for murder were black, as were 76 percent of those executed for robbery and 91 percent executed for rape. Whites accounted for 75 percent of commutations and 80 percent of the reversals on appeal. It was claimed that blacks made up 52 percent of homicide victims, but only 13 convicted killers were on death row for killing blacks. "The fact is that a black life is worth less than a white life in our society," asserted a witness at senate hearings.[102] Another witness testified that while blacks make up only 12 percent of the U.S. population, 57 percent of the condemned are black.

A 1946 *Lansing State Journal*[103] article noted Michigan's one hundredth year without capital punishment. An international movement away from the death penalty was noted in 1957.[104] According to a local newspaper,[105] both Canada and England were struggling with an issue that Michigan had resolved 117 years ago. A death penalty opponent noted that Michigan was the first English-speaking government to abolish capital punishment.[106] One hundred and twenty-seven years of abolition in Michigan were also noted.[107] A Detroit public defender testified during Michigan senate hearings in 1985: "Why kill when you [Michigan] have shown the world for 140 years that there is an alternative? You can read in other languages all over the world 'Michigan' because it was the first government to abolish the death penalty."[108] A state senator claimed: "The Michigan constitution has served as an example to many societies and to other states as kind of a leading light in the nineteenth century when capital punishment was still very, very much prevalent."[109] In an interview in 1985, the editor of the *Detroit Free Press* said that in Michigan a "tradition exists that worries about social justice." This history is frequently noted in the press and mentioned by opponents of the death penalty.[110] Frequent reference by the press to this history of abolition coexists with widespread editorial opposition to capital punishment.

Nevertheless, between 1846 and 1985 there were sixty-two legislative and four petition attempts to reinstate the death penalty. The amount of legislative activity had increased during the 1960s and 1970s. From 1973 to 1986 there was a nearly continuous effort to reinstate the death penalty through initiative petitions. As their frequency increased, the press predictably gave more editorial attention to this issue. A collection of newspaper editorials found in government files dating back to 1950 was compiled, together with all editorials from the *Detroit News* from 1976 to 1985. These statements suggest that death penalty editorials have, since 1975, become both much more common and, since 1980, increasingly opposed to such legislation (see Table 2.1).

In 1929, the Michigan governor vetoed a death penalty bill and demanded instead a bill that called for a statewide referendum:

> If a bill ever justified a referendum[,] this is the bill. It legislates on a subject on which most people have fixed opinions, and it is so drastic that it will never work out unless there is strong public sentiment in back of it.[111]

A death penalty bill last passed both legislative houses in 1931. Opponents of the bill had such trust in popular opposition that they supported the bill on the condition that it contain a referendum clause, while the sponsor of the bill bitterly opposed a referendum.[112] Legislators supporting a referendum won out and a statewide referendum proposing the death penalty was held that year. It failed by nearly 100,000 votes.[113] Retaining this strategy, death penalty opponents attached a referendum to a 1943 death penalty bill.[114] In 1947, supporters of the death penalty remained suspicious of public opinion and thus were opposed to a referendum clause being attached to death penalty legislation.[115] A supporter of yet another death penalty bill in 1952 voiced similar opposition to a referendum amendment.[116]

By 1973, however, death penalty supporters both inside and outside the state legislature viewed public opinion as an ally. Consequently, they organized a series of initiative petitions calling for a referendum on the death penalty.[117] The 1973 petition effort failed to secure the necessary number of signatures to put capital punishment on the No-

TABLE 2.1
Michigan Newspaper Positions on Capital Punishment, 1950–1985

YEAR	CAPITAL PUNISHMENT POSITION		
	Positive	Neutral	Negative
1950–54	0	0	0
1955–59	1	0	0
1960–64	0	0	1
1965–69	0	0	0
1970–74	1	1	1
1975–79	10	5	10
1980–85	7	2	21

vember 1974 ballot. The effort netted only 180,000 of the 265,000 signatures required.[118] The 1976 petition drive failed by 17,000 signatures.[119] In 1979, yet another petition drive was begun, this one initiated by the father of a thirteen-year-old female murder victim.[120] Although the necessary number of signatures was delivered to the secretary of state, many of the petition signatures were found to be invalid by the state election board after a challenge by the Michigan Coalition Against the Death Penalty. Thus, capital punishment did not appear on the 1982 ballot.[121] The 1984 petition effort to put the death penalty question on the 1986 general election ballot also failed. As in 1982, many petition signatures were declared to be invalid because they were judged to be over 180 days old, a violation of state referendum legal requirements.[122] These events suggest that it is more difficult to get public support for death penalty initiatives than one might imagine from the results of public opinion surveys. The director of the Michigan Council on Crime and Delinquency observed: "If people in this state were really into capital punishment they would sign petitions."

Increasing numbers of legislative and petition efforts give the impression that Michigan has gradually moved closer to reinstating a death penalty. In fact, however, a death penalty bill passed both houses of the state legislature only in 1929 and 1931, and a single referendum was submitted to the voters in 1931. An effort in 1973 to allow a full house vote on the death penalty by discharging it from committee was defeated by a fifty to fifty-six vote.[123] In the first full senate vote since

. . . .

1931, a Republican-controlled senate could muster a total of only six votes in favor of a 1986 death penalty resolution. Moreover, the 1963 state constitutional prohibition made reestablishment considerably more difficult. The constitutional prohibition requires either a two-thirds vote of both legislative houses followed by a majority vote of the electorate, or a successful initiative petition drive putting the issue on the ballot followed by a majority vote of the electorate, which would then allow, but not require, the legislature to reinstate capital punishment. In reality, there is no evidence that Michigan is on the verge of reinstating the death penalty. A leading Republican opponent of the death penalty noted in a 1985 interview that the constitutional prohibition was passed in recognition of shifts in public opinion and was designed to make legislative expression of this opinion more difficult.

The Contradiction of Traditional Elite Resistance to Capital Punishment

By the time Michigan first experienced significant population heterogeneity, there had been no death penalty in Michigan for nearly a century. Moreover, murder rates did not dramatically escalate until the 1960s. Thus, early Michigan history provided an environment conducive to the development and maintenance of abolition, not unlike that in other early abolitionist states. Additionally, it has been noted that once abolitionist laws are in place, the tradition of abolition develops a power of its own. Zimring and Hawkins note, for example, that states that had no death penalty prior to the *Furman v. Georgia* decision, typically did not pass one later and that those with a death penalty prior to this decision, did pass one later.[124] The influence of legal tradition is recognized by those on both sides of the abolitionist debate in Michigan. Nonetheless, a general theory of legislative tradition does not adequately explain the Michigan situation. Contrary to Zimring and Hawkins's contention that popular support for capital punishment in abolitionist states decreases over time, public opinion polls suggest that the support for capital punishment has never been greater in Michigan.

Continued abolition through the second half of the twentieth century is even more difficult to explain. There is no indication that unique characteristics of the state legislature account for its frequent rejection of death penalty bills. There is no evidence, for example, that key committee chairs have been responsible for blocking death penalty bills in committee and thereby preventing them from reaching a vote in the legislature. Rather, legislative leadership has been relatively united in opposition to reestablishing capital punishment, just as Bruxton has observed in England, where "in the case of capital punishment, legislators still lead from the front."[125] Yet political leaders in Michigan have not had to operate alone. The assistance of the mass media is an especially important part of the equation because the "news is an ally of legitimated institutions." Unlike politicians, "the 'average' man or woman does not have such access to the media."[126] Thus, reporting helps maintain the status quo. In this way the media's effect on the political agenda is by "magnifying movements that have already started, as opposed to originating those movements."[127] The press has largely controlled public discourse on the issue of capital punishment and has contributed to the definition of capital punishment as uncivilized and racist, making public support for reinstatement very difficult. Citizens are reluctant to sign initiative petitions and the few politicians who endorse capital punishment have short and unsuccessful careers.

Moreover, there has been nearly unanimous rejection of capital punishment by the leaders of religious, labor, and professional organizations. Elite preference for less coercive statutes is consistent with the observation that to "the extent conflicts of attitudes become widespread in contemporary American society, it is dominant groups that are more likely to endorse the more tolerant viewpoints."[128] Similarly, Zimring and Hawkins have noted that considering that the legal and medical professions have largely opposed capital punishment, "there is a tradition of deference to the organized legal and medical professions in matters of moral judgment that might be influential and exploitable in this connection."[129] Bedau indicates how a wide range of elites are involved in the abolitionist movement in the United States even though they have nothing personal to gain from such activity and the direct beneficiaries of abolition are the "lumpenproletariat of America: the poor, the nonwhite, the uneducated, the unemployed."[130] Yet the alleged altruism of these elites seems inconsistent with their positions on other issues.

. . . .

The Contradiction Resolved

Many observers have noted that on the issue of capital punishment elites often put benevolence above class interests. The question remains whether elite opposition to capital punishment in Michigan spills over into other criminal justice policies. Helfman argues that from 1847 to 1861, convicted murderers in Michigan were treated more cruelly than if they had been executed.[131] They were sentenced to life in solitary confinement at hard labor. Worse yet, labor was never provided, and visits were restricted to prison staff and visiting clergy. In 1859, for example, four of the twenty-two lifers died and three became insane. Prison personnel estimated that eight years of "unmixed suffering and misery" was the average life expectancy of persons sentenced to solitary confinement. Even more recently there has been some questioning of the humaneness of Michigan's criminal justice system. In 1987, the state ranked fifteenth in the percentage of its citizens imprisoned.[132] A ratio based on the "total index crime rates" compared with "total control rates" placed Michigan thirteenth in punitiveness. Studies from the 1950s to the 1980s of the state's massive state prison in Jackson describe it as among the worst in the nation.[133]

The isolation of Michigan's death penalty abolition from other portions of the state's criminal justice policies suggests that there is not necessarily any contradiction between abolition and elite class interests. The elites' alignment with religious leaders on this cause dramatizes the moral superiority of the status quo. Edelman has observed that elites have often endorsed humane and progressive legislation in an effort to protect their self-interest.[134] In considering executions, Foucault reasoned that "a confused horror spread from the scaffold. . . . [I]t was always ready to invert the shame inflicted on the victim into pity or glory[;] it often turned the legal violence of the executioner into shame."[135] Even as early as the eighteenth century, many began to "doubt the efficacy of [the ritual of] public hanging as a deterrent" to crime and instead recognized that this practice seemed to generate disrespect and defiance of law in general.[136] Such an explanation does not contend that Michigan's abolitionists were necessarily motivated by punitive sentiments. The abolitionist coalition has been heterogeneous and motivations among individuals may vary. Even so,

. . . .

the perceptual significance of abolition may extend beyond criminal justice. As with any symbolic legislation, the audience of the law is a significant consideration. In this case it appears that the elite abolitionists not only attempt to convince others of their general moral virtue, but in so doing they appear to convince themselves.

Whatever the motivations involved, it must be said that there is much to admire in Michigan's continuing abolition of capital punishment. The leaders in the state clearly recognize the irony of a democracy adopting a legal practice identical to that found in murderous dictatorships such as China and Iran. Michigan leaders hold out against a growing tide of executions elsewhere in the nation. Between 1977 and 1999, there were 598 executions in thirty American states. Considering that by the end of 1999, thirty-eight states had laws that provided for capital punishment, most observers expect that the pace of executions will soon quicken. By the end of 1999, a total of 3,572 prisoners were under a sentence of death in the United States.[137]

Postscript

Throughout the 1990s, there was no significant movement toward reinstatement of the death penalty in Michigan. This was due in part to the leadership of popular three-term Republican Governor John Engler, who was recently quoted as saying, "I think Michigan made a wise decision 150 years ago. . . . We're pretty proud of the fact that we don't have the death penalty."[138] The governor went on to say that he was not swayed by public opinion polls showing most Michigan citizens favored capital punishment since "100 percent would not like to pay taxes."[139]

. . . .

CHAPTER

3

**The Death Penalty
and Social Policy
in Wisconsin**

In 1853, Wisconsin became the first state to abolish capital punishment for all crimes. Six years earlier, Michigan abolished the death penalty for all offenses except treason. When the United States Supreme Court ruled in 1976 that death penalty statutes could be constitutionally permissible, many states rushed to reinstate. Wisconsin has not, however, even in the face of Jeffrey Dahmer's serial murders, which became public in 1991. Dahmer committed fifteen gruesome murders, dismembered the bodies, and practiced necrophilia on his victims. In analyzing public policy changes, Kingdon[1] defined policy windows as "those opportunities for action on given initiatives." If there was ever an event of sufficient magnitude, or "an opportunity for action" sufficient to move the legislators of Wisconsin to restore capital punishment, the Dahmer case was it.

This chapter examines the structural foundations and cultural dispositions that shaped death penalty politics in Wisconsin from January 1991 through December 1995. This time frame provides a natural laboratory in which to analyze the legislative response to Jeffrey Dahmer, arguably the most infamous serial murderer in American history. The significance of this research lies in its social policy implications for eliminating the death penalty. Through Wisconsin's death penalty politics, society might learn how to manage crime and violence without capital punishment.[2] Our research tells the story of Wisconsin's 146-year history of death penalty abolition. A complete description of the research methods used here can be found in the Appendix.

Levels of violence, population homogeneity, and economic crisis are associated with death penalty abolition. From 1989 to 1996, murder rates in Wisconsin ranked at least 50 percent below the national average.[3] Low murder rates tend to reduce popular support for capital punishment. From 1990 to 1994, the nonwhite population was 7 percent; that proportion reached 8 percent in 1995.[4] Abolitionist states tend to have small nonwhite populations.[5] Wisconsin's rate of unemployment matched the national average in 1980 and 1985 at 7.2 percent. In 1990, however, Wisconsin's unemployment rate fell below the national average, 4.4 percent; by 1996, it had dipped to 3.5 percent.[6] Vigorous economic circumstances are further conducive to death penalty abolition. Wisconsin's unobtrusive level of murders, small minority population, and relatively low unemployment rate are all characteristics conducive to long-term death penalty abolition.

Cultural Dispositions

Cultural dispositions are reflected in opinions of interest groups on either side of the death penalty issue. The concept of cultural dispositions implies a type of ethos that a people are *disposed* to act out. A newspaper correspondent attending the legislative session in which capital punishment was abolished, succinctly outlined the moral importance of death penalty abolition:

> So passage of this law tells clearly that our people have risen above the barbarities of the old statute; have progressed into a higher, clearer, and purer atmosphere of moral and mental life. . . . [M]ay we continue to progress, as I know we shall, until we realize fully the condition of brotherhood, when justice shall be here, and love shall prevent and eradicate all wrong.[7]

To understand Wisconsin's reaction to capital punishment it is necessary to take into account Wisconsin's cultural traditions of progressive liberalism, especially in the figure of Governor Robert LaFollette. LaFollette was elected governor three times and was chosen to serve four terms in the U.S. Senate.[8] LaFollette was a person ahead of his time, who lobbied against caucuses and conventions for the selection of candidates and for the introduction of direct primaries.[9] He argued in 1897 against political machines, bossism, corporate influence, and corruption. He argued for fairer tax laws and "the need to make political parties responsive to the electorate through the adoption of his direct primary bill."[10] In 1917, Senator LaFollette and nine other members of the state's congressional delegation voted against President Wilson's declaration of war, which preceded U.S. involvement in World War I.[11]

This progressive spirit was also found in the 1990s when 85 percent of the state's prosecutors preferred a life sentence without parole to capital punishment.[12] A *Capital Times* editorial characterized Wisconsin's perspective on the death penalty. The editorial cited the opposition of a religious leader, the Reverend Tim Kehl, who claimed that people in his state were not "destroyers of life." He also claimed that the people of Wisconsin see capital punishment as "an inhumane policy that makes neither moral nor financial sense."[13]

The Organization of Legislative Action

Each legislative session in Wisconsin lasts for two years. The "work horses" of the legislature are its committees. "Committees perform a gate keeping function for the legislature. [For example,] out of 1,709 regular and special session bills introduced in the 1991 session, 979 (or 57 percent) never left the committee to which they were originally referred."[14] The *Wisconsin Blue Book* explains that "In some cases, bills dealing with highly controversial issues are sent to committee and intentionally ignored. As an example, death penalty bills rarely received a public hearing."[15] Moreover, only a legislator or a legislative committee can introduce a bill in the state legislature. "Unlike many other states, Wisconsin does not have an initiative process on the state level that allows citizens to bypass the legislature," and as a consequence, capital punishment cannot be reestablished in Wisconsin without legislative acquiescence.[16] By contrast, in Oregon, citizens have voted on capital punishment seven times during the twentieth century with differing results.[17]

Another category of legislative documents used in this analysis is the fiscal estimate. "Since 1955, Wisconsin has required fiscal analysis of all bills that increase or decrease state revenues (often referred to as a 'fiscal note')." The Wisconsin legislature was the first state in the nation to require this type of analysis.[18] In theory, Wisconsin legislators weigh the benefits of passing a death penalty bill against the financial cost of its administration and implementation. Fiscal notes play a prominent role in maintaining death penalty abolition in the state.

Historical Background

Before the geographical area currently known as Wisconsin became a separate territory of the United States, executions were carried out under Native American tribal laws, military law, and previous territorial law.[19] In 1839, the first codified laws of the Wisconsin Territory specified hanging as the punishment for murder.

> Section 1. That every person who shall commit the crime of murder, shall suffer the punishment of death for the same.
> Section 2. That every person who shall, by previous engagement or appointment, fight a duel within the jurisdiction of this Territory, and in so doing shall inflict a wound upon any person whereof the person injured shall die, shall be deemed guilty of murder.[20]

Specifying the exact execution history of Wisconsin is difficult. Espy and Smykla report that only one person has been executed in Wisconsin since 1680.[21] Cropley reports that after Wisconsin became a separate territory in 1836, four executions were performed, as well as four others while it was still a part of the Michigan Territory.[22] A state of Wisconsin "Informational Bulletin" states that five persons were executed under "Wisconsin's own territorial and state laws."[23] Whatever the precise number, the frequency of executions in Wisconsin is relatively low by U.S. standards.

Pendleton and Renfert report that Wisconsin held its first constitutional convention in 1846, where a provision prohibiting the death penalty was discussed.[24] The proposal had considerable support among delegates and was extensively debated in the territory's newspapers. The proposal was narrowly defeated. Capital punishment did not become an issue again until the John McCaffary case made front-page headlines in 1851. The *Kenosha Telegraph* reported on July 23, 1850, that the "Horrid Murder" of Bridget McCaffary had been perpetrated by her husband, John.[25] Ultimately, John McCaffary was tried, found guilty, and hanged. McCaffary's execution triggered moral concerns among legislators and citizens, and laid the foundation for the move to abolish capital punishment in Wisconsin. The McCaffary trial was marred by accusations of ethnic discrimination. His botched execution was widely described in the newspapers.[26] Before McCaffary was hanged, several Wisconsin newspapers expressed their displeasure with the death penalty. In 1851, "*The Kenosha Telegraph*, edited by Latham Sholes, ran a series of editorials favoring its abolition."[27]

To carry on his fight against capital punishment, Sholes stood for election to the state assembly and was elected in the fall of 1851. Describing McCaffary's death on the hanging platform, Sholes wrote:

> He continued to struggle in space for five minutes. After he had been suspended eight minutes, the physicians were called upon the stand to examine his pulse, at which time his pulse was slightly reduced, and continued to beat for about ten minutes longer, at which time life was extinct and the prisoner was let down into the coffin. There were from 2,000 to 3,000 people to witness the execution.[28]

Sholes also wrote, "We hope this will be the last execution that shall ever disgrace the mercy-expecting citizens of the state of Wisconsin."[29]

By January 1852, petitions asking for the abolition of capital punishment had been presented to the legislature. "The petitions were referred to a committee consisting of Sholes, Utly, and Barber, all men in favor of [death penalty] abolition."[30] A newspaper correspondent observing the legislative session reported:

> So this legislature will wipe this most objectionable statute from the books, to which I am sure it will return no more. The gratifying feature of this is that it indicates distinctly a step in progress. Legislation on such subjects is never in advance of popular opinion, so the passage of this law tells clearly that our people have risen above the barbarities of the old statute; have progressed into a higher, clearer, and purer atmosphere of moral and mental life. Let the law of bloodshed perish . . . and may we continue to progress . . . until we realize fully the condition of brotherhood, when justice shall be here, and love shall prevent and eradicate all wrong.[31]

. . . .

Sholes's 1852 bill to abolish capital punishment was rejected by the assembly, twenty-five to thirty-six.

Before abolition, the only sentence a judge could impose for those convicted of willful murder was death. This requirement provided a further incentive to abolish capital punishment. A well-argued case of murder was presented against William Radcliffe in 1852. The evidence was convincing, but the jury refused to convict Radcliffe of murder. Later, "[i]t was reported that the jury did not convict . . . partly as a result of at least one juror's opposition to the death penalty."[32] There were two more trials in Waukesha County in the early 1850s where the defendants were not convicted of willful murder; again, these outcomes were reportedly due to anti–capital punishment sentiment among jurors.[33]

In 1853, Edward Lees introduced a bill to abolish capital punishment in Wisconsin, assembly bill 67 (AB 67). It passed the assembly, without discussion, by a margin of thirty-six to twenty-eight. Later, the senate passed the bill by a vote of fourteen to nine. Governor Leonard Farwell signed the bill into law on July 10, 1853. The outcome of AB 67 was in all likelihood influenced to some degree by the establishment of a state prison at Waupun in 1851. Before that time, prisoners were housed in county jails, clearly unsuitable places for incarcerating a person for life.[34]

Early Attempts to Reinstate the Death Penalty

Several lynchings and the murder of a Milwaukee banker in 1855 triggered a large majority of Wisconsin newspapers to favor reinstatement of the death penalty. In 1857 and 1866, legislators introduced bills supporting the repeal of the 1853 abolitionist law.[35] Both failed. The next attempt to restore capital punishment came seventy-one years later.

By 1937, the kidnap and murder in New Jersey of Charles Lindbergh's baby triggered the introduction of an assembly bill to establish the death penalty for kidnapping. It was later withdrawn by its author after it became apparent that there was no hope of passage.[36] In 1949, an assembly joint resolution called for an advisory citizen referendum on the death penalty for first-degree murder. The resolution was rejected by a vote of forty-nine to thirty-three. In 1955, a multiple murder in Milwaukee led Assemblyman Arthur J. Balzer to introduce a bill to establish the death penalty for first-degree murder. As in 1937, "the bill was returned to him at his request."[37] Another legislative attempt to reestablish capital punishment in Wisconsin was not made until 1973. That year three bills were introduced (senate bill 186, senate joint resolution 37, and assembly bill 33). Since 1973, at least one death bill has been introduced in every session of the Wisconsin legislature. From 1973 through 1990, twenty-four death penalty bills were introduced in the assembly or in the senate. All twenty-four of those bills died in committee. Motions were made in the 1975–76 and 1981–82 legislatures to forcibly remove death penalty bills from their respective committees and schedule them for consideration by the full assembly. Those efforts were defeated by substantial margins.

A Colossal Triggering Event

On Monday, July 22, 1991, Jeffrey Dahmer was booked on suspicion of homicide after he had confessed to multiple murders.[38] Between the time he was taken into custody and the end of the month, Dahmer had confessed to seventeen murders.[39] Authorities searched Dahmer's apartment and found a little house of horrors: photographs of mutilated males, severed heads in his refrigerator and freezer, skulls in his closets and file cabinets, severed genitals, and headless torsos in a vat found in his bedroom. The Milwaukee County medical examiner confirmed that five full bodies and parts of six others had been recovered from Dahmer's apartment.[40]

Public reaction to Dahmer's crimes was so intense that six months after Dahmer's sentencing "more than 500 people marched through downtown Milwaukee . . . in memory of the eleven males whose body parts were found in Dahmer's apartment and the other men police say Dahmer has confessed to killing."[41] Dahmer's crimes generated intense public reaction and interest in the press. One article noted the brand names of products Dahmer used. He drank Budweiser beer and smoked Camel cigarettes. He carried a skull to work in a Samsonite

cosmetic case. Dahmer cooked a bicep in Crisco shortening and sea-
soned it with A-1 Steak Sauce. He stored Arm and Hammer Baking
Soda next to a severed head in the refrigerator. He preferred Ruffles
potato chips and sometimes poured Bailey's Irish Creme into a coffee-
drug mixture that he would offer his victims before strangling and dismembering them.[42]

As noted by McGarrell and Castellano,[43] heinous crimes can be considered "triggering events capable of producing crime legislation and
policy." Predictably, the Dahmer murders generated calls for reinstatement of the death penalty in Wisconsin. A Republican member of the
assembly said that the "Dahmer episode has convinced many people
in this state that the death penalty is long overdue for Wisconsin."[44]
Soon after Dahmer's arrest, a senator reported that an informal telephone poll of 6,700 Wisconsin residents asking the question, "Should
Wisconsin have a death penalty?" found 84 percent said "yes."[45]

Public reaction to Jeffrey Dahmer's crimes was so great that legal
authorities became concerned about the cost of protecting him during
his trial. To save the county money, a trial judge requested a shield to
separate the courtroom audience from Dahmer.[46] "Potential jurors
were warned that they may hear reports of human carnage, mutilation,
cannibalism, necrophilia and more."[47] Evidence was expected to include reports that "Dahmer tried to lobotomize some of his victims
and turn them into zombies by drilling holes in their heads and pour-
ing in a fluid to deaden their brains."[48] On February 15, 1992, "a jury
decided that the 31-year-old Dahmer was sane when he killed 15
young men and boys he had lured to his home."[49] "The serial killer was
denied the possibility of parole [and was] sentenced to 15 consecutive
life terms in prison . . . the maximum sentence the judge could give
Mr. Dahmer for killing and dismembering [the] boys and young men
to fulfill his sexual desires."[50]

Dahmer's first year in prison was spent in protective isolation, away
from the general inmate population. However, the next year, authorities deemed it safe enough for him to be integrated into the general
inmate population.[51] "Safe enough" was actually not safe enough for
Dahmer. On Monday, November 28, 1994, at approximately eight A.M.,
a guard found Dahmer bleeding on the floor.[52] He was pronounced dead

. . . .

within an hour. The story of Dahmer's infamy began in 1991 and largely ended in 1994 with his death.

While the Dahmer murders triggered calls to reinstate capital punishment, drops in crime rates made it difficult to present rational arguments for reinstatement. In October 1995, the *Milwaukee Journal Sentinel* reported: "Murder, rape and robbery rates dropped sharply in Milwaukee during the first six months of 1995, leading a statewide decline in nearly all categories of crime, according to a report released Tuesday by the Wisconsin Office of Justice Assistance."[53] The trend toward lower murder rates in Wisconsin continued in 1996 when the number of murders reported by Wisconsin police departments showed a 4 percent drop from the year before, the lowest total since 1989 when 176 murders were reported.[54] In addition to declining murder rates, in 1988, Wisconsin passed a murder penalty stipulating "life means life" without parole, a tough and certain alternative to capital punishment.[55]

Recent Legislative History, 1991–1996

During the course of three legislative sessions spanning February 6, 1991, through February 23, 1996, assembly and senate members introduced twenty-two bills and resolutions to reinstate the death penalty: five bills or resolutions in the 1991–92 session, nine bills or resolutions in the 1993–94 session, and eight bills or resolutions in the 1995–96 session.

The 1991–1992 Legislative Session

As the Wisconsin legislature opened the 1991–92 session, an article titled "Death Penalty Erodes Struggle for Humanity" appeared in the *Madison Newspapers, Inc.*, which succinctly summarized the dominant political views of the press.[56] The article acknowledged that "Dahmer's case has given new impetus to the movement for adding capital punishment to Wisconsin's repertoire of punishments." However, the "heart of the debate is whether society acting through the government ought to deliberately take the life of another human being."[57] In 1991, that debate began with five death penalty statutes introduced into the Wisconsin legislature: two senate bills (SB 44 and SB 125), two assembly bills (AB 588 and AB 985), and one senate joint resolution (SJR 15). No legislative action was taken on AB 985, SB 44, or SB 125. All three bills died in committee. SJR 15, which called for an advisory referendum on capital punishment in the 1992 general election, suffered the same outcome. AB 588 received more legislative attention.

Nearing the Christmas season, "two Republican legislators announced that an assembly committee would hold a public hearing on December 12. . . . We need to send a clear message that the most abhorrent crimes can be punished by the ultimate penalty," claimed Representative Susan Vergeront, one of AB 588's authors.[58] Lawmakers opposed to reinstating capital punishment were equally vocal. A *Madison Newspapers, Inc.* article titled "Lawmaker Vows to Kill Death-Penalty Bill" reported: "The chairman of a legislative committee scheduled to consider the bill to allow the death penalty in Wisconsin under certain conditions vows to kill the measure."[59] Committee chairman, State Representative Wayne Wood, D-Janesville, noted that "the bill will not get out of the committee because 'it cannot guarantee that innocent defendants will not be executed.'" Chairman Wood also argued that:

> It's my policy to give the author a public hearing. It's also my policy to call for a vote and move along any bill if I get a sense that a clear majority of the committee members want to do that. But some bills are so flawed, and this is one of them, that even if the committee members wanted the bill out, I would exercise my power as committee chair and hold it up.[60]

The public hearing on AB 588 did not create nearly as much press attention as the Jeffrey Dahmer trial. Appearing in opposition to the death penalty bill were eight citizens, as well as representatives of several religious, labor, and civil rights organizations. These groups included the Wisconsin ACLU, the Wisconsin Catholic Conference, Amnesty International, the University of Wisconsin Law School, Act-Up Madison, the Lutheran Office for Public Policy, and the Jewish Defense League. Also registering their opposition to reinstating capital punishment were two members of the assembly, as well as a representative of the Wisconsin attorney general's office and two representatives of the AFL-CIO. Two senators, along with twenty-one citizens, registered in support of the bill. Representative Vergeront argued that capital punishment "was needed to deal with the most horrific, most offensive kind of murders . . . [calling] capital punishment a 'legitimate function of the state to punish certain killers and to prevent killers from killing again.'"[61] In an article titled "Death Penalty Debate Rages," Representative Vergeront further reasoned that "some horrible crimes deserve a greater penalty than life in prison."[62] In spite of Representative Vergeront's argument, this hearing was the last action taken by the 1991–92 legislature on capital punishment.

The 1993–1994 Legislative Session

Undaunted by their failure to pass death penalty legislation in the 1991–92 legislative session, Wisconsin's pro-death legislators introduced nine proposals to reinstate capital punishment in 1993—eight were killed in committee and one failed to pass a floor vote in the senate. Reflective of an increased interest in such legislation, public hearings were held on three of those bills. The Judiciary and Insurance Committee held a public hearing on SB 23 on June 16, 1993.[63] Senator Alan Lasee, along with five private citizens, appeared at the hearing in support of the bill. Those testifying against SB 23 included an attorney, two private citizens, and many of the same organization representatives as in 1991: the Wisconsin Catholic Conference, the Lutheran Office for Public Policy in Wisconsin, the Wisconsin ACLU, the Wisconsin Conference of Churches, and a public defender. A representative of the Wisconsin AFL-CIO, three citizens, the Reverend Alan G. Newton, and Kelly Kennedy for Attorney General James Doyle registered their opposition.[64] At the public hearing on SB 23, a representative for the Wisconsin Catholic Conference said that they "regard any efforts to revive the death penalty in the state as detrimental to the consistent life ethic they preach."[65] The Milwaukee Jewish Council representative asserted: "We believe that capital punishment is no greater a deterrent to crime than other forms of punishment."[66] According to the spokesperson for the United Methodist church, "In spite of a common assumption to the contrary, 'an eye for an eye and a tooth for a tooth' does not give justification for imposing the death penalty."[67] The spokesperson for the National Council of the Churches of Christ in the USA said that "it reaffirms its opposition to the death penalty, with particular reference to executing juveniles."[68]

"First Vote on Death Penalty Since 1857 Likely in Senate," read an October 5, 1993, headline in the *Wisconsin State Journal.* Referring to the historic milestone represented by SB 23, the article reported that "[f]or the first time since 1857 the state senate will face a vote . . . on whether to reinstate the death penalty in Wisconsin."[69] "Death Penalty Debate Emotional in Senate" was the headline of an article reporting the senate debate preceding the vote.[70]

SB 23 received serious bipartisan criticism. Republican Senator Alberta Darling expressed her views on the upcoming bill saying she would vote against it. She also stated that "it was no deterrent to crime, cost too much to implement and maintain, and put[s] the state in the 'very negative role' of sanctioning killing. . . . [I]ndividuals are going to pay more if we have the death penalty."[71] Correspondingly, the *Wisconsin State Journal* reported: "State fiscal analysts contended that trying to execute criminals would cost Wisconsin taxpayers more than imprisoning them for life,"[72] noting that it costs up to $3.2 million to execute each prisoner and only $26,000 per year for incarceration. Another Republican, Senator Peggy Rosenzweig, argued that "reinstating the death penalty would teach children to answer violence with more violence. Government should not sanction killing. By placing the state in the role of executioner, we . . . lower ourselves to the level of the murderer."[73] Longtime Democratic Senator Risser asserted, "the death penalty does not deter violent crime. . . . Thirty-six states have the death penalty, and more than 30 of them have worse violent crime records than Wisconsin."[74] On a vote of twenty-one to twelve, the Wisconsin senate voted to table SB 23 indefinitely.[75]

Records suggest that six of the 1993–94 death penalty proposals (AB 358, AB 835, AB 170, AB 123, SB 30, and AB 30a) received only minimal consideration by their respective legislative committees. These bills suffered the same end as do most capital punishment bills in Wisconsin, death at the committee level without a public hearing. The practice is so embedded in the death penalty politics of the Wisconsin legislature as to appear routine. Nevertheless, early in 1994,

. . . .

two senate joint resolutions concerning the reinstatement of capital punishment were scheduled for public hearings.

On February 9, 1994, a public hearing was held on SJR 42. Senator Alan Lasee, Senator Andrea, the deputy district attorney of Winnebago County, and five private citizens made appearances in support of SJR 42. Appearing in opposition to the resolution were six private citizens and representatives of organizations similar to those that testified against SB 23: the Public Defender's Office, Project Hope to Abolish the Death Penalty, the Wisconsin Association of Criminal Defense Lawyers, the Wisconsin Catholic Conference, the Lutheran Office for Public Policy in Wisconsin, the Wisconsin Coalition Against the Death Penalty, and the Wisconsin ACLU. The resolution was killed in committee. The Committee on State Government Operations and Corrections held the 1993–94 session's third, and final, public hearing on capital punishment. The hearing on SJR 43 included the same cast of characters as the public hearings on SB 23 and SJR 42. In the end, SJR 43 died in committee.[76]

Three public hearings on the death penalty in one session suggest that public sentiment was pressuring the legislature to reinstate capital punishment. Existing evidence, however, does not support that conclusion. While Governor Tommy Thompson did say that he would sign a limited death penalty bill if he received one, he admitted, "I still don't see a ground swell for passing it. . . . I think opinion leaders and the press are opposed to it. I'm not pushing it."[77] One reason for a turning away from capital punishment may be found in the FBI's 1992 crime figures. "Wisconsin had less crime than the national average. Wisconsin had the 13th lowest crime rate in the nation. Moreover, the murder rate in Wisconsin ranked 16th lowest among U.S. states, 4.4 per 100,000" while the national murder rate at that time was 9.3 per 100,000.[78]

The Wisconsin attorney general's race between James Doyle and Jeff Wagner in 1994 reflected the inconsequential attitude that a majority of the state's electorate placed on reinstating capital punishment. In 1993, Attorney General James Doyle argued that "resuming the death penalty in Wisconsin after 140 years would be an expensive, ill-suited solution to frustration over violent crime."[79] Doyle also claimed that Wisconsin's murder penalty stipulating "life means life" without parole provides "a much more certain system."[80] Speaking to the costs of what a new death penalty law would generate, Doyle reported: "Certainly in this department [we] better be prepared to give a significant number of new positions to handle death penalty appeals. . . . There also would be added expense in the public defender's office."[81] While Doyle conceded that computing the costs of a death penalty over lifetime incarceration is "very murky," he also said:

> Those costs for the state Justice Department will rise if the state adopts a capital punishment bill. . . . Justice departments in states of similar size that have the death penalty have five to 15 new assistant attorney generals who don't do anything except death penalty cases. . . . In fiscal year 1993 it cost $20,579 to house a prisoner, according to the Wisconsin Department of Corrections. In Florida the cost of a death penalty case has been pegged at $3.2 million, while in Texas the cost is placed at $2.3 million.[82]

Attorney General Doyle also argued that "if you do have the death penalty, you run the risk that an innocent individual is going to be prosecuted."[83]

Jeff Wagner, a Republican candidate for the office of Wisconsin attorney general, hired Rick Jones, father of a twelve-year-old Wisconsin girl slain in September 1994, to star in his political commercial to promote the death penalty. In the half-minute commercial, "Rick Jones criticized Democratic Attorney General James Doyle for opposing the death penalty. Doyle was among those who led the fight to enact the 'life means life' law."[84] In the political ad, Jones began with pictures of his daughter, Cora Jones, and asks, "How can Jim Doyle oppose the death penalty for someone who killed my daughter? Jeff Wagner will support the death penalty and see that justice is done for Cora."[85] Doyle said that "[t]he ad was very misleading in the sense that it suggests the attorney general would decide whether there would be a death penalty in Wisconsin, and the legislature decides that."[86] "Wagner's position seems to be accepted by a solid majority of Wisconsin's residents, according to a 1994 *Milwaukee Journal* poll. The poll of 525 likely voters showed 70 percent favored reinstating the death penalty."[87] While everything seemed to be in place for a Republican victory, as well as for the reinstatement of capital punishment, the paper added that these polls do not "necessarily translate into votes."[88]

Just as the newspaper speculated, incumbent Attorney General Doyle defeated Wagner in the November 1994 election. As noted above, a poll conducted by the *Milwaukee Journal Sentinel* of 525 voters found that 70 percent of those polled supported reinstating the death penalty.[89] During the election day, Voter News Service conducted an exit poll based on 1,700 interviews outside precincts around the state. Again, although the findings showed that "72 percent of Wisconsin voters favored the death penalty and 24 percent opposed it," the voters "brushed aside an attorney general candidate who supports capital punishment in favor of an incumbent who opposes it."[90] The contrast between what voters say they believe and what voters do at the polls demonstrated an aspect of the protracted political conflict and normative ambivalence found in many states with long-term traditions of abolition.[91] That ambivalence is consistent with the cultural dispositions reflected in a *Wisconsin State Journal* article that reminded its readers of the John McCaffary case and reported that in Wisconsin:

> Opponents see capital punishment as a remnant of barbarous times when "an eye for an eye" guided self-appointed seekers of justice. Poor and minority members of the population most often receive the death sentence, according to studies then and now.[92]

Yet Wisconsin's abolition forces remained under attack during the second half of the 1993–94 legislative session. A staffer with the Wisconsin assembly Democratic caucus expressed his dismay when the Democratic speaker of the assembly switched his position on capital punishment. He reported: "Progressive Democrats had slept poorly the night of Assembly Speaker Walter Kunicki's bombshell announcement that he will bring a capital punishment bill to the floor of the Assembly next session."[93] Disillusioned by what he considered Kunicki's "betrayal of democratic values," the Wisconsin assembly Democratic staff person stated: "I'm not abandoning faith in my neighbor's ability to wake up one election day and choose the government they really deserve—one made of people who represent our highest, not our meanest, aspirations."[94]

The defection of Speaker Kunicki was highlighted in a *Madison Newspaper, Inc.* article titled "Playing Into GOP Hands." According to the September 21, 1994, article:

> Kunicki, who as Assembly Speaker leads legislative Democrats, stunned his colleagues. . . . After a close call in the Democratic primary in his south Milwaukee district—more than 40 percent of voters offered to trade away Kunicki's "power"—he ditched his historic opposition to the death penalty and announced that he would lead the fight in the coming legislative session to make Wisconsin a death penalty state. . . . Kunicki's obsession with avoiding criticism from the other side of the aisle is so pervasive that he has now embraced the most evil tool in the bag of Republican tricks—capital punishment.[95]

One Democratic nominee for an open assembly seat "sighed when she considered what could well be the toughest question she will face. . . . Will you support Wally Kunicki's death penalty initiative?" Two members of the assembly—both "passionate foes of the death penalty"—expressed shock at the political move made by the assembly speaker. Democrat Frank Boyle said, "He's got to understand that there is an implication that his view represents the view of the Democratic caucus, and it does not."[96] Democrat Tammy Baldwin—questioning Kunicki's motivation—reasoned that "while it may now be somewhat more difficult—[legislative] candidates can still make a case against what Boyle calls 'social legalization of murder.'"[97] A *New York Times* article titled "Support Builds for Death Penalty Wisconsin Banned Nearly 140 Years Ago" reported: "The public's anger over violent crime is turning politicians around."[98] Two killings in September 1994 led Democratic Assembly Speaker Walter J. Kunicki to throw his hat in the ring with legislators who supported capital punishment reinstatement. The first crime was the disappearance and death of a twelve-year-old girl; the second crime was the random killing of a Milwaukee police officer. In reaction to these murders, a University of Wisconsin Law School professor stated: "It's quite likely we're going to have a death penalty."[99]

The 1995–1996 Legislative Session

As was the case in 1989, legislative failures during the 1991 and 1993 legislative sessions did not dampen the resolve of death penalty supporters in Wisconsin's senate or assembly. In fact, the spirits of pro-death legislators were bolstered because "GOP leaders, in full control of the Legislature for the first time since 1970, ended the Fall session . . . and immediately began plotting their January legislative strategy."[100] Republicans held a "one-seat majority in the 33-member Senate and a two-seat majority in the 99-member Assembly [and they had the votes] to push through almost everything they sought to do."[101]

Wisconsin legislators introduced eight death penalty proposals into the 1995–96 legislative session: one senate bill and one senate joint resolution (SB 1, SJR 51); three assembly bills (AB 298, AB 352, AB 937); and three assembly joint resolutions (AJR 9, AJR 10, AJR 84). Public hearings were held on SB 1 and SJR 51. Senator Alan Lasee and other senators sponsored both bills. While the *Bulletin of the Proceedings of the Wisconsin Legislature* does not provide data on the public hearings for SB 1, a report issued by the *Prison Activist Resource Center* provides some information on the testimony given during three days of public testimony (January 17 and 18, 1995, and May 17, 1995) on the desirability of reestablishing capital punishment in Wisconsin. The *Prison Activist Resource Center*[102] reported that the earlier hearing (January 17 and 18) was more evenly divided between proponents and opponents of the death penalty. During the May 17 hearing, "the overwhelming majority (perhaps 85 percent) testified or registered against Senate Bill Number 1, demonstrating their strong opposition to re-introduction of the death penalty in Wisconsin." SJR 51 called for an advisory referendum on the question of enacting the death penalty. The public hearing on SJR 51 was not held until February 29, 1996.[103]

Senator Alan Lasee, a veteran death penalty advocate (authoring bills in the 1985–86, 1987–88, 1989–90, 1991–92, 1993–94, and 1995–96 legislative sessions), had said that "he believes the Legislature will pass a capital punishment measure this year."[104] Senator Lasee's moral entrepreneurship was also captured in a *New York Times* article published March 19, 1995. Commenting on his legislative proposal

(SB 1) to limit the death penalty to "cases where the victim is under age 16," Lasee alluded to two 1994 child murders and said, "[t]hese young people were brutally murdered . . . [and] [l]ife imprisonment is not sufficient. The judiciary should have had the option of the death penalty."[105]

Governor Tommy Thompson, Senator Lasee, and other death penalty supporters became even more optimistic about getting a death penalty bill through the Wisconsin legislature after the bombing of the Alfred P. Murrah Federal Building in Oklahoma City in April 1995. A poll showed that 71 percent of Wisconsin's residents favored the death penalty. Governor Thompson said:

> Absolutely, I'd say if that bill came up today [4/21/95], it probably would pass the Legislature. . . . People are just fed up with the mayhem, and then this bombing of these poor kids. . . . [C]an you imagine putting a bomb below a day-care center? Those people don't deserve to live. They're murderers. Cold [and] calculating.[106]

The *Green Bay Press-Gazette* concluded that "the bombing of a federal building in Oklahoma City enhances the chances for a death penalty in Wisconsin, the Legislature's leading death-penalty advocate says. Senator Lasee . . . said a bill to create the death penalty for murderers of children will gain support as a result of the Oklahoma City tragedy."[107]

With the opening of the 1995–96 legislative session, anti-death forces also renewed their defense of death penalty abolition. The *Wisconsin State Journal* ran the headline, "Prosecutors Speak Against Death Penalty." In the accompanying article prosecutors for the state's two largest counties argued that "[c]apital punishment is a costly, moral abomination that should not be re-enacted in Wisconsin."[108] Dane County District Attorney Bill Fouse was quoted as saying, "It is simply wrong to take the life of another human being. I did not run for office to sink to the level of the people I prosecute." Likewise, Milwaukee County District Attorney E. Michael McCann said that "he favored 'life means life' sentences, which allow a judge to send a convicted criminal to prison without any hope of release."[109] McCann also said that "he opposed the death penalty because it was a permanent sentence that couldn't be changed if the convicted individual was found to be innocent years later."[110] To make his point, McCann cited a Milwaukee case "in which new law enforcement techniques proved the innocence of a man sentenced eight years earlier to life in prison."[111] The chair of the Wisconsin State Bar Association's criminal law section, Waring Fincke, said his group "opposed restoration of the death penalty and the current bill before the Legislature for several reasons. Among them, the measure allows a simple majority of the jury to impose the death penalty and a judge may overturn a jury's decision not to impose it."[112]

In March and April 1995, the Wisconsin State Bar Association conducted a survey of prosecutors statewide. Pat Schneider of the *Capital Times* reported: "Concerns over morality, mistaken executions, lack of deterrence and racial disparity in application of the death penalty lead most Wisconsin prosecutors to favor life in prison instead of executions."[113] As noted earlier, even Jeffrey Dahmer's prosecutor, Milwaukee County District Attorney E. Michael McCann opposed the death penalty. During one of the three public hearings debating the merits of SB 1, McCann found significant comparisons in the Deep South: "Texas has the highest murder rate and they're also leading the nation in executions. . . . In other states, such as Florida and Georgia, that have had the death penalty for some time, their murder rate is two to three times our murder rate."[114] The press also recorded strong opposition to death penalty legislation from other than the legal community. In "Churches Fight Death Penalty," William Wineke reported that the "Wisconsin Conference of Churches, an organization of nine Protestant church bodies . . . launched a state campaign to fight capital punishment."[115]

A headline, "Lawmakers See Greater Interest in Death Penalty," appeared in the April 30, 1995, edition of the *Appleton Post*. The corresponding article discussed the rising optimism of legislators who favored passage of a new death penalty law.[116] On May 1, 1995, the *Wisconsin State Journal* published similar articles titled "Death Penalty Support Mounts" and "Lawmaker Leads Crusade to Amend Constitution" as a means of reinstating capital punishment. The Wisconsin legislature, however, did not return to the death penalty issue until

1996.[117] On March 12, 1996, SJR 51 was released from the Committee on State Government Operations and Corrections by a four to one vote and was scheduled for consideration by the full senate.[118] On March 28, 1996, the Wisconsin senate rejected SJR 51. The resolution was indefinitely tabled on a vote of twenty-one to twelve.

On April 4, 1996, SB 1 was killed in the Joint Committee on Finance.[119] The legislative future of SB 1 was no doubt hurt by the various fiscal estimates on the cost of implementing the death penalty. The Wisconsin Department of Justice projected that it would cost the state $96,667 for attorney salaries for each death penalty case they tried. Significant cost increases were also projected for the State Crime Laboratory, the Division of Criminal Investigation, and local district attorneys' staffs. The Wisconsin Department of Corrections estimated that it would have to build and staff a twelve-cell death row to implement SB 1, with a projected cost to state government of $2 million for construction, plus an annual $458,000 for staffing and maintenance.[120] The 1995–96 legislative session began with press headlines expressing unparalleled optimism among politicians favoring the return of capital punishment in Wisconsin. In the end, however, nothing changed. Anti-death cultural sentiments, anti-death newspapers, and the anti-death organizations of Wisconsin were simply too strong and too prestigious.

Conclusion

During the 1990s, several circumstances appeared to threaten death penalty abolition in Wisconsin. In 1991, Jeffrey Dahmer surfaced as one of the most infamous serial killers in Wisconsin or U.S. history. In 1994, a Republican candidate for Wisconsin attorney general attempted to unseat the incumbent Democrat by attacking his abolitionist position. In the same year, the assembly speaker deserted the ranks of death penalty opponents. In 1995, the Republican party secured control of the Wisconsin senate and assembly for the first time in numerous years. Yet legislators were not ready to reestablish capital punishment. The long-term low crime rates enjoyed by Wisconsin moved state legislators to view the Jeffrey Dahmer case as an anomaly rather than a reason to reestablish the death penalty. Year after year, Wisconsin's crime rates are among the lowest in the nation. On a practical level, the money necessary to implement capital punishment clearly outweighs any political benefit associated with reestablishing capital punishment. The homogeneous nature of the state's population also disposes Wisconsin toward continued abolition. Leaders of religious, labor, and civil rights groups publicly line up against capital punishment. Reinstatement has no such organized endorsements.

Additionally, the structure of legislative processes in Wisconsin has acted to facilitate death penalty abolition. A strong committee system and the lack of a citizen referendum process has kept death penalty debates largely confined to committee settings. Introducing death penalty bills and referring them to legislative committees where they die after receiving little or no attention, has become a ritual. In summary, Wisconsin aptly illustrates Zimring and Hawkins's observation that a history of executions in a state provides residents with the assurance that executions are acceptable. With fewer than ten territorial and state executions in its history, such a precedent does not exist in Wisconsin. The long history of abolition in Wisconsin has created a moral ambivalence toward executions.[121] Thus, Wisconsin is in little jeopardy of reinstatement. The population diversity, economic circumstances, and levels of crime found in the state do not threaten that moral ambivalence.

Postscript

Prominent, senior elected officials continue to oppose reinstatement of the death penalty in Wisconsin. The longtime prosecuting attorney from Milwaukee, Michael McCann, was recently quoted as saying, "To participate in the killing of another human being, it diminishes the respect for life. Period. Although I am a district attorney, I have a gut suspicion of the state wielding the power of the death penalty over anybody."[122] Likewise, Democratic Senator Fred Risser, the president of the Wisconsin state senate, said:

. . . .

I take some credit [for] abolition in that I've been in the legislature for 42 years, 6 years in the Assembly and 36 years in the Senate. I've been president of the Senate for a good share of the time and the president of the Senate has considerable discretion and power in the referral of bills to committee. There's a million ways to kill a bill and only one way to pass it.[123]

The Power of History
Death Penalty Abolition
in Maine

A Short History of Executions in Maine

When Maine entered the Union in 1820, prisoners could be executed for treason, murder, arson, rape, burglary, or robbery. In 1829, the punishment for rape, burglary, or robbery was reduced to life imprisonment. Only treason and murder remained capital offenses. Less than a decade later, Maine legislators placed further restrictions on the use of capital punishment. Motivated by the highly publicized execution of Joseph Sager in 1835, an 1837 bill required that condemned persons be held in prison for a minimum of one year and a day before the sentence of death could be carried out.[1] The governor—after reviewing the legal proceedings surrounding each capital conviction—was given the responsibility of determining who lived and who died. Condemned persons were held under a sentence of death until the governor either signed their death warrant and delivered it to the hangman, or commuted their death sentence. The bill placed so much responsibility on the governor that another execution did not take place in Maine until 1864.

Since the 1837 bill placed no time limit on gubernatorial deliberations, it was not unknown for condemned persons to be imprisoned under a sentence of death for twenty years.[2] In 1867, with ten persons awaiting execution, the governor petitioned the legislature to abolish capital punishment or to alter the statute and require the governor to issue a death warrant, pardon, or commute a death sentence within a specific period of time. The 1837 law was indeed altered by an 1875 amendment requiring the governor to issue a death warrant within fifteen months of sentencing.[3]

Given these circumstances, it is not surprising that only four abolitionist states (Wisconsin, North Dakota, Alaska, and Michigan) have
executed fewer persons than Maine. Nine executions were carried out
in Maine after statehood was achieved: two between 1820 and 1863,
and seven between 1864 and 1887.[4] Including pre-statehood years,
twenty-one executions have taken place in the geographical area now
known as Maine.[5] As in other parts of the United States, racial minorities and recent immigrants were disproportionately subjected to the
gallows.

Racial Bias: A Question of Guilt and Brutality

In 1749, several white men assaulted a number of Canabas Indians.
During the attack, one Native American was killed and two were se-
verely wounded. Three white men were indicted for the crimes. The
first man who stood trial was acquitted. The court was so dissatisfied
with the verdict that a change of venue was ordered for the remaining defendants. These men, however, were never tried. "So strongly
seated was the feeling of resentment against the Indians, that no white
person, even in times of profound peace, could be convicted for killing one of them: it being found impossible to impanel a jury not
containing some members who had suffered from savage depreda-
tions, either in their persons, families, or estates."[6] The tendency to direct capital punishment toward outsiders did not end with statehood.
Among the last seven persons executed in Maine were one black man,
a Prussian immigrant, and two Italian immigrants.

The 1869 execution of a black man for the murder of two white
women was viewed by many Mainers as blatant racism.[7] The editor of
the *Daily Eastern Argus* wondered why Governor Chamberlain signed
Clifton Harris's death warrant on the very day he commuted the sentence of two white men who had been under a sentence of death for
twelve years. Harris had been under a sentence of death for less than
two years. The editor of the *Maine Farmer* questioned why Harris was
subjected to a barbarous punishment which—with the exception of a
single execution for the killing of a prison warden—had "slumbered
upon our statute book" for thirty years.[8] Maine's attorney general also

. . . .

spoke in opposition to Harris's execution. He questioned the ethics of executing Harris while the individual that likely carried out the killings (Luther J. Verrill) remained a free man. Verrill was initially found guilty of murder but his conviction was later overturned through appellate review.[9] Immediately following Harris's hanging, additional evidence was found that further supported Harris's claim that Verrill was actually the murderer.[10]

Six years after Harris's execution, the claim of innocence was raised again by Louis F. H. Wagner, a Prussian immigrant convicted of first-degree murder. Wagner's execution became one of Maine's most famous cases. Convicted of killing two women on a small island known as Smutty Nose, Wagner maintained his innocence until the end.[11] His assertion of innocence was widely accepted. Even the warden of the prison where he was executed expressed doubts concerning his guilt: "I have tried to shift the matter and come to see some other conclusion, but I cannot rid myself of the conviction that he is innocent."[12] Wagner's fate was immortalized in the poetry of Edna St. Vincent Millay. In the early 1920s, Millay used the supposedly wrongful conviction of Wagner in an attempt to save two Italian immigrants, Sacco and Vanzetti, from the gallows in Massachusetts.[13]

Problems associated with executions in Maine did not end with racial bias and claims of innocence. Published accounts of nearly every execution that took place after 1820 told extremely graphic and gruesome tales of human torture. Selective accounts of executions badly carried out no doubt exist in every state. In Maine, however, the majority of hangings were botched. Newspaper accounts of the executions of John True Gordon and Daniel Wilkinson were especially troubling.[14] John True Gordon, who was executed beside Wagner in 1875, attempted to stab himself to death in his cell immediately before being led to the gallows. Since he was not yet dead, Gordon's cut, bleeding, barely conscious body was carried to the gallows where he was held over the trap door and hanged. Seventeen reporters witnessed the executions.[15] Before the trap door opened, one of those observers reported Wagner looking down on Gordon: "Miserable looking wretch, the ghastly face with the bright sun showing up the hideousness, the deep groans, the bloody, limp form held by the officers and said, 'poor Gordon, you are almost gone.'"[16] Accounts of the execution of Gordon and Wagner were promptly published in most of Maine's daily and weekly newspapers.

The final days of Daniel Wilkinson, who was executed in 1885, were chronicled by an industrious reporter: "Hangings were big news and the reporter pulled all the stops in creating a sort of *you were there* routine for the readers."[17] In the end, the reporter filed a word-by-word proceeding of Wilkinson's execution that was published in daily and weekly newspapers across Maine:

> Three minutes after falling, his pulse was 96, four minutes after, 84. In five minutes the heartbeats were unsteady and scarcely distinguishable, at five and one-half minutes, the pulse was 72, and very irregular; at six and one-half minutes the pulse was barely felt at the wrist beating perhaps at 43. At 13 minutes the heart was beating at the rate of 20; and at 15 minutes it had ceased to beat.[18]

Apparently the hangman had bungled the job.[19] Mainers struggled with the same injustices that plagued states where executions were more common: racial bias, possible innocence, and brutality.

Abolition, Reinstatement, and Re-Abolition of the Death Penalty

Formal efforts to end executions in Maine are as old as the state of Maine itself. Petitions to end executions were presented to the state's first legislature by members of Maine's Quaker community.[20] In 1835, Senator Joseph R. Abbot of Bassalboro, with the support of the Society of Friends, submitted a legislative document calling for the abolition of capital punishment. Morality, lack of deterrence, judicial error, and the bias of jurors against the accused were cited as reasons for abolition.[21]

In 1835 and 1836, legislative committees appointed to study the feasibility of abolishing capital punishment issued reports supporting abolition. The first report challenged the notion that Christian scripture required the execution of murderers, noting that some of the greatest human tragedies had taken place in man's mistaken zeal in following God's law: "Even our puritanical fathers to whom we are so deeply

. . . .

indebted for the valuable religious and political institutions we enjoy, could argue themselves into believing that the Scriptures enjoined it upon them as a duty to extirpate heresy, by taking the life of the heretic."[22] The report went on to argue that governments do not have the right to take life unless "public safety demands it"; deterrence does not allow societies to prevent people from offending "by any means"; innocent persons can be executed; and capital punishment decreases the chances of convicting guilty persons. Harsh and inhumane punishments, according to the authors of the report, "contribute largely . . . to the formation of that savage and ferocious character which prepares men for the commission of the most shocking and atrocious crimes."[23] In 1836, Tobias Purrington, one of Maine's most famous and articulate supporters of death penalty abolition, authored a *Report on Capital Punishment.* Building on the previous legislative study, the Purrington report reasoned that:

1. Determinism in human behavior rendered executions useless;
2. "[M]an has no right to think of inflicting vengeance";
3. The sole purpose of punishment is deterrence;
4. Prisons do allow government to protect society without executions;
5. Promptness and certainty are more important than severity in deterring crime;
6. Milder punishments reduce the barbarous tendencies of individuals while harsher punishments stimulate disrespect for government; and
7. The death penalty had been successfully abolished in the past.[24]

Attached to the 1852 edition of Purrington's legislative report were messages from Michigan and the Boston Prison Discipline Society. According to Michigan's secretary of state, death penalty abolition had not increased the number of homicides. According to the Boston Prison Discipline Society's report, severity of punishment had little to do with levels of crime: "Massachusetts where seven crimes are punished with death, is no more secure in person and life, than Pennsylvania, where only one, and New Hampshire, where only two crimes are punished with death."[25] Thus, by the mid-nineteenth century, the no-tions of Enlightenment thinkers, practical experience, and scientific data had altered the taken-for-granted support of capital punishment among Maine's religious and political leaders. No executions were carried out between 1836 and 1868.

Ending the Informal Moratorium on Hangings and Eventual Abolition

The threats and actions of Governor Chamberlain during the 1860s turned the largely philosophical debate over the morality and efficacy of the death penalty into a practical problem. In January 1868, Chamberlain informed legislators that, unless they formally abolished the death penalty, he was going to begin signing death warrants:

> Nothing can be more plain than that the law contemplates the death penalty as the extreme punishment. It declares even the method, and requires the judge to pronounce the awful sentence, but leaves a weak place in providing for its execution by which a Governor, if so disposed, can shirk a painful duty. It begins a tragedy and ends a farce. . . . I . . . shall either see that the law is duly executed or shall interpose the Executive prerogative of commuting the sentence to imprisonment for life.[26]

Chamberlain wasted little time carrying out his threat. He signed Clifton Harris's death warrant in 1869. Senator John Stevens responded by introducing a bill to abolish capital punishment. In remarks to the Senate Judiciary Committee, Stevens reminded legislators of the moral implications of the Harris hanging and recommended that if executions were to be continued that they be reserved for whites:

> Shall the conviction and sentence of Clifton Harris be the means of fully emancipating the people of the State from the delusions and mischief of the death penalty forever? . . . Let the hangman exercise his stern vengeance, which belongs to the Almighty alone, on some tough, gnarled, large-brained villain of Anglo-Saxon blood.[27]

Stevens ended his testimony before the Senate Judiciary Committee by stating that he had not heard demands from any sectors of society wanting to resume executions.[28] The senator's attempt to abolish capital punishment and thereby save Harris was unsuccessful. Stevens's bill died in the legislature and Harris died on the gallows. Six years later, Louis Wagner and John Gordon were hanged. The words of Senator Stevens proved to be prophetic. In January 1876, the legislature of Maine, on the strength of a seventy-five to sixty-eight vote of the house and an eighteen to eleven vote of the senate, abolished capital punishment.[29] In the words of one observer:

> The strong minority opposed to the death penalty, had much to do with its non-enforcement from 1837 to 1867, and the enforcement of the law from the latter date until 1876 had more to do with its abolition; since the executions during this period awakened discussion and debate upon the subject.[30]

Reestablishing and Re-Abolishing the Death Penalty

Maine's association with the gallows did not end in 1876, however. Less than ten years following abolition (1883), the governor reported that an unusually high number of "cold blooded murders" had taken place in Maine over the past two years. The death penalty was immediately reestablished. Records suggest that there was little opposition to reinstatement.[31] The 1883 reinstatement bill allowed three additional executions to take place in Maine—two in 1885 and one in 1887. As was the case in 1876, these hangings were instrumental in undoing capital punishment in Maine. The brutality of the 1885 and 1887 executions were painfully described in newspapers across the state.

In addition to the brutality, hangings did not prove to deter murders.[32] The words of Maine's attorney general succinctly described the effect that reestablishing capital punishment had on Maine's murder rate:

> If there is any argument to be deduced from [these data], to my mind it sustains the position that when a person commits the crime of homicide, either premeditated or in the heat of passion, and especially as the result of an attempt to commit another crime, the question of the results of such acts is but little thought of, and the murderer little expects being brought to justice and sentenced when the crime is committed.[33]

Thus, in 1887, the death penalty was once again abolished in Maine. "Republicans, some Democrats, farmers, merchants, lawyers, Congregationalists, Universalists, Methodists, Freewill Baptists, religious liberals, and Unitarians banded together to rid Maine of the death penalty."[34]

Death Penalty Dormancy, 1888–1972

For the years 1888 through 1972, we reviewed legislative records and newspaper articles found in the death penalty clipping files located in the Maine State Library, the *Blethen, Maine, Newspaper* library, and the *Bangor Daily News* library.[35] Legislative documents and thirty newspaper articles (four in favor and twenty-six opposed to capital punishment) offer insight into the dynamics of death penalty abolition in Maine during the last decade of the nineteenth century and most of the twentieth century. These data suggest that Mainers of this period were firmly opposed to reinstating the death penalty. Newspaper accounts of the small number of executions that took place in Maine during the nineteenth century undoubtedly influenced this sentiment.

At the turn of the twentieth century, pamphlets published by Maine's attorney general and the secretary of state noted that the sentiments of Maine residents were so strongly opposed to capital punishment that it could be safely assumed that it would never again be enacted in Maine.[36] While it was noted that Maine was one of only eight states that had formally abolished capital punishment, an article published in the *Portland Evening Express* argued: "It is doubtful if the Legislature of Maine can be prevailed upon to restore capital punishment. The sentiments of the greater number of the population is, or appears to be, distinctly against it."[37] Similar arguments were published again in the *Portland Evening Express* and in the *Portland Press Herald*.[38] Additionally, three of the four newspaper articles published between 1888 and 1972 that favored capital punishment acknowledged that public sentiment was not on their side.[39]

Available evidence suggests that the strength of anti–death penalty sentiments between 1888 and 1972 was nourished by an ongoing discussion of innocent persons being executed and of badly botched executions. Half (i.e., fifteen) of the death penalty articles found in the capital punishment clipping files with publication dates from 1888 through 1972 discussed the potential or actual execution of an innocent person and the brutality of hangings. The *Bangor Daily News* discussed the likelihood that Clifton Harris was wrongly executed.[40] The *Portland Sunday Telegram* concluded that three persons convicted of murder during Maine's initial period of abolition would have been wrongfully executed if capital punishment had been in effect between 1875 and 1887.[41] The *Portland Evening Express,* the *Portland Sunday Telegram,* and the *Portland Press Herald* discussed the possibility that Louis Wagner was wrongly executed.[42] The horrid executions of John Gordon and Daniel Wilkinson were reviewed in the *Portland Sunday Telegram* and the *Portland Press Herald.*[43] Any attempt to reestablish capital punishment in Maine would have to neutralize a history of wrongful, inhuman, and brutal executions.

The forces of history, however, were not strong enough to prevent two death bills from being introduced in Maine's legislature between 1888 and 1972. The first bill was introduced in 1925. No legislative action was taken on the bill. The second attempt to reinstate the death penalty occurred during the 1937–38 legislative session. This bill was motivated by some particularly brutal murders that took place in South Paris, Maine. However, the 1937–38 bill met the same fate as the 1925–26 bill. Editorials written at the time expressed unenthusiastic reactions to the bill. The *Portland Evening Express* reacted negatively to a *Boston Post* editorial reasoning that the South Paris murders required the establishment of capital punishment in Maine by pointing out that murders increased rather than decreased when Maine first attempted reinstating capital punishment in the nineteenth century.[44]

Early attempts to bring back capital punishment brought to the surface an additional factor that has reinforced death penalty abolition in Maine, a relatively low murder rate. In the words of a journalist in the 1930s, "We know that the homicide rate in Maine is much lower than the average throughout the country or in states where the death penalty prevails. We know that it has been no higher in Maine since we abolished the death penalty some fifty years ago than before."[45] Similar statements were published in 1937 in the *Portland Evening Express* and the *Portland Press Herald,* and in 1971 by the *Portland Press Herald.*[46] In all likelihood, attempts to reestablish capital punishment would have had more impact if more homicides had taken place in the state.

Beginning the Reinstatement Debate, 1973–1984

A bill to reinstate capital punishment in Maine was introduced in the 1973–74 legislative session—the first legislative attempt to reinstate capital punishment in thirty-five years. Seventeen legislative sessions had passed without a single death penalty bill. The 1973–74 death bill began a trend in Maine politics. Capital punishment legislation was introduced, debated, and defeated during the 1975–76, 1977–78, and 1979–80 sessions. A citizens' initiative petition calling for the reinstatement of capital punishment was introduced in 1980.

The revival of Maine's death penalty debate was no doubt stimulated by events outside Maine. A *Portland Press Herald* article noted that legislatures across the country were debating capital punishment, "even in Michigan which abolished capital punishment in 1846. . . . Air hijackings and sensational murders like the Manson case in California also are involved in the shift of public attitudes, which two years ago opposed capital punishment."[47] Maine, however, did not reestablish capital punishment during the 1970s and early 1980s. In addition to Maine's history of wrongful executions and the low murder rate, the pervasive sentiment among the political, religious, and media elites was that the death penalty was unnecessary, irreversible, inhumane, and racist.

The strength of the anti–death penalty sentiment among legislators was evident in the manner in which the 1973 death penalty bill was introduced, debated, and defeated. It called for the execution of persons that kill law enforcement officers. The sponsor of HB 979, Democratic Representative Fecteau, rather than actively endorsing his own legislation, disavowed any personal support for reestablishing capital punishment.[48] According to Representative Fecteau, HB 979 was introduced solely as a courtesy to a group of high school students residing in his district. There is, however, a more compelling explanation for Fecteau's decision to introduce his death penalty bill "by re-

. . . .

quest"—an unwillingness on his part to challenge openly a dominant political sentiment of his legislative colleagues.

Representative Fecteau was well advised to respect the pervasiveness and depth of anti–death penalty sentiments among Maine's legislators. Of the twenty-one representatives who participated in the debate that preceded the vote on HB 979, only two representatives spoke on the side of capital punishment. After Fecteau's testimony, one anti-death legislator openly accused him of attempting to conceal his personal support for reinstatement by falsely contending that the bill was introduced by request. One death penalty supporter in the Maine house of representatives alleged:

> [In s]ome of the southern states that do have it [capital punishment], the proof is in the pudding. You see how many bank robberies they have in Georgia, and I think you will find that there [aren't] any, . . . but people from Georgia have gone to New York and New Jersey and Connecticut and rob[bed] banks. . . . Georgia strings a rope around their necks and drops the scalpel and this is a deterrent.[49]

The limited support capital punishment did receive during the debate tended to reinforce the negative, stereotypically Southern images that Maine legislators had of those favoring capital punishment. In the end, HB 979 was defeated ninety-four to forty-two, and without debate the senate rejected the bill nineteen to five.[50]

Support for capital punishment was equally wanting outside the legislature. Not a single newspaper article or editorial in the clipping files between 1973 and 1974 favored death penalty reinstatement. On the other hand, the *Portland Press Herald* reminded Maine residents of Gordon, Wagner, and Wilkinson.[51] The same article reported that the sponsor of HB 979, a Baptist radio evangelist, and a number of high school students were the only persons who testified during a public hearing. During that hearing Representative Fecteau once again stated that he was personally opposed to capital punishment, and that he had introduced the bill merely as a courtesy to the students who were about to testify before the committee.

In 1974, capital punishment was once again brought before Maine legislators. The bill would have allowed Mainers to vote on the desirability of reinstating capital punishment. According to death penalty advocates, shifting the death penalty debate from a legislative to a referendum issue increased the chances of reestablishing capital punishment. Pro-death forces reasoned that a larger number of Maine's legislators would support a referendum on the death penalty than would vote in favor of actually reestablishing capital punishment; and that if given a chance, the people of Maine would vote to reestablish capital punishment. The first assumption was correct. The 1974 bill authorizing a referendum on the death penalty lost by only a seven-vote margin in the house of representatives.[52] Thus, the second assumption was not tested. Nevertheless, an editorial in the *Kennebec Journal* expressed shock to see only seven votes separating those favoring from those opposing reestablishment of the death penalty.[53] Thereafter, the referendum became an ongoing strategy of reinstatement efforts in Maine. The belief that Mainers would support reinstatement at the ballot box has motivated advocates and opponents of the death penalty into the twenty-first century.

The Laffin Years

Attempts to reinstate capital punishment occurred in the 1975–76, 1977–78, and 1979–80 legislative sessions. All three bills had the same legislative sponsor, Republican Representative Stanley "Tuffy" Laffin. Unlike the sponsor of the 1973–74 death penalty bill, Laffin said he did not care what his fellow legislators thought of him.[54] Without Laffin, it is unlikely that capital punishment would have been a persistent legislative issue in Maine during the 1970s. In the words of a *Kennebec Journal* reporter: "[Laffin] is hardly known in legislative halls for anything but his single-minded devotion to getting a death penalty law in Maine. The issue remains in the news thanks to . . . [him], and vice versa."[55] According to the *Bangor Daily News*, "We are not under great pressure from the people to enact this bill. If the sponsor wasn't here, it wouldn't have the death penalty."[56]

In a 1975 press conference, Laffin suggested that those who disagreed with his pro-death perspective were in favor of "cop killers. . . . Cop killers are not wanted in Maine."[57] The following day, Laffin responded—with an equally disparaging insinuation—to a motion to postpone indefinitely his bill: "I am sure that nobody endorses cop killers in this legislature. I am hoping they don't."[58] Later that year he repeated one of his most memorable statements in a house debate: "[T]his country was founded on capital punishment: the West was settled on capital punishment, and the day that we restore capital punishment in Maine, it will be our finest hour. And I want those words to go back to the . . . newspapers of this state."[59] At a 1977 hearing on his death penalty bill, "Laffin made an emotional presentation in favor of his bill, charging at one point that many persons at the hearing in opposition to his bill also supported abortion. 'And that's murder,' he shouted, waving his arm at the committee."[60] In 1978, Laffin informed other house members that "the streets of Maine are nothing more now than a shooting gallery."[61] To end the violence, he stated that he was "willing to pull the first switch."[62]

Juvenile murderers, Laffin reasoned, were "a nuisance to society. We'd be better off if we got rid of them anyway."[63] Laffin was unconcerned with the possibility that Maine might administer capital punishment in a biased fashion or that Maine might execute an innocent person: "We are not talking about poor people being railroaded, we are not talking about black people being railroaded, we are talking about justice and equality for the living people; that is what we are talking about."[64] "Not one innocent person has ever been sent to death. . . . [D]oes [anyone] really and truly believe, . . . that the people of Maine, that the judicial system that we live under, would allow an innocent person to be put to death in 1977?"[65] Commenting on the cost of keeping convicted murderers in prison, he reasoned: "I would rather spend it [money] on an unwed mother with five children than housing a convicted murderer."[66] Thus, the primary proponent of capital punishment often reinforced the notion, inside of and outside of the legislature, that capital punishment and its advocates were inhumane and biased.

Newspapers did more to harm reinstatement efforts than simply broadcast Laffin's hyperbole. In the years 1973 through 1984, the print media were nearly single-minded in their opposition to reestablishing the death penalty in Maine. A substantial proportion of their efforts noted errors in Laffin's assertions. We could identify only four newspaper publications in the clipping files, published between January 1975 and December 1980, which supported reestablishing capital punishment in Maine. On the other hand, seventy anti–death penalty articles and editorials were identified during that period. Twenty-nine of these publications belittled Laffin's statements.

An editorial in the *Portland Press Herald* noted that "the mere idea of executing a human being is something unpleasant to contemplate. The suggestion that there is something so glorious about enacting a death penalty as to provide a state its finest hour is repugnant."[67] Commenting on Laffin's cavalier attitude toward racial bias, an editorial in the *Portland Press Herald* printed a George Wallace quote: "There are a lot of bad white folks and a lot of bad black folks who ought to be electrocuted."[68] The editorial went on to express "worry and fascination" with Wallace's and Laffin's enthusiasm with executions: "The difference between George Wallace and Stanley Laffin is that the former wants to be president."[69] Journalists seemed never to tire of informing the public that a police officer had not been murdered in Maine for fifteen years.[70] The *Portland Press Herald* pointed out that Laffin was wrong when he said murder was growing more prevalent in Maine.[71] In the words of a *Kennebec Journal* article,[72] Laffin, in an "emotional, shouting, finger-jabbing speech[, argued that] the streets are nothing more than a shooting gallery. [Yet] state police statistics indicate that murder is not on the rise in Maine, but has held steady at around 30 annually for the last few years." The newspapers continued to keep early Maine executions in the public eye. The history of wrongful executions in Maine was reviewed in twelve articles published between 1975 and 1980.

How Successful Was Laffin as a Death Penalty Legislator?

If one examines the legislative record of the 1975–76, 1977–78, and 1979–80 bills, it appears that legislative support for reinstating capital punishment increased significantly from 1975 to 1980. The Committee on Judiciary voted eleven to two to report out the 1975–76 bill with an "ought not pass" recommendation.[73] The full house voted ninety-two to thirty-seven to postpone the bill indefinitely.[74] The senate did not debate the issue. During the 1977–78 legislative session, the Committee on Judiciary voted twelve to one in favor of reporting out Laffin's death penalty bill with an "ought not pass" recommendation.[75] The vote in the house of representatives to accept the "ought not pass" recommendation, however, was somewhat less lopsided than in the previous session: eighty-seven representatives voted in favor and forty-four representatives voted against indefinite postponement.[76] The senate voted seventeen to eleven against the 1977–78 death penalty bill.[77]

The 1979–80 death penalty bill was once again reported out of committee with an "ought not pass" recommendation. However, this time the committee vote was considerably closer than the two previous legislative sessions, with eight "ought not pass" and five "ought to pass" recommendations.[78] The vote of the full house on the "ought not pass" recommendation narrowed once again in a vote of eighty-one to sixty-one.[79] The senate vote remained nearly the same, sixteen to twelve.[80] Some members of the legislature believed that capital punishment was gaining strength. Laffin told a *Kennebec Journal* reporter that in the past he had to seek out representatives to co-sponsor his capital punishment bills. This year, "legislators are coming to him."[81] Before the Maine legislature took up the death penalty debate in 1979, the cochairs of the Joint Committee on Judiciary reasoned that the death penalty could be reinstated during the 1979–80 legislative term.[82]

The 1977–78 and 1979–80 house votes on the death penalty overstated the emerging strength of death penalty advocacy among Maine legislators. The 1977–78 and 1979–80 bills were relatively more successful because the bills contained a referendum. In short, a belief in the referendum process rather than changing death penalty sentiments accounted for increased legislative support for the bills. Representatives willing to speak in favor of reestablishing capital punishment did not increase their numbers significantly between 1975 and 1979. Of the eleven representatives who participated in the 1975–76 house debate on capital punishment, Laffin and one additional representative spoke in favor, while eight others spoke in opposition.[83] Among the eleven representatives who spoke during the 1977–78 house debate, Laffin and two other representatives favored reinstating capital punishment, while five representatives spoke in opposition.[84] Ratios were strikingly similar during the 1979–80 debate.[85] The small and consistent number of representatives willing to publicly endorse capital punishment, in conjunction with the fact that the 1977–78 and 1979–80 death penalty debates took place in largely empty chambers, suggests that support for capital punishment in the house increased little during the Laffin years. Circumstances were similar in the senate. The 1975–76 and 1979–80 death penalty bills were rejected by the senate without debate.[86] Of the four senators who testified during the 1977–78 debate, only one was openly in favor of reinstating capital punishment.[87]

Only two officials voiced support for any of Laffin's efforts to reinstate capital punishment. The support capital punishment received from Governor Langley during the 1977–78 legislative session was limited to a single statement that capital punishment might deter drug pushers.[88] During the same legislative session, the secretary of state openly embraced capital punishment as a political strategy against Attorney General Brennan, a vocal proponent of death penalty abolition. Both men were seeking the Democratic party's nomination for governor.[89] In the end, Brennan was elected governor. As governor, Brennan continued his opposition to capital punishment. He openly threatened to veto the 1979–80 bill if it passed the legislature.[90]

Tuffy Laffin's legislative career was succinctly summarized by one of his legislative colleagues:

> People would say that Tuffy is off-the-wall—he gets carried away. But he does say what the common man, the man with the lunch pail, is thinking. But he only had the ranting and raving to bring to the situation and not anything more sophisticated, nor any strategies for dealing with other members of the legislature or building coalitions to make something happen. He did not have the skills.[91]

Laffin and the Community

Laffin also found it difficult to gain organizational support for his death penalty measures outside government circles. Support for reinstating capital punishment among the clergy was limited to a single fundamentalist evangelist. Consequently, Laffin openly struggled to keep religion out of Maine's death penalty debate. Before the 1975

house vote on capital punishment, Laffin reminded legislators who opposed capital punishment on religious grounds that their churches did
not elect them: "You were elected by the people of the state to fulfill
the laws for the betterment of the people of this state. We have a separation of church and state."[92] Laffin even failed to secure the support
of Maine's Police Chiefs Association. Following the execution of Gary
Gilmore in Utah, the president of the association refused to comment
on the execution or capital punishment, noting that "I wouldn't touch
the topic with a 10-foot pole."[93] On January 31, 1979, the lack of organizational support for capital punishment was succinctly summarized
by Laffin himself in the *Bangor Daily News* when he said, "there are no
high Mucka-muck groups supporting us."[94]

Laffin's appeal to reinstate capital punishment was not as popular
among Mainers as several nonscientific polls had suggested.[95] Upon
the defeat of his 1979–80 death penalty bill, Laffin decided to take the
death penalty issue directly to the people in the form of a citizens'
initiative petition: "The real issue is whether or not the people of
Maine have the right to vote in a referendum on the death penalty."[96]
Laffin needed 37,046 signatures to get the issue on the ballot.[97] On
February 22, 1980, the *Portland Press Herald* reported that he fell 9,000
signatures short, and that capital punishment would not be an issue on
the next election ballot. Laffin blamed his defeat on technical issues
and lack of money.[98] Ten years later, the sponsor of the 1991–92 death
penalty bill would explain the failure of the citizens' referendum by
citing history: "[A]n innocent person was hanged. Thus it was difficult
to get people to sign the petition."[99] Other evidence suggests that
many Mainers simply did not want capital punishment to be reinstated
in their state. A statewide scientific telephone poll in 1979 found that
Mainers were evenly split on returning the death penalty.[100]

The Death Penalty after Laffin

Laffin was not reelected in 1980, and death penalty bills were not
introduced in the 1981–82 and 1983–84 legislative sessions. Newspaper articles and editorials show that the Maine press continued to ve-
hemently oppose the idea of reestablishing capital punishment in

Maine. Of the twenty-four articles and editorials found in the clipping files, nineteen opposed capital punishment and only two favored reinstatement. Five articles refreshed the public memory that innocent people could be convicted and that executions were simply uncivilized.[101] In the end, Laffin managed to make capital punishment a legislative issue in Maine for nearly a decade, but he failed to sway the political, religious, and media leaders of Maine. Even more unexpected was the fact that Laffin had little effect on the opinions of most Mainers. In short, Laffin failed as a "moral entrepreneur."

Death Penalty Activity, 1985–1994

The brutal murder of a young child revived the capital punishment debate in Maine during the 1985–86 legislative session. Death penalty bills were also introduced in the 1987–88, 1991–92, and 1993–94 legislative sessions. The legislative outcomes of these bills were strikingly similar. Each bill was reported out of the Joint Committee on Judiciary with a unanimous "ought not pass" recommendation and died without further legislative action. The 1991–92 and 1993–94 bills were also similar to earlier or pre–Laffin death penalty bills; they were introduced "by request." At a public hearing, Republican Senator Linda Brawn told committee members that she did not personally favor the death penalty but believed it was "worthy of debate." Even the person who asked Brawn to introduce the death penalty bill stopped short of endorsing the death penalty.[102] Republican Senator Charles Bagley, sponsor of the 1993–94 death penalty bill, likewise told legislators: "I do not support the death penalty, but I believe strongly in the democratic right my constituent has to submit the bill."[103] No legislator was willing to challenge the anti–death penalty sentiments of the legislature, to fill the vacuum left by Tuffy Laffin's departure.

Organized Opposition Grows

While records suggest that the 1985–86 death penalty bill died without debate, the same cannot be said about three later bills. The Judiciary Committee held public hearings on capital punishment in 1987, 1991, and 1993. These hearings partially account for the brief life span these bills enjoyed in the legislature. Nine citizens testified at the 1987 hearing on capital punishment. Seven witnesses testified in opposition to the bill. Only the bill's sponsor and the radio evangelist argued in favor of the bill. Among those opposing capital punishment were the executive director of the Maine ACLU; the president of the American Baptists; and representatives from the Catholic Diocese of Portland, the Maine Council of Churches, Amnesty International, and the Society of Friends.[104] The 1991 public hearing on the death penalty was similar to the Committee on Judiciary's 1987 hearing on the topic. Sixteen persons testified. Four persons testified in favor of capital punishment: the bill's sponsor, a private citizen, the evangelist, and a state representative who was a retired state trooper. Twelve organizational representatives spoke in opposition and eight groups sent letters of opposition to the committee. Noticeable additions to the opposition were representatives from the National Association of Social Workers, Maine's Psychiatric Association, and the Lewiston, Maine, Police Department.[105]

The 1993 Judiciary Committee hearing was even more lopsided. Sixteen people testified. All sixteen witnesses argued that the death penalty was barbaric and unchristian; that innocent persons are sometimes executed; that capital punishment discriminates against the poor, uneducated, and minorities; and that capital punishment does not deter.[106] The effect that anti-death witnesses had on the capital punishment debate during these years was succinctly summarized by a co-chair of the Committee on Judiciary: "I was quite impressed with the quality of testimony against the bill."[107] Comments by Representative Lebowitz, cosponsor of a 1988–89 death penalty bill, suggest that the size, organization, and sophistication of anti–death penalty forces deterred citizens from publicly supporting capital punishment legislation.

> Just to appear in front of a committee is threatening to some people. I think a lot of people who may have felt that this issue was something that they would have liked to see in statute were that type of person. Organized opposition to capital punishment is intimidating to those in favor of capital punishment and to members of the committee. They get

hordes of people to appear and it looked like everybody is opposed to a bill.[108]

Conservative Politics and the Death Penalty in Maine

To understand fully the success of anti–death penalty forces in Maine, one must also review the decisions and actions of Maine's most affluent conservative groups. In 1985, the Maine Republican party refused to take a position favoring a referendum on the death penalty. Before that decision was made, "Republican members of the Legislative Judiciary Committee had unanimously supported the idea of allowing a public referendum on the reinstatement of the death penalty, and the majority of the GOP caucus appeared ready to support the plan earlier."[109] In 1987, the Christian Civic League of Maine, probably the state's most active conservative political organization, did not have the death penalty on its political agenda. The group's executive director explained: "I think if you polled our membership you'd probably find a great many people support it, at least in certain situations. But it's never been discussed in any official way in our organization."[110] The sponsor of the 1992–93 death penalty bill explained that there was nothing in the Republican platform to bring back capital punishment: "Capital punishment is not a strong issue for Democrats or Republicans."[111]

Press Opposition Remains Strong

Finally, anti-death forces during the late 1980s and early 1990s benefited from a press that remained staunchly committed to death penalty abolition. Death penalty clipping files contained 110 newspaper articles and editorials published from 1985 through 1994. Thirty of those publications simply disseminated information concerning legislative bills, United States Supreme Court decisions, and executions. Seventy-eight of these publications opposed death penalty reinstatement. Only two publications endorsed reinstatement. The quotes in the next paragraph come from a series of editorials appearing in the *Portland Evening Express.*

On August 28, 1985, an editorial titled "Death: Getting to Be Routine" informed Mainers that the number of persons awaiting execution in America had grown to 1,540 inmates, 14 percent of whom were on death row in Texas:[112] "Earlier this month, the crush of scheduled executions got so heavy [there]—four in two days—that the director of the Texas Department of Corrections asked the courts to do a better job of coordinating the deaths."[113] On June 28, 1986, an editorial informed its readers that the United States Supreme Court was being asked to determine whether states could legally execute people who had grown insane while being held on death row.[114] The editorial reviewed the case of Florida death row inmate Alvin B. Ford, one of a dozen condemned persons who claimed they had grown insane while on death row. On February 25, 1987, an editorial complained that the United States Supreme Court was being asked to decide the fate of an Oklahoma death row inmate who was fifteen when he had committed his offense.[115] On April 14, 1987, the newspaper warned Mainers that executions in Texas and Florida had increased to the point of "butchery."[116] Later that year, the *Portland Evening Express* reported that murder rates were not declining in states that were executing the most, Texas and Florida.[117] Thus, reasoned the writer, the only justification for capital punishment was revenge: "Maine is not yet ready to trade off its own humanness for a barren policy of retribution from which there is no ultimate appeal and which renders error uncorrectable."[118] Some time later, an editorial wondered how Texas could execute a person with the mental development of a seven-year-old and the emotional maturity of a ten-year-old: "Perhaps [this case] can help refocus attention on the moral poverty of the death penalty. . . . As it is, it has little to recommend it. Used to snuff out the life of what is effectively a child-offender, it has nothing to recommend it whatsoever."[119] An editorial on May 21, 1990, informed Mainers that "in Florida, witnesses were horrified when the head of a convict caught fire, during an electrocution."[120] A month later, the newspaper lamented the expanding number of states carrying out executions: "It's been more than a century since Maine has executed anyone. The examples being set by Arkansas and other states today give us no reason to suspect that we were wrong to put a stop to the official bloodletting here."[121] On November 16 of the same year, the newspaper reported that Louisiana officials had asked the United States Supreme Court for permission to give death row inmates "mind-altering medicine" to make them sane enough to execute—"a gruesome exercise for a society that calls itself civilized."[122]

Conclusion: The Power of History

The class, ethnicity, and race of those persons executed in Maine demonstrate that the political will to execute cannot be disassociated from the public fear of "dangerous classes," even among states that have lengthy histories of death penalty abolition.[123] The selection and execution of Harris—a black man—in 1869 is illustrative of that association in nineteenth-century Maine. A member of Maine's house of representatives and an outspoken critic of capital punishment during the Laffin years believed that the interrelationship between xenophobia and the will to execute remained intact.

> Maine is the second or third whitest state in the country. So we don't have minority groups to stir up things—quite frankly. And if people were stereotyping—worried about the Willie Hortons of the world—it's conceivable there might be a little more energy to do it [bring back executions in Maine]. But there aren't symbolic classes that are getting out of hand. Nobody would say that, but . . . I suspect that if there were, Maine legislators might be more inclined to institute the death penalty.[124]

While stories of brutal and wrongful executions characterize the death penalty history of many abolitionist states, such tales have exerted a far greater influence on death penalty dynamics in Maine. For more than one hundred years, local newspapers have kept brutality and the possibility of error in the public's mind. The political consequences of that publicity have been considerable. The sponsor of a 1992–93 death penalty bill explained the tenacity of death penalty abolition in Maine succinctly: "Supposedly a person was executed and later it was found out that he was innocent. From that point on Maine has been reluctant to reestablish capital punishment."[125] According to a Bowdoin College sociologist, "the century-old story of how Maine abolished the death penalty after the execution of a man who was wrongly accused of murder has become a part of the state's folklore." That folklore may be why Maine has not reinstated capital punishment. "It is a powerful argument whether it is true or not."[126]

Similar to circumstances in Michigan and several contiguous New England states, the religious and political leadership in Maine began to question the morality and utility of capital punishment early in the nineteenth century.[127] The strength and pervasiveness of Enlightenment reforms and the anti-slavery, temperance, and anti-war ideology among Maine's religious and political elites provided the cultural authority necessary to abolish the death penalty. The transformation of Enlightenment ideology into pragmatic political change was facilitated by several nineteenth-century executions. Brutality, in the sense that innocent persons were executed, provided Maine legislators with the will to abolish capital punishment. Maine legislators abolished the death penalty a second time in 1887. They were moved by newspaper accounts of three executions and by practical experience. The number of murders increased the year after the death penalty was reestablished: Four people were murdered in 1882 and in 1883, and in 1884, the number of people murdered in Maine increased to thirteen.[128]

The effects of Enlightenment ideology did not end with death penalty abolition in 1887. The notion that capital punishment is inhumane, uncivilized, and unnecessary became the taken-for-granted doctrine among Maine's political and religious leadership throughout the twentieth century. In that respect, the abolitionist states of Maine and Michigan are remarkably similar. The strength of Enlightenment ideology accounts for 113 years of death penalty abolition in Maine and 154 years of abolition in Michigan.[129] At the end of the twentieth century, the Enlightenment ideology concerning the death penalty was largely the same as that espoused by the dominant educational, religious, and political institutions in both states. Newspapers in Michigan and Maine were instrumental in perpetuating and reinforcing anti–death penalty sentiments among their readers. The press in both states has tended to associate capital punishment with inhumanity, racism, and the Deep South. At the end of the twentieth century, however, the death penalty debate in Michigan differed in at least one significant way from the debate in Maine; Enlightenment ideology and death penalty abolition were considerably stronger in Maine.

During the early twentieth century, the evolving automotive manufacturing industry fundamentally altered Michigan society. Large numbers of people arrived from the South. Along with them came urbanization, high murder rates, population diversity, and a Southern perspective on capital punishment. Maine, on the other hand, remained largely unaffected by either industrialization or Southern migration. The homogeneous, rural, low-crime-rate environment that nurtured Enlightenment ideology and death penalty abolition in both states has remained relatively untouched in Maine. Strong anti–death penalty sentiments continued to dominate the religious and political scene in Maine through the last decades of the twentieth century. For thirty years, only one religious leader has spoken in favor of capital punishment at public hearings, an individual described by one representative as "a self-anointed preacher. He would read from the Old Testament. It was amazing[—]just one religious person."[130] Legislative support for capital punishment has been equally lacking. Of the seven capital punishment bills introduced in Maine's legislature between 1970 and 1993, three were introduced by Representative Laffin, who openly boasted that he did not care what his colleagues or the press thought of him,[131] and three were introduced "by request." In short, the sponsors of the 1973–74, 1991–92, and 1993–94 death penalty bills were unwilling to publicly support their own bills. The cochair of the Committee on Judiciary characterized the sponsor of the 1991–92 death penalty bill as "sheepish."[132] The legislative sponsor of the 1993–94 death penalty bill painfully summarizes his experiences as a death penalty advocate in Maine:

> I called the individual that requested the bill and asked if he still wanted to pursue the bill. He said that he did. I called him several times after that—informing him of the date and place of the hearing. At the same time I had reporters calling me, asking why I was doing this. At the hearing, I was the only one there who, supposedly, was on the side of the bill. The person that wanted the bill introduced did not come—and philosophically I was opposed to capital punishment. Probably 25

people were there representing various organizations opposed to capital punishment. It was a little embarrassing. After the hearing I must have heard from ten people who said they favored capital punishment, I asked them why they did not attend the hearing.[133]

At the end of the twentieth century, support for death penalty abolition remained strong among Mainers. Those opposed to capital punishment remained largely unchallenged among Maine's institutional elites. Legislators who did challenge the cultural authority of death penalty opposition suffered frustration, isolation, and embarrassment. Over the past fifty years, death penalty bills have been more numerous, more widely sponsored, and better supported in Michigan than in Maine.

In conclusion, death penalty abolition was accomplished in Maine through a number of structural and situational factors that coalesced during the nineteenth century. Enlightenment ideology, problematic executions, and population homogeneity remained key ingredients in the political and social processes that kept Maine free of capital punishment throughout the twentieth century. Death penalty abolition in Maine will likely be maintained into the foreseeable future. The sponsor of the 1993–94 death penalty bill voiced similar conclusions:

> The legislature at this time will not pass a capital punishment bill. There is not enough serious crime committed that would get the public excited about capital punishment. We don't have a major crime problem in this state. We are probably 48th or 49th in the country. We do not have the urban crimes you read about. We have our murders, mostly domestic crimes. I don't see anything in the next decade that would bring capital punishment back.[134]

Postscript

In 1999, a death penalty bill was introduced in Maine's house of representatives by a Republican legislator. The cosponsor of the bill was the wife of Maine's only state trooper killed in the line of duty. During a public hearing held by the legislative Judiciary Committee, the bill was strongly criticized by religious and peace groups. Anti–death penalty proponents sent state legislators over 2,000 emails outlining their opposition to reestablishment. The bill, which contained a referendum, had little chance of success. If by chance the bill would have passed both legislative houses, the governor had threatened a veto. Death penalty abolition appears secure in Maine.

CHAPTER 5

Abolition and Attempted Reinstatement in Minnesota, 1911–1923

The Progressive Era in America was a period of numerous legal reforms, including the abolition of capital punishment. During this period, ten U.S. states abolished the death penalty (Arizona, Washington, Oregon, Colorado, Kansas, Tennessee, Missouri, South Dakota, North Dakota, and Minnesota), but only North Dakota and Minnesota failed to quickly reinstate this punishment.[1] After abolishing the death penalty in 1911, succeeding generations of Minnesota legislators have maintained that ban for over ninety years. Fear of crime, social disorder, and lynching—while moving most Progressive Era abolitionist states to reestablish capital punishment—has been unable to alter Minnesota's anti-death history. Changing demographics, economic circumstances, and evolving cultural traditions in Minnesota, as in other Northern Central abolitionist states (Wisconsin, Michigan, North Dakota, and Iowa), work to negate pro-death sentiment among Minnesota's legislators.

Executions in Minnesota

When Minnesota entered the Union in 1858, state and federal authorities, along with numerous private citizens, were actively waging war on the lives and property of the indigenous peoples of Minnesota. The plight of the Santee Sioux provides a particularly gruesome example. Two deceptive treaties cost the Santee 90 percent of their territory. Traders and government reservation agents cheated them out of the rest.[2] As if all that were not enough, Governor Ramsey (a former agent for the Santee reservation) told white Minnesotans: "The Sioux

Indians must be exterminated or driven beyond the borders of the state."[3] Conditions for Santee Sioux people did not improve after their 1862 uprising; the following year Minnesota began paying $25 for Sioux scalps.[4] The Minnesota settler who shot the leader of the uprising, Little Crow, received the regular bounty plus $500 for Little Crow's scalp. Between 1680 and 1911, records show that sixty-six executions were carried out in the geographic territory now known as Minnesota.[5] Among the states whose legislatures have abolished capital punishment, only West Virginia has carried out more executions.

Of the executions attributed to Minnesota, forty were carried out under the authority of the federal government. Twenty-six were carried out under state authority. All persons executed under federal authority were Native Americans. One of the persons executed under state authority was black; the remaining were white. All forty Native Americans were executed between 1862 and 1863. On December 26, 1862, the largest known mass execution in U.S. history took place outside Mankato, Minnesota.[6] On that day at "[a]bout ten o'clock, the thirty-eight condemned men were marched from the prison to the scaffold. They sang the Sioux death song until soldiers pulled white caps over their heads and placed nooses around their necks. At a signal from an army officer, the control rope was cut and thirty-eight Santee Sioux dangled lifeless in the air."[7] If it were not for the intervention of President Lincoln, 303 Santee Sioux would have been hanged that day.

Evidence suggests that the prime motivation for the hangings was to satisfy the hatred of white settlers. Evidence of individual guilt was all but nonexistent at the military trials.[8] Preceding the executions, two attempts were made by Minnesotans to lynch Santee prisoners. "Governor Ramsey demanded authority from the President to order speedy executions of the 303 condemned men, and warned that the people of Minnesota would take 'private revenge' on the prisoners if Lincoln did not act quickly."[9] At the hangings three thousand Minnesotans cheered as thirty-eight Santee Sioux fell to their deaths.[10] The last Native Americans executed in Minnesota were Shakopee and Medicine Bottle, two Santee Sioux leaders. In December 1863, the Minnesota militia kidnapped both in Canada. As did the executions of 1862, their hangings had little to do with guilt or innocence. According to the St. Paul *Pioneer:* "We do not believe that serious injustice will be done by the executions tomorrow, but it would have been more creditable if some tangible evidence of their guilt had been obtained. . . . No white man, tried before a jury of his peers, would be executed upon the testimony thus produced."[11]

Executions directly under Minnesota state authority were less numerous and less dramatic. Executions occurred on a relatively consistent basis through the latter part of the nineteenth century and early twentieth century. For example, one execution occurred in 1901, 1903, 1904, 1905, and 1906. The 1906 execution of William Williams was to be Minnesota's last. Williams was convicted of killing a boy and his mother. Inflammatory news accounts of the killings, "complete with denunciations of a suspected 'unnatural relationship' between the murderer and the boy," were pervasive.[12] It the end, however, the execution of twenty-eight-year-old William Williams provided anti–death penalty advocates in Minnesota with the final measure of momentum necessary to abolish capital punishment.

Original Abolition

Minnesotans were uneasy with the death penalty long before they abolished it. In the 1860s, fences were built around the state's gallows to remove executions from public view.[13] Perhaps in part as an outgrowth of the mass public hanging in Mankato, in the 1880s the Minnesota legislature passed a law requiring that executions be carried out behind prison walls during the very early hours of the morning.[14] The midnight assassination law—as the newspapers of the day labeled it— also prohibited press coverage of executions. Nevertheless, journalists generally found ways to circumvent the law and report the gruesome details of a hanging. One enterprising writer went so far as to disguise himself as a priest. During the 1906 execution, the weight of Williams's body stretched the rope to the point where his toes touched the ground. It took nearly fifteen minutes for him to die of strangulation. In spite of the legal prohibition against it, newspapers published grisly accounts of the ordeal.[15] The press was prosecuted and convicted; however, the judge imposed only a token fine.

Minnesota's governor reacted to newspaper accounts by launching an investigation into the botched hanging. He threatened to resign rather than preside over another execution. He also announced that he would recommend abolition of the death penalty to the next session of the state legislature.[16] This began a six-year movement to abolish capital punishment. Republican Representative George MacKenzie from Gaylord became the leading advocate of abolition among legislators. Representative MacKenzie, along with other legislators, supported unsuccessful abolition bills in 1905 and 1909. On his third attempt in 1911, MacKenzie gave a speech in support of abolition that journalists of the day labeled "the most eloquent anti–death penalty speech ever given in the House chamber."[17] "Let us bar this thing of vengeance and the furies from the confines of our great state. Let not this harlot of judicial murder smear the pages of our history with her bloody fingers, or trail her crimson robes through our halls of justice, and let never again the great seal of the great state of Minnesota be affixed upon a warrant to take a human life."[18] Representatives applauded MacKenzie's effort and voted overwhelmingly in favor of the bill HF 2 to abolish capital punishment, with ninety-five in favor and nineteen opposed. Not long after, the senate likewise voted to abolish capital punishment, with thirty-five in favor and nineteen opposed. Governor Adolph O. Eberhart signed the bill into law.[19]

Reinstatement Efforts

Newspaper accounts and legislative records reveal that only three notable legislative efforts in 1913, 1921, and 1923 to reinstate capital punishment have taken place since Minnesota abolished capital punishment during the Progressive Era. Since 1923, death penalty bills either have died in a house or senate committee or have been returned to their author.

Adjusting to Abolition, 1912–1913

During the months preceding the first serious legislative threat to death penalty abolition, a number of murders were reported in the

. . . .

Minneapolis Morning Tribune. Evidence suggests, however, that these crimes had little to do with the 1913 reestablishment effort. Murders described in newspaper accounts tended to be domestic homicides, crimes where the offender killed a family member or a lover. One such crime involved a university professor who fatally wounded another man. According to his confession, he killed out of jealousy. He was unhappy that his wife had been receiving attention from this man.[20] During court proceedings, the professor remained calm, contending that an "unwritten law" allowed him to shoot the man.[21] In another case a man shot and killed a woman after she refused to marry him. He had threatened to kill her and her family if she did not marry him after receiving a divorce from her husband.[22] "Domestic troubles" were also the cause of an attempted double homicide in Hastings, Minnesota. A man shot his wife and sister-in-law, then killed himself by slashing his throat with a razor.[23] Several additional murder-suicides were chronicled in the *Minneapolis Morning Tribune* during the latter half of 1912 and the early months of 1913. Such murders, however, did not seem to generate strong demands in the press for reinstating capital punishment. Many viewed such murders as quasi–private matters, and hence of little public concern. There were no discussions in the *Morning Tribune* of uncontrollable street crimes requiring capital punishment to protect the general community. Moreover, domestic murderers—as the volume of murder-suicides demonstrates—often imposed more severe punishment on themselves than allowed by law.

Early in 1913, the *Morning Tribune* reported that an innocent man had been lynched in Mississippi. According to the article, a mob wrongly killed a black man for the murder of a white woman. Later, in apparent recognition of its mistake, the same mob killed another black man for the same murder. The second man was chained to a post, covered with tar and straw, and burned alive.[24] The newspaper's disgust in describing these events was obvious.

On February 2, 1913, bill HF 416 reinstating the death penalty in certain cases was introduced in the house. HF 416 left the decision to impose the death penalty up to the jury.[25] On February 11, a senator from Minneapolis introduced capital punishment bill SF 336. It provided for the execution of an individual "who is already under a life sentence and who commits an assault upon anyone."[26] The bill also proposed altering the method of execution in Minnesota from hanging to the electric chair.[27] On March 8, 1913, the house ended the year's death penalty debate by narrowly defeating HF 416, with forty-nine in favor and fifty-one opposed.[28] The senate bill was never released from committee.

The Scourge of Banditry Emerges, 1920–1921

A June 27, 1920, article published in the *Morning Tribune* reviewed the confession of a man who admitted being a member of a trio of bandits reputed to have been involved in at least forty-two robberies.[29] The same issue of the *Morning Tribune* chronicled the holdup of the Great Northern State Bank in which over $10,000 was taken. The police commissioner and the chief of police contended that the people who committed the crime were part of a crime cabal from New York and other Eastern cities who planned to start a "wave of organized crime" in St. Paul.[30] Thirty-nine additional police officers were assigned to duty in the city.

On September 4, 1920, an article described a "wave of holdups in St. Paul causing widespread indignation and apprehension in all parts of the city."[31] Among the many citizens calling for "drastic measures" was a judge who endorsed capital punishment for holdup men "whether they shoot or not."[32] A state representative said that he was proud to be one of the few who had voted against the abolition of capital punishment and would continue to fight to reinstate it. Another judge in favor of these drastic steps said that "the deterrent effect of the law seems to have been lost to some people since the war but it can readily be brought back by capital punishment and life sentences."[33] On November 10, 1920, a series of articles began on what the *Morning Tribune* labeled the "kerchief bandits."[34] According to these articles, two bandits—their faces covered with silk handkerchiefs—"for more than two weeks . . . carried out a program of banditry unparalleled in Minneapolis."[35] It was reported in the *Morning Tribune* that there was "considerable talk among legislators" regarding the return of capital punishment in the state.[36] Yet Governor Burnquist was not enthusiastic about capital punishment. He recommended that a thorough investigation be conducted to determine if murder was, indeed, less frequent in states that employed the death penalty. He also called for "a compilation of figures in Minnesota to show whether there has been an increase in the number of murders since capital punishment was abolished."[37]

On October 25, 1920, the Ramsey County delegation to the state legislature met to consider "laws to stem the tide of crime and the reestablishment of capital punishment."[38] Their meeting to "halt [the] wave of crime . . . had been prompted . . . after [they] had been convinced that there [was] a popular demand for more adequate legislation to ensure the safety of citizens."[39] A grand jury, charged with ascertaining, "if possible, what measures might be suggested to assist in preventing crime and apprehending criminals," held that "unsettled industrial conditions, [and] reactions from the war" were responsible for the crime wave.[40] A national crime wave was now the state's problem.[41] To protect the citizens of Minnesota, the grand jury also recommended "that capital punishment be restored as an optional penalty, to be imposed by the jury, for murder in the first degree."[42]

On January 14, 1921, the *Morning Tribune* reported that a capital punishment bill introduced in the house had the endorsement of the mayor of Minneapolis.[43] On January 22, the State Association of County Attorneys adopted a resolution urging the state legislature to restore capital punishment.[44] At the third annual conference of the state's mayors in Minneapolis on February 8, 1921, the officials attending the meeting visited the state legislature to urge the return of the death penalty.[45] At this point the return of capital punishment seemed imminent.

Lynching and Community Response

In Duluth, Minnesota, on June 16, 1920, three black men were lynched for allegedly assaulting a seventeen-year-old white female. The mob stormed the police station where the victims and three other black suspects were being held.[46] One mob participant blamed the impending lynchings on state government: "We don't have no electric chair or hanging in Minnesota. . . . Then what happens to the niggers?"[47] As was the case with the 1862 hanging of the Santee Sioux some decades earlier, individual guilt or innocence was not the central concern.[48] Thirty minutes after the mob gained access to the six black men, three had been lynched. Between five thousand and ten thousand onlookers, or approximately one tenth of Duluth's citizens, witnessed the event.[49] To help restore order, two companies of the state national guard from Fort Snelling were immediately called out by Governor Burnquist.[50] The governor announced that leaders of the mob would be charged with "inciting to riot" and requested a military investigation of the police in Duluth.[51] The governor wanted to determine why police discipline had broken down and why the rioters met with so little resistance.[52]

Several local judges and the county attorney called for an immediate session of the grand jury to investigate the incident.[53] The Duluth Kiwanis Club demanded the punishment of mob leaders. Community leaders deplored the actions of the men arrested for the assault on the young woman, but said that the city of Duluth had been "disgraced before the world, and every decent citizen has been made to hang his head in shame because of the horrible crime perpetrated by a mob of Duluth men."[54] They also "condemn[ed] the lawless mob . . . as disgraceful, barbarous and criminal, and denounc[ed] every individual who participated therein as unworthy of law and civilization to which they now look and have looked for protection."[55] The Fifth Ward Republican Club in Minneapolis also condemned "the members of the mob as criminals and demand[ed] the strictest investigation and the most stringent prosecution of the persons guilty of taking the law into their own hands" and held that the lynchings "besmirched" the name of Minnesota.[56]

The *Morning Tribune* noted that mob participants "brought disgrace upon this commonwealth [and action must be taken] to properly punish the leaders of the mob. . . . Constitutional authority has been overridden. . . . Restoration of authority and the supremacy of the law is of prime importance."[57] The *Minneapolis Journal* reasoned that "it was the color of the three prisoners that made them victims of the mob. Had they been white they might have been the objects of reprobation for the crime for which they were charged, but would have no doubt been left to the processes of the law."[58] In the week following the lynchings, negative editorial reactions were also published nationally. "In fact, the leading newspapers throughout the North vilified residents of Duluth for having stained their city's good name and castigated them for being no better than Southern racists."[59] The *New York Times*, the *Chicago Tribune*, and the *New York World* were especially critical.

District Court Judge W. A. Cant, who had convened the special grand jury that investigated the Duluth lynchings, declared "that the laws of God, of man, [had] been defiled, set at naught. In our midst, from this time forth the laws of God will be less sacred, life will be less safe, property [will] be less secure and humanity itself of every character [will] be held more cheaply. Instead of pressing constantly forward, we have taken a long step backward."[60] He called the Duluth killings "the most atrocious crime in all of [Duluth's] history."[61] Calling the assault of the seventeen-year-old woman "heinous," he still believed that they deserved full protection under the law. He characterized the acts of the mob leaders as unusual and excessively brutal.[62] He also asked that the jurors "let every one know that notwithstanding those incidents [Minnesota] has a citizenship which denounces such outrages and which will do its utmost to discover and punish the perpetrators."[63] Some time later, the county attorney concluded that two of the three men lynched were innocent of the crime for which they had been punished,[64] and it was ultimately determined that the third lynching victim was also innocent.[65]

Meanwhile, deputy sheriffs and others who were thought to know the identity of the mob leaders testified before the grand jury. The county attorney said that he did not care if it took "half the population," that they would question as many witnesses as necessary.[66] The grand jury was forced to postpone temporarily its investigation on June 19, 1920, amidst rumors that another mob was forming in Duluth. The governor called up more troops from Fort Snelling, and those guarding the suspects held in connection with the sexual assault were ordered to shoot if necessary to prevent additional lynchings.[67] The next day there was no sign of mob activity.[68]

A resolution presented to the county commissioners asked that Governor Burnquist offer "a substantial reward for evidence leading to the arrest and conviction of one or more participants in the disturbance."[69] The New York State branch of the NAACP offered Governor Burnquist its assistance in the apprehension of the mob leaders. (Burnquist was the president of the St. Paul branch of the NAACP.) The NAACP said it would do "anything in its power with its 328 branches and membership of 100,000 to help [track] down the lynchers."[70]

The *Morning Tribune* reported on June 26, 1920, that the authorities had six people implicated in the lynchings in custody.[71] Four days later, three members of the lynch mob were indicted and charged with first-degree murder, and the first conviction came approximately two months later.[72] Eighteen other persons were indicted on charges of rioting and faced second indictments of first-degree murder.[73] The assistant county attorney said that "Duluth's reputation for law and order [was] at stake."[74] The *Morning Tribune* reported that the conviction of rioting in connection with lynching was one of only a few in the history of the nation.[75] In the end, nineteen men were indicted.

With the Duluth lynching fresh in the minds of Minnesotans, the *Morning Tribune* published an editorial condemning Tulsa, Oklahoma, for a race riot that had occurred there. It called the mob rule, resulting after a black man allegedly assaulted a white woman, "inexcusable lawlessness." The editorial accused Tulsa of being "under a heavy shadow of disgrace, [and] made themselves criminals when they took things into their own hands and ran amuck with weapon and torch. Race riots never cure racial prejudices. They serve only to intensify them."[76] In a similar vein, a *Morning Tribune* editorial condemned the light sentence given a white planter who murdered a black sharecropper in Georgia.[77] Earlier, a *Morning Tribune* editorial criticized an episode of West Coast racism in which the white residents of the Pacific Coast were described as opposed to the negotiations between the Japanese and American governments: "Situated in the north central part of America, freed from the vexations of any particular race problem, it is rather difficult for us to enter sympathetically into the fears which our countrymen on the Pacific coast are voicing."[78]

. . . .

Divided Opinion and Ambivalence about Capital Punishment

After the lynchings and the convictions of the mob leaders, several editorials appeared in the *Morning Tribune* that were indecisive and ambivalent about capital punishment. The burgeoning street crime obviously pushed editorial opinion toward capital punishment; on the other hand, the decisive legal reaction of reinstatement did not seem necessary to prevent further lynching in Minnesota. One *Morning Tribune* editorial favored life in prison over capital punishment because abolition encouraged citizens to respect human life.[79] On December 3, 1921, however, another *Morning Tribune* editorial declared that "no punishment less than death should be meted out to the perpetrators of so horrible and unwarranted a crime [as murder]. If it is necessary to go back to the death penalty to prevent such crimes, so be it."[80] On March 1, 1921, yet another *Morning Tribune* editorial suggested that the state should either restore capital punishment or stop the practice of pardoning and paroling persons serving life sentences. The editorial reasoned that a sentence of irrevocable life imprisonment might do more to deter potential murderers than the death penalty. In addition, juries would be more likely to impose a sentence of life in prison rather than death.[81]

According to a March 1, 1921, editorial in the *Morning Tribune*, "one of the liveliest verbal skirmishes" in a series of open forum lunches and discussions held by the Civic and Commerce Association was the informal exchange between the Minneapolis mayor and a rural county attorney over capital punishment.[82] The mayor favored reinstating capital punishment as a crime control measure. The county attorney opposed reinstatement because it did not respect human life: "We cannot uproot Christianity and substitute brutality," he reasoned.[83]

On March 1, 1921, the press reported that a senate capital punishment bill "calling for capital punishment for murder in the first degree" was likely to die in committee.[84] The story recounted that a similar bill had already been killed. On March 4, 1921, the *Morning Tribune* observed that capital punishment was indeed dead.[85] The problems of criminal behavior, however, were yet to be solved. A March 21, 1921, *Morning Tribune* article titled "Crime Wave Taxes State Reformatory"

. . . .

89

reported that the state reformatory at St. Cloud was nearly filled to capacity.[86]

Robberies and Murders Continue, 1923

On January 3, 1923, police arrested a man for robbing four grocery stores and holding up several women. The arrest added to an ever-growing list of men accused of robbing pedestrians.[87] On January 14, a *Morning Tribune* article discussed a series of crimes in which a trio of bandits had robbed an office, a home, a dairy, as well as a grocery robbed twice in two hours.[88] One week later, it was reported that several bandits were arrested in connection with the robbery of a local bank[89] that resulted in the injury of bank employees.[90] On February 10, the *Morning Tribune* published a series of articles on the murder of a shop owner who was a war veteran and Shriner.[91] A crowd of four hundred turned out at the courthouse to get a glimpse of the shop owner's accused killers during the defendants' initial court appearance.[92]

Developing Press Support for Capital Punishment

In the midst of this violent lawlessness, a January 6, 1923, editorial published in the *Morning Tribune* stated that capital punishment was supported "by a very considerable share of formulated public opinion."[93] The editorial expressed belief in the deterrent effect of capital punishment and voiced support for the death penalty in cases where murders occur while offenders are committing other felonies, such as burglary: "There ought to be no quarter of tolerance for the further existence of the rational person who tops his lesser felony with the arch felony of murder."[94] An editorial on January 13, 1923, referred to the number of capital punishment bills before the legislature: "[T]he bill shower [indicates] that there has developed in the state a widespread sentiment in favor of more drastic punishment for some kinds of crimes, notably murder."[95] The editorial also specified that executions should be carried out behind prison walls. According to the editorial, open executions could stimulate outrage and violence among the viewing public; however, the "'brutalizing' nature of public hangings are reduced to an inappreciable minimum when executions are carried out in the quiet and seclusion of the state penitentiary."[96] On January 22, 1923, yet another *Morning Tribune* editorial discussed a bank robbery in which one of the suspects was a former police officer. The offender was out on parole after serving a year and a half in prison for an earlier offense.[97] The editorial pointed out that the bank robbery came on the heels of several capital punishment bills making their way through the legislature: "Bandits of this type are well aware that under existing laws the worst fate they invite is imprisonment for life, and that the chances are good, if they receive life sentences, of their being released after a few years in the name of penal reform."[98] In the final death penalty editorial published by the *Morning Tribune* during January 1923, the newspaper chastised those citizens of Minnesota opposed to capital punishment. It recognized that death penalty opponents in the state represented an important political force. A protest at the state capitol by those opposed to reinstating capital punishment was called ironic. The gist of the editorial can be summarized by the following excerpts: "On the subject of taking human life we Americans are the most sentimental and childish on the face of the earth. . . . As a race, we are indifferent to the taking of human life—except the murderer's life, the very mention of which may always be trusted to arouse a storm of indignant protest."[99] In response to this editorial position on reestablishing capital punishment, an anonymous letter to the editor criticized the newspaper's dramatic reversal on the issue.[100]

Community Opposition to the Ku Klux Klan, the South, and Lynching

The alarm expressed by journalists and political leaders over street crime was equaled by their overt revulsion for lynching and racial discrimination. On January 15, 1923, a newspaper article discussed the Minneapolis City Council's investigation into the activities of the local KKK. The heads of some city government departments were charged with being affiliated with the KKK. Reports suggested that the secret organization had been enlisting members in the police department and that KKK meetings had been held in the courthouse.[101] The mayor stated that any city employee would be forbidden from joining the KKK. As with the Duluth lynchings, public sentiment favored rooting out any shred of barbaric Southern culture.

Two editorials on lynching appeared in the *Morning Tribune* in January 1923. One editorial criticized the state of Texas for the volume of lynchings that had occurred in the state—eighteen in one year.[102] The editorial read in part that "Texas has taken one pennant for 1922 which is not a matter for state pride—the pennant for contributing more lynchings than any other state in the union."[103] It also reported that for 1922 "the skirts of the North are clear [from lynchings]," but admitted that fourteen such crimes had already occurred in Northern states, not including the lynchings in Duluth three years earlier.[104] The other *Morning Tribune* editorial continued this theme: "[T]he lynchings recorded by the Tuskegee Institute were saturated with horror, but they do not encompass the whole ghastly story of mob lawlessness. The lynchings were a mockery of American confession of ideals."[105]

Divided Elites: Public Debate on the Death Penalty

In the wake of continued banditry, support for capital punishment was becoming increasingly evident. On February 3, 1923, the Second District Editorial Newspaper Association joined the *Morning Tribune* and "adopted resolutions asking the state legislature to restore capital punishment."[106] On January 19, 1923, the *Morning Tribune* also reported that the Minnesota State Sheriffs' Association favored reinstating capital punishment,[107] and on the 20th, the County Attorneys' Association unanimously agreed to support reestablishing capital punishment in Minnesota.[108] At the same time it reported that "legislators expect an insistent demand from women's and church organizations opposing adoption of capital punishment."[109] The *Morning Tribune* discussed an informal debate on capital punishment sponsored by the Calhoun Commercial Club between a woman who "opposed the enactment of a death penalty on the grounds that it is 'retrogressive and un-Christian,'" and a state senator who "upheld the proposed law as a 'stern necessity.'"[110] The Minnesota Federation of Women's Clubs was so divided on the question of capital punishment that club members decided to take no action in order to avoid a split in the organization.[111] The Hennepin County sheriff suggested that women did not fully understand or appreciate the necessities of crime control: "[T]here would be no opposition to the resumption of [capital] punishment if the women of the state realized the seriousness of the crime situation."[112] One letter to the editor published in the *Morning Tribune* reasoned that "women's clubs as well as individual 'sob sisters' who oppose capital punishment . . . delight in crime and . . . admire crime and weakness."[113] On January 25, 1923, the *Morning Tribune* printed excerpts from a public hearing on capital punishment where a majority of the three hundred people in the audience were opposed to the death penalty. The hearing was sponsored by the Crime Prevention Committee of the house. At the hearing, an attorney representing the St. Paul Spiritualist and Theosophical Societies presented a petition opposing the death penalty that had been signed by 1,200 St. Paul residents.[114]

The Minnesota Crime Commission, appointed by the governor in 1922 to make recommendations to state government on crime control, made "no specific recommendations on capital punishment [although] a majority report of this commission . . . opposes capital punishment on the grounds that it is brutal and that it is not effective" as a deterrent.[115] In their final report, the majority concluded that the legal provisions requiring private executions attest to the brutalizing effect of executions. The majority also concluded that capital punishment was "out of harmony" with Christian traditions. The ineffectiveness of capital punishment was reflected in the fact that states that relied on capital punishment, including Georgia, were swamped with homicides.[116]

Divided Elites: Legislative Debate on Capital Punishment

Five death penalty bills (four in the house, one in the senate) were introduced in the 1923 Minnesota legislature. One house bill provided "death for a murderer who committed the crime while engaged in committing a felony and specified that the execution shall take place

. . . .

at the state penitentiary at Stillwater."[117] On January 9, 1923, a death penalty bill calling for execution for first-degree murder was submitted to the senate.[118] On January 10, two additional death penalty bills were introduced in the house.[119] On February 4, yet another capital punishment bill, "designed to quiet critics," was introduced in the house. Hoping to remove much of the criticism that arose regarding the possible restoration of capital punishment, the February 4th bill provided "death for first degree murder, but would give the trial judge authority to change the penalty to a life sentence if he believed that circumstances warranted."[120]

On February 7, a Senate Judiciary Committee hearing on the death penalty triggered "bitter verbal clashes" between those for and against the punishment. "The feeling became so intense at one time that calling of names and sharp, sarcastic rejoinders became general."[121] A senate author of one of the capital punishment bills defended the legislation by saying, "the people who come here opposing this bill haven't red blood in their veins . . . [and have a] maudlin sentiment [for criminals]." Opponents of the bill were called "soft hearts," while proponents of the bill were called "soft heads."[122]

By February 15, the various capital punishment bills had been collapsed into one, SF 20, and a majority of the Senate Judiciary Committee recommended that it pass. To appease death penalty opponents the author of the legislation suggested amending the original bill, giving juries the sole responsibility of determining whether persons found guilty of murder were to be executed or sent to prison for life. "Offering the amendment apparently weakened opposition to the bill, judging from the reception it received."[123] Nevertheless, the bill was amended in yet another way, specifying that no person could be sentenced to death when the conviction was "obtained wholly or in part on circumstantial evidence."[124] The full senate considered the much-amended senate capital punishment bill on February 27, 1923.[125] Even with its numerous amendments, the bill remained unacceptable to the majority of senators. According to the *Journal of the Senate*, the 1923 death penalty bill was rejected by a vote of twenty-six to forty-one.[126] Never again has Minnesota come this close to reinstating capital punishment.

Conclusion

Understanding death penalty abolition and its longevity in Minnesota requires an examination of demographics, crime trends, cultural factors, and economic circumstances.

Demographics

Minnesota entered the United States in a virtual state of war with its native peoples. Formal and informal executions played a key role in the "ethnic cleansing" of Minnesota. The plight of the Santee Sioux who survived the 1862 uprising is illustrative: "Previous treaties were abrogated, and the surviving Indians were informed that they would be removed to a reservation in Dakota Territory. Even those [Santee] leaders who had collaborated with the white men had to go."[127] By the beginning of the twentieth century, Native Americans were no longer a significant economic, political, or social threat to white Minnesotans. The size of Minnesota's black population was, and continues to be, among the smallest in the nation.[128] Thus, as Minnesota moved into the twentieth century, it took on the traits conducive to death penalty abolition: a homogeneous and primarily rural state, with low murder rates and few perceived internal or external threats.

Crime Trends and the Threat to Personal Security

Press reports and surviving police records indicate that shortly after abolition was passed into law, murder in Minnesota primarily involved domestic homicides and was little threat to the general public. The situation began to change dramatically following World War I. By the late teens and early 1920s, murder in Minnesota became a public problem involving frequent armed robberies and the killing of police officers. "It was a time of economic uncertainty, a time when people were polarized along lines of intense patriotism, or pressing for social reform, a time when racial and religious distrust was on the rise, that volatile clashes were not only possible, but inevitable."[129] Similar to other states, a spate of lynchings occurred in Minnesota in full view of

. . . .

thousands of spectators who did nothing to intervene to stop them. Ultimately, the *Morning Tribune* decided to support capital punishment, as did other influential groups, including a newspaper editors' association and the organizations representing the state's county attorneys and sheriffs. But opinion remained divided among legislators.

Cultural Factors

A central difference that distinguished Minnesota from other U.S. states was the response of local leaders to lynching. When three innocent black men were lynched by an angry mob in 1920 after being accused of raping a young white female, community leaders in Duluth were uniformly outraged and authorities vowed to punish the lynchers to the fullest extent of the law. Lynching was seen as a central symbol of the violence and bigotry of Southern culture. Local leaders all agreed that such vigilantism was contrary to local traditions. Governor Burnquist immediately called in the state's national guard to restore order. Mob leaders were quickly located, apprehended, tried, convicted, and sentenced to prison. During abolitionist periods in Colorado, Arizona, Tennessee, and Missouri, there was no punishment of lynch mobs and this undoubtedly played a significant role in reinstating the death penalty in those states, where it was generally assumed that it had to be one or the other, capital punishment or "mob rule."[130] On the other hand, Minnesota's political leaders did not see the reinstatement of capital punishment as the only alternative to mob violence. Indeed, a second round of anticipated lynchings was quickly aborted when the presence of the military became clear.

It is instructive to note that prior to abolition, the *Morning Tribune* opposed capital punishment and had defied a law that required secrecy in executions. Later, when the paper advocated reinstatement of capital punishment, it supported private executions. By its actions on both occasions, the *Morning Tribune* risked offending local sensibilities.

The Minnesota experience demonstrated that even when capital punishment had the support of prominent citizens, including political leaders and the press, quick legal action against lynch mob leaders quelled potential lynchings, and with it, the reinstatement of capital punishment.

. . . .

During the first quarter of the twentieth century, lawmakers and other community leaders continued to be deeply divided on the question of the reinstatement of capital punishment. Editors of the *Morning Tribune* had been of three minds: at times opposed to executions, at other times ambivalent about executions, and at other times in favor of capital punishment. Ultimately, the Northern Central abolitionist states seem to share cultural traditions inconsistent with capital punishment. Attitudes expressed in the press and among political officials toward lynching, the KKK, and the South seem to have sealed the fate of capital punishment. In Minnesota, comparison with the South provided a powerful symbol of Minnesota's perceived cultural superiority based on its respect for human life. This self-assured, collective self-concept is similar to the moral superiority that was felt by Protestants of the early twentieth century in relation to the behavior of Roman Catholics who drank alcohol.[131] In any case, while the anti-Southern ideology did not preclude isolated lynchings, it did prevent collective acquiescence to lynching. The Minnesota governor's swift response was not really surprising since he was a leader of the Minnesota NAACP. The fact that the Minnesota governor was a leader of the NAACP reflects in turn the well-known liberal traditions in the state.[132] The anti-Southern ideology helps explain why the legislatures in five contiguous Northern Central states—North Dakota, Minnesota, Iowa, Wisconsin, and Michigan—have abolished capital punishment.

Economic Circumstances

There is no doubt that cultural factors played a significant role in the abolitionist history of Minnesota. Nevertheless, it is important to note that factors beyond "moral righteousness" played a role in the legal outcome of the Duluth lynchings. Black residents of Duluth were placed squarely between two competing economic interests. Much of the uneasiness between blacks and whites in 1920 Duluth can "be traced to the strike-breaking tactics of U.S. Steel which imported blacks to maintain the hourly wage for all workers at twenty-five cents. Perhaps upwards of a hundred southern blacks were recruited by the company from plantations to work at the Duluth mill. It was not a difficult decision for the blacks to leave their homes. The offered wage more than doubled their present ten-cent dole, so they came north with the promise of employment at good pay."[133] Given existing prejudices, working class residents of Duluth inevitably came to view black labor as a threat. "On the other hand, well-to-do whites in the city welcomed the influx of more blacks. Cheap domestic labor [similar to cheap factory labor] was not an easy commodity there, and the grand large homes and private clubs were in constant need of help, routinely assigned to black workers."[134]

There is little evidence that racial attitudes among the upper-class residents of Duluth differed significantly from the attitudes of working-class residents. For example, during the early twentieth century, several dozen Haitians were held in Duluth with statuses akin to indentured servants. Lacking an understanding of the English language and the law, they spent years working for slave wages.[135] In short, the struggle between the black and white residents of Duluth reflected—in part—economic interests. Unlike economic circumstances in Southern states, the elites in Duluth had a direct interest in rejecting mob rule to guarantee a ready supply of cheap labor. Moreover, allowing mob rule under any circumstance would have given the wrong message to the primary enemies of Minnesota's economic elite: the socialists, anarchists, and trade unionists of the day. The economy of most Southern states provided no such economic incentive. On the contrary, encouraging and maintaining racism, executions, and lynchings protected the economic interests of elites tied to sharecropper agriculture.[136] Thus, long-term abolition in Minnesota reflects the commitment and work of numerous anti–death penalty advocates. Their efforts have, no doubt, been facilitated by the demographic, social, and economic foundations of the state.

Postscript

In recent years, death penalty bills have received opposition not just from the liberal Democrats in the state legislature, but from conservative Republicans as well.[137] In 1989, a death penalty bill was overwhelmingly defeated by the House Judiciary Committee on a two to twenty-one vote. In 1992, the Senate Judiciary Committee defeated a bill—two to fifteen—calling for death by lethal injection for certain heinous crimes.[138] At the present time, death penalty abolition in Minnesota appears to be firmly entrenched in Minnesota's legal culture. Minnesota's colorful independent governor, Jesse Ventura, is publicly opposed to capital punishment, making reinstatement even less likely.[139]

Un–American Activities in North Dakota
The Continuing Abolition of Capital Punishment

In 1865, the Dakota Territory adopted the penal code of New York State. Under that law, punishment for murder was not designated by degree. Hanging was the sentence for anyone convicted of murder. In 1883, the territorial legislature altered the definition of murder and expanded the list of punishments that juries could impose. Under the new code, punishment for first-degree murder was death or life imprisonment. For those convicted of second-degree murder, the sanction was imprisonment for ten to thirty years. In the early twentieth century, North Dakota juries found capital punishment so troublesome that it was seldom utilized.[1] A citizen's petition submitted to the 1915 legislature reflected the sentiments of many in North Dakota:

> Whereas, the death penalty is barbarous, ineffective in checking crime, contrary to the dictates of humanity, and violates the sacredness of human life we, the undersigned, protest against the infliction of the penalty and make this appeal for the abolishment of capital punishment.[2]

That year the North Dakota house of representatives passed house bill 33 abolishing the death penalty for murder by a unanimous vote. Later, the senate passed HB 33 by a vote of twenty-eight to twelve, and Governor Louis B. Hanna signed the bill into law.[3] The North Dakota legislature retained capital punishment for treason and for murder committed by an inmate already serving life for murder.[4] These last vestiges of capital punishment were not repealed until 1973. That year overwhelming majorities in both houses—with no floor debate—passed a new criminal code without capital punishment.[5]

Systemic Violence in North Dakota

Relations between Native Americans and European Americans on the Northern Plains remained peaceful during the first half of the nineteenth century. Native trappers and hunters were heavily involved in the fur trade. By the mid-1860s, circumstances had changed dramatically. Violent confrontations along with the decimation of the Northern Plains bison herds forced the majority of nomadic Dakotas onto reservations to avoid starvation. When President Benjamin Harrison approved the admission of North Dakota to the Union on November 2, 1889, the Northern Plains tribes were no longer a military threat to the growing white population.

Lynching was not an uncommon event on the Northern Plains during the latter part of the nineteenth and early twentieth centuries.[6] At least sixteen persons were lynched in North Dakota between 1882 and 1930. Available evidence suggests that law enforcement officials did not attempt to punish any persons who participated in these lynchings. According to Espy and Smykla, since 1680, only eight legal executions have taken place in the geographical area now known as North Dakota.[7] North Dakota has not held a public execution since 1894.

Demographic Patterns

Spurred on by the 1862 Federal Homestead Law, farming settlements sprang up all across North Dakota. Between 1879 and 1886, in excess of 100,000 people entered the territory. During its second settlement boom, North Dakota's population grew from 190,983 in 1890 to 646,872 in 1920. The majority of new immigrants were of Scandinavian or Germanic origin. In 1915, over 79 percent of North Dakotans were either first- or second-generation immigrants.[8] In 2000, the statewide total population was remarkably similar at 643,949.[9] Since the beginning of the twentieth century, North Dakotans have been leaving the farm at the rate of between 3 and 10 percent per decade. In 1890, 94 percent of the population lived in the country, but by 1990, more than half of North Dakota's residents lived in towns.[10]

There were 86,000 farms in North Dakota in 1933. At the end of the twentieth century, that number had declined to 30,500.[11]

Historically, the proportion of North Dakota's population classified as nonwhite has been extremely small. In 1920, only 0.93 percent of the population was classified as nonwhite. In 1999, approximately 5.58 percent of North Dakota's population was nonwhite, but only 0.62 percent of the state's population was African American (see Table 6.1). Currently, there is little migration into the state. According to the census of 1990, only 56,071 of North Dakota's residents were living outside the state in 1985.[12] Peirce and Hagstrom observe that: "Except for West Virginia, they [both North Dakota and South Dakota] have the highest percentage of people living in small villages and farms among all the states. The agrarian mentality still dominates, because almost three-quarters of the people either live on farms or grew up there."[13]

Economics

Historically, North Dakotans have also suffered from their nearly total dependence on agriculture: "When agriculture has a big year, the rest of the state reaps the benefits. Rural towns, big cities. It doesn't matter. They all feel the ripple effect of agriculture."[14] Farming during the late nineteenth and early twentieth centuries was characterized by cycles of boom and bust. During this period, large numbers of North Dakota's farmers blamed their less-than-secure economic circumstances on distant elites. According to Remele:

> The distant leadership of rail and commodities were often arrogant and unresponsive to the needs of their customer, and . . . rural people were often taxed out of proportion to their means. Most galling, however, was the frequent evidence that out-of-state corporate interests dominated North Dakota government, using it to further private goals rather than the general welfare of the citizens.[15]

North Dakota's greatest political insurgency, the Nonpartisan League, "united progressives, reformers, and radicals behind a platform that called for many progressive reforms, ranging from improved state ser-

TABLE 6.1
Population Diversity in North Dakota, 1920–1999

YEAR	AFRICAN AMERICAN		NONWHITE		WHITE	
	Number	Percentage	Number	Percentage	Number	Percentage
1920	†	N/A	6,000*	.93	640,000*	99.07
1930	†	N/A	9,000*	1.32	672,000*	98.68
1940	201	.03	10,270	1.60	631,464	98.37
1950	257	.04	10,931	1.76	608,448	98.19
1960	777	.12	12,131	1.92	619,538	97.96
1970	2,494	.40	15,782	2.55	599,485	97.04
1980	3,000*	.46	24,000	4.33	626,000*	95.21
1990	4,000*	.63	28,500	4.48	604,000*	94.89
1999	4,000*	.62	42,551	5.58	598,791	92.80

*Rounded to nearest 1,000.
†Less than 500.
Sources: Bureau of the Census, 1999. Population Estimates Division, September. Historical Statistics of the United States: Colonial Times to 1970, Part 1, 1975: 32. *Statistical Abstract of the United States*, 1962, 1972, 1982–83, 1992.

vices and full suffrage for women, to state ownership of banks, [grain] mills and elevators."[16]

While progressive reforms improved the economic circumstances of most North Dakotans, local political and economic action could not negate the catastrophic effects of the 1920 collapse of wartime grain prices, a drought in western North Dakota, and the Great Depression of the 1930s. During these times, thousands of North Dakotans lost their farms. In the 1930s, an estimated 70 percent of the state's population required some type of public assistance; however, by the 1940s, crop yields and commodity prices were strong once again. In 1945, North Dakota led the nation in per capita bank deposits.[17]

A February 7, 1975, front-page article in the *Bismarck Tribune* attested to the economic strength of that day: "North Dakota's new wealth, money created by North Dakota enterprises in 1974, is more than $2.75 billion. . . . Agriculture, generating 82 percent of the 1974 value, continues to be the dominant component of the new wealth produced in the state."[18] "The dollar value of goods and services produced in North Dakota increased from $1.3 to $4 billion between 1960 and

1973, according to a University of North Dakota study."[19] Per capita income, cost of living, low crime rate, low unemployment rate, air quality ranking, divorce rate per 100,000, and educational spending per pupil are just some of the economic and social characteristics lauded in a *Bismarck Tribune* editorial.[20]

According to the *Bismarck Tribune*, however, during the 1980s and 1990s, droughts and depressed crop prices hit North Dakota agriculture very hard, accelerating the exodus from the state's farms. The new millennium did not seem any brighter. In 2001, the newspaper reported: "Last year, for example, ended with nearly $400 million in crop losses, which translates into a $1.2 billion economic hit to the state."[21] For a time in the 1980s, it appeared that oil drilling would be the economy's salvation, but slumping oil prices led to massive layoffs.[22] North Dakota's economic history has been succinctly written as follows:

> When North Dakota entered the Federal Union in 1889, its leaders prophesied a glorious future for the Northern Prairie State. Great cities and prosperous farms, said the promoters, would make Dakota the "jewel" in the crown of Democracy. The ensuing century has proven the "boomers" both right and wrong. North Dakota has enjoyed prosperity, but it has also seen devastatingly hard times. . . . [Today] the essential problem remains the same as a century earlier—finding the capital necessary to provide services and benefits of a modern society to a far-flung population. As it was in 1889, North Dakota remains a social, cultural, and economic colony, a producer of raw materials . . . and an exporter of educated young people.[23]

Crime Rates

North Dakota routinely has a homicide rate between one-fourth and one-eighth the national average. In 1974, the nationwide murder rate was twelve times higher than North Dakota's homicide rate. Circumstances changed little during the 1980s and 1990s (see Table 6.2). Among abolitionist states, only Iowa has a lower murder rate than North Dakota.[24]

Most crime-related articles published by the *Bismarck Tribune* provide a relatively clear picture of North Dakota's crime problem. A 1976

TABLE 6.2
Homicide Rates in North Dakota and the United States

Year	North Dakota	United States
1938	2.1	6.8
1939	1.9	6.4
1975	.8	9.6
1977	.9	8.8
1978	1.2	9.0
1979	1.5	9.7
1989	.6	8.7
1995	.9	8.2
1999	1.6	6.3

Sources: *Uniform Crime Reports,* 1938, 1939, 1999. *Statistical Abstract of the United States,* 1977, 1979, 1980, 1991, 1997.

headline read, "Serious Crime Decreases in Bismarck."[25] According to the accompanying statistics for the state capital in 1975, there were no cases of murder, three cases of forcible rape, eleven cases of robbery, and twenty-three cases of aggravated assault. The general nature of North Dakota's crime problem was further revealed by two 1978 headlines: "Vandalism, Theft Reported at Bismarck High School" and "Shoplifting Main Juvenile Offense."[26] At times metaphors used by *Bismarck Tribune* staff to describe criminal behavior gave the impression that crime in North Dakota was a good deal more serious than data suggested. For example, in December 1975, the paper reported a "Local Crime Wave Puts a Chill on Christmas Spirit."[27] The "crime wave" consisted of some twenty complaints of property damage, three burglaries, three stolen cars, nine larcenies, three assaults, several peace disturbances, and four Volkswagen tip-overs.

The structure of North Dakota's overall criminal justice system during the mid-1970s suggests that a majority of North Dakota's legislators did not consider crime a serious threat. In 1975, only four counties in North Dakota had full-time prosecutors. In response to an initiative to establish a district attorney system, the North Dakota Association of State Attorneys voiced strong opposition to the idea, questioning whether the growth in crime warranted such a system.[28] During the same year, state officials announced that they planned to discontinue a four-year-old public defender pilot program that provided free legal counsel to indigents in a ten-county area.[29] In 1976, state officials decided to drop the idea of developing a modern, computerized, law enforcement database. The proposed statewide system, which would have gathered and stored law enforcement information, was abandoned following a decision by the Federal Law Enforcement Assistance Administration to exempt North Dakota from developing such a system.[30] Such federal regulations would have required North Dakota to become a central repository and to conform to new standardized methods of record keeping.[31] Finally, a 1975 news article reported: "North Dakota's agrarian nature and enlightened judiciary system have helped produce the lowest penitentiary population, per capita, of any state."[32] In 1975, the prison population was 164 inmates.

Attempts to Reinstate Capital Punishment in North Dakota

Since 1915, relatively few legislative attempts have been made to reestablish the death penalty. Nevertheless, the legislative efforts of 1927, 1977, and 1979 seriously threatened abolition in North Dakota.[33] As was the case in Minnesota—the other successful Progressive Era abolitionist state—demographics, an agrarian economy, low levels of violent crime, and cultural dispositions mediated against death penalty reestablishment efforts in North Dakota.

Reinstatement Bills, 1926–1927

As the second quarter of the twentieth century began to unfold, death penalty debates were heating up in North and South Dakota. Residents of both states looked to the other as a bellwether of their own death penalty future. Given the proximity and "similarities between the Dakotas,"[34] and the fact that both states abolished their death statutes during the Progressive Era, it was reasonable to assume that if one state reinstated capital punishment, the other state would likely follow. On February 3, 1927, death penalty abolition in South Dakota was seriously threatened. A front-page story with the headline

. . . .

"Death Penalty Bill Passed by S.D. Lower House" appeared in the *Bismarck Tribune.*[35] Five days later, a follow-up article reported that a capital punishment bill had passed both houses of the South Dakota legislature. The front-page headline read "Death Penalty in S.D. Is Up to Governor."[36]

Death penalty abolition appeared equally threatened in North Dakota. From January 1, 1926, through December 31, 1927, the *Bismarck Tribune* published thirty-seven articles favoring reestablishing the death penalty. Another front-page story reported the following:

> The need for the return of the death penalty is obvious [according to Attorney General George Shafer and was needed] to protect the state from the depredations of professional criminals. . . . The promise of a life sentence to the penitentiary is not nearly as effective in halting deliberate and planned murder as the prospect of death in the event of capture and conviction.[37]

Support for a proposal to restore the death penalty as a punishment for murder was voiced by the legislative committee of the North Dakota Association of State Attorneys.[38] In early January 1927, the North Dakota legislature considered a bill to reinstate the death penalty. One North Dakota senator favoring reinstatement stated that he "wanted to go back to the middle ages or further if necessary to . . . dish out to some of these criminals what they have coming."[39] But expressing his opposition to reinstating the death penalty, another senator argued: "I am opposed to capital punishment because it is shutting the door of mercy against the offender. I don't want to close that door even against a murderer. I want that right of mercy for all my fellow men."[40]

Reflecting the prominence of domestic disputes in the state, a member of North Dakota's house observed that "the leniency shown to women slayers . . . inspired other women to take lethal action to rid themselves of their spouses."[41] A North Dakota senator reached the opposite conclusion. He reasoned that the death penalty should only apply to men: "[I]f a woman kills a man, the chances are he should have been killed long ago anyway."[42] While some legislators saw the death penalty as "a deterrent to crime," others viewed the punishment as "legalized murder."[43] In spite of significant legislative support and favorable public opinion, a January 26, 1927, front-page article reported that the senate voted thirty to nineteen against reinstating the death penalty.[44] In an attempt to overcome legislative opposition, North Dakota sheriffs went on record in favor of capital punishment for first-degree murder.[45] In February 1927, however, North Dakota's house followed the senate's lead and killed capital punishment.[46] Death penalty abolition in both North and South Dakota survived the scare of 1927.

A Major Trigger Event Sidestepped by North Dakota: South Dakota Reinstates

On July 29, 1938, the *Bismarck Tribune* ran a story titled "South Dakota Girl Slugged: Second Disappears."[47] On August 2, the paper reported that Betty Schnaidt's body had been found, "bound hand and foot, a gag thrust into her mouth and towel knotted around her throat."[48] "Andrew Earl Young, a fugitive from Pennsylvania also wanted in four states for robbery, kidnapping, rape and murder [was] killed . . . in a gun fight with police,"[49] and "was the man wanted for the kidnap-murder of Betty Schnaidt in Sioux Falls."[50] According to the news reports, Young was slain in a battle with police in Hot Springs, Arkansas. In reaction to the Schnaidt case, South Dakota reinstated capital punishment after a twenty-four-year period of abolition.[51] Even though the Dakotas are historically, politically, and culturally very similar, the tragedy of the Betty Schnaidt murder failed to generate a legislative initiative to reinstate capital punishment in North Dakota. However, an editorial in the *Bismarck Tribune* stated that for Schnaidt's murderer, "[h]ot lead is an excellent treatment for such a human rat as this man was."[52]

More Reinstatement Efforts, 1977–1979

Two front-page articles describing a double murder hit North Dakota's streets on July 12, 1976.[53] Both articles reported that "the manager of the McIntosh County Bank . . . and his wife have been killed in a robbery of the bank." The murdered bank officer and his wife were

. . . .

found partly buried in a gravel pit not too far from their town of Zee-land, North Dakota.[54] A July 15, 1976, newspaper article attested to the victims' prominence in their community. Over seven hundred people attended their funeral.[55] In the end, David Feist, twenty-one, Sebastian Feist, eighteen, and Gregory Huber, eighteen, were convicted of the killings and sentenced to life in prison with eligibility for parole after ten years.[56]

The Zick case, in conjunction with United States Supreme Court rulings that capital punishment could be constitutional, awakened legislative efforts to reinstate the death penalty in North Dakota. In 1977, representatives introduced house concurrent resolution 3074 calling for a legislative council study to explore the "feasibility and constitutionality" of reestablishing the death penalty.[57] Thus, it was not a death penalty bill per se, but an effort to determine whether enough support existed to launch a successful death penalty reinstatement effort. In a survey conducted by eleven North Dakota weekly newspapers, 75 percent of North Dakotans stated that they favored a law providing capital punishment for those found guilty of first-degree murder.[58] On February 15, 1977, the House Judiciary Committee held a hearing on the resolution. Representative Wilbur VanderVorst argued that his constituents in Zeeland demanded reinstatement because of the Zick murders. Attorney General Olson contended, however, that capital punishment would not deter murder. In any case, the Committee on Legislative Resolutions failed to support the measure and it was defeated on the house floor, thirty-four to fifty-three.[59]

The push to reinstate the death penalty in North Dakota was renewed in 1979 with the introduction of a bill by Senator Theron Striden allowing judges to impose the death penalty in murder cases where deaths are caused during the commission of felonies such as robbery or arson.[60] Senator Striden viewed executions as a deterrent and as a way to eliminate dangerous criminals from society.[61] Senate bill 2169 designated the warden of the North Dakota State Penitentiary to serve as executioner, although Senator Striden expressed concern about the heavy burden that the role of executioner would place on the warden. In response, Warden Joe Havaner claimed that he neither favored nor opposed the death penalty: "You get yourself in the frame of mind that it's not you that's executing the person, but the state is. It's not personal."[62] He went on to say, however: "If this thing were reversed, if I were over in Germany, this could be me."[63] Other state officials were not as neutral. Deputy Agriculture Commissioner Lynn Clancy was quoted as saying: "I cannot believe that taking a life because someone else has taken a life will in any way make the situation better."[64]

Attorney General Olson and the deputy warden of the North Dakota State Penitentiary, Dr. Kenneth Johnson, also expressed opposition to such legislation. Attorney General Olson did not see the death penalty as an effective deterrent to serious crime, and the deputy warden reasoned that "the death penalty has been misused in this country, noting that historically many have been executed for crimes less serious than murder, but nearly all of those were black."[65] Republican Senator Ernest Sands characterized the death penalty as "cruel and severe punishment which does not prevent murders and is more likely to be imposed on poor defendants who can't hire expensive attorneys. . . . In most of these cases the offender and victim were friends. . . . These are not pre-planned murders that might be deterred by a death penalty. It is wrong to kill and two wrongs don't make a right."[66] In 1979, the neighboring South Dakota legislature approved a new death penalty bill using guidelines provided by the United States Supreme Court in Gregg v. Georgia.[67] The North Dakota legislature remained unmoved, however, in light of opinion both for and against reinstatement. North Dakota's legislative effort to reenact capital punishment failed in the senate by a margin of fourteen to thirty-six.[68]

Reinstatement Efforts, 1990–1999

During the 1991 legislature, Democratic Senator Dale Marks suggested he might introduce a capital punishment bill on behalf of a constituent. He admitted, however, "I wasn't very excited about doing that. I didn't think it would fly here in North Dakota. Maybe people here just like to give a person a second chance, or a third chance."[69] There was an extensive debate during a 1995 public hearing on a proposal to reinstate capital punishment.[70] Responding to a kidnap and murder, the proposed bill's sponsor, Democratic Senator Meyer Kinnoin, told reporters: "You've got these people, what I call the scum of the earth, taking in these young girls and raping them and murdering them, and then they turn them out and they do the same thing."[71] North Dakota Attorney General Heidi Heitkamp was not convinced: "Many states that have the death penalty have the highest incidence of murder."[72] Despite boasting the lowest crime rates in the nation, the Senate Judiciary Committee agreed to hold hearings on reinstatement. Death penalty supporter Representative Tom Freier told members of the Senate Judiciary Committee: "North Dakota doesn't have as high a crime rate as other parts of the country, and this bill would keep it that way. The bill would send a message to all would-be criminals in our state and outside our borders." Correspondingly, Senator Russell Thane warned his colleagues against complacency and reminded them that "we have two interstate highways and entrances on each side. Who is to say that a criminal from another state is entering?"[73] If crime rates did not compel the return of capital punishment, a local citizen argued that it was justified on moral or religious grounds. Stanley Hughes claimed: "It is God's judgment that [murderers] should be executed. The man who bears the sword by the sword shall he be slain." North Dakota Roman Catholic Bishop Kenny, among others, testified against the bill: "My opposition to the death penalty comes from our belief that each person is created in the image of God. . . . [The death penalty] denies the sovereignty of God over life."[74] A statement presented by the North Dakota Conference of Churches argued that the death penalty "does not deter murder, abrogates rehabilitation and forgiveness, may lead to the execution of innocent persons, is deeply discriminatory against minority groups, does not save money, [and] diminishes the dignity and humanity of the community."[75]

Other persons testifying against senate bill 2097 raised additional moral concerns. Senator Lafountain reasoned that

> [I]n the state of North Dakota about a third of the [prison] inmates are Native Americans. . . . [According to] the parole division, the warden, the attorney general . . . nine out of ten times . . . they are sentenced to

more severe penalties. And in many cases they come from an economic background where they don't have the resources to contest the information, so this is a grave concern for me as a Native person.

A representative of the North Dakota Trial Lawyers Association reasoned that "the risk of having innocent persons executed is way too high."[76] Senator Carolyn Nelson spoke to the sentiments of anger and vengeance:

> I do not want my do not pass recommendation to imply that I do not have sympathy for those who've lost folks, because I've been there too. . . . It's been fifteen years since my sister was killed and it isn't something that leaves you. I heard a lot of "I need justice" or some sort of vengeance. There's some sort of anger . . . but I don't think this [death penalty] is the proper way to go.[77]

According to testimony from the warden of the North Dakota State Penitentiary, Tim Schuetzle, capital punishment harms prison staff morale since it is difficult to kill someone after working with them for many years. Capital punishment also makes inmate control more difficult and is not a deterrent to murder. Further, the "cost of processing a death sentence ranges between 1 to 3 million dollars per case, with most of these costs coming from the cost of trials and appeals. This money, he argued, could be better spent on other—more needy—areas of the criminal justice system."[78] The chief justice of the North Dakota Supreme Court, Gerald W. VandeWalle, testified that "I am concerned about the issue of finances."[79]

Several persons testifying in opposition to reinstatement combined the moral and economic costs of capital punishment. In a written statement the director of North Dakota's Department of Corrections, Elaine Little, told Senate Judiciary Committee members:

> I believe the 1 to 3 million dollars required to process each death penalty case can be spent much better elsewhere in the criminal justice system. States that have the death penalty claim that high costs associated with it actually decrease the funds available for normal law enforcement and crime prevention efforts. . . . Executing an inmate who has been on death row for an average of nine years is very traumatic for a Department and its staff. . . . Finally, I do not believe a state should be in the

business of violence, and an execution, regardless of the method, is a violent act.[80]

One witness reasoned: "I have been a prosecutor for five years and seven years a United States Attorney for the District of North Dakota. I have served on the state Parole Board for six years. . . . I have defended criminal cases. And I have been a professor of law. . . . If the legislature wants to reduce crime it should spend more money on relieving poverty" and increase the use of probation and parole, which "are cost-effective." Former North Dakota Governor Arthur Link also testified and submitted a written statement recommending against reinstatement. He discussed the high costs of capital trials and the problems of "a mistaken conviction. . . . [However, the] overriding moral and ethical beliefs of one's religion that denies the taking of another person's life [he argued] may be all the reason that one needs to oppose the death penalty."[81] Thus, moral and fiscal objections to reinstating the death penalty were voiced by a broad coalition of political and religious leaders. As in the case of the other abolitionist states, few spoke in support of capital punishment.

The Senate Judiciary Committee voted five to zero to report out SB 2097 with a "do not pass" recommendation. Three days later, the senate responded by defeating the bill fourteen to thirty-three. Eleven Republicans and three Democrats voted for reinstatement of the death penalty. Seventeen Republicans and sixteen Democrats voted in opposition to the reinstatement of the death penalty.[82]

Conclusion

Today, the majority of North Dakotans can trace their origins to Western European immigrants who settled in the region in the late nineteenth and early twentieth centuries. The second wave of settlers brought with them socialist politics, a mistrust of government, and a familiarity with the relationship between totalitarian government and capital punishment. The social and political sentiments of these early North Dakotans helped move the state toward death penalty abolition in 1915. The *Minot Daily News* reported that: "The old Farmer-Labor populist tradition . . . continues to play a role in North Dakota's failure to re-establish capital punishment."[83] The "boom and bust" nature of North Dakota's economy is similar to the economies in the abolitionist states of West Virginia and Alaska. Populations in all these states tend to view themselves as colonies, societies that provide the raw materials for industrially developed states and get little in return. Distrust of government and fear of distant elites shape their understanding of everyday life. Under these circumstances, granting the state power over life and death is simply too intimidating to the general population.

The common economic, social, and political experiences of the past century have molded residents of the Northern Plains into a homogeneous population that tends to resist executing "one of their own." In the words of another prison warden, Winston Satran: "North Dakotans would have a hard time accepting an execution in the state, even though they may say they support the concept. The death penalty would be extremely shocking. . . . We don't have the anonymity that you have in other states. It would be a very personal punishment."[84] Additionally, death penalty abolition is furthered by consistently low homicide rates. Although the Zick murders in 1976 inspired legislative efforts to reinstate the death penalty as did a kidnapping in 1994, those efforts were unsuccessful. The Schnaidt murder and reinstatement of capital punishment in South Dakota in 1939 had no apparent impact on North Dakota's abolitionist tradition. This can be explained by the fact that although North Dakota and South Dakota are very similar, it is well-known that the former is much more liberal than its neighbor to the south. Indeed, North Dakota has been celebrated as one of the most liberal states in the Union.[85]

The *Minot Daily News* reported in a November 25, 1990, article that 75 percent of North Dakota's citizens supported the death penalty. This appears to be a common characteristic in abolitionist states. Reflecting a populist concern over the current and historical injustices suffered by Native Americans, North Dakota will probably maintain their abolitionist tradition. Entering the twenty-first century, North Dakota's position on the death penalty continued to echo the sentiment expressed in a 1915 citizens' petition: "Whereas, the death penalty is barbarous, ineffective in checking crime, contrary to the dictates of humanity, and violates the sacredness of human life, we, the undersigned, protest against the infliction of the penalty and make this appeal for the abolishment of capital punishment."[86]

Postscript

The 1995 Senate Judiciary Committee hearings show the powerful coalition assembled against capital punishment that would probably take decades to unravel. On March 27, 1995, the North Dakota legislature also passed SB 2496, which made the punishment for first-degree murder life without the possibility of parole, making reinstatement seem even less necessary to protect the community.

The History of Death Penalty Abolition in Alaska

To understand the origins and maintenance of death penalty abolition in Alaska, one has to examine the relationship between political repression, crime levels, economics, and capital punishment in Alaska. Data presented here contradict the notion that death penalty abolition occurs only in states with relatively homogeneous populations. Alaska boasts one of the most diverse human populations in the United States. Data presented here also contradict the notion that death penalty abolition is dependent upon low levels of violence. When capital punishment was abolished in 1957, Alaska's murder rate ranked eleventh among all U.S. states. Among abolitionist states, Alaska has often had the highest murder rate (see Table 7.1). Data presented here also contradict the notion that death penalty abolition occurs only during times of economic expansion. Alaska abolished the death penalty during a severe, long-term, economic downturn. The data presented here illuminate the structural foundations and situational factors that led one state government—despite horrific murders and ongoing calls by moral entrepreneurs to reestablish capital punishment—to reject the death penalty. A unique political and economic history, relatively powerful minority populations, a sparsely populated landmass, and a poorly funded state government provide the structural foundations for that rejection.

Social, Economic, and Political Context of Abolition

The Russian Years

Russia established and maintained a fur-trading industry in Alaska a century before selling the colony to the United States in 1867. During

TABLE 7.1
Average Murder Rates per 100,000 Among Abolitionist States

State	1955–64	1965–74	1975–84	1985–94
Alaska	8.1‡	10.9	12.9	8.0
Michigan	3.7	8.7	10.0	10.7
Hawaii	2.4‡	4.4	6.0	4.2
West Virginia	4.1*	5.4	6.1	5.6
Massachusetts	1.5*	3.1*	3.7§	3.7
Rhode Island	1.2*	2.6*	3.5§	4.0
Wisconsin	1.3	2.3	3.0	3.9
Maine	1.7	2.3	2.5	2.2
Vermont	1.0†	2.0	2.8	2.3
Iowa	1.1*	1.7	2.3	1.9
Minnesota	1.2	2.2	2.1	2.8
North Dakota	1.1	1.0*	1.3	1.2

*Death statute existed at this historical point.
†Statistics not available for 1955 or 1956.
‡Statistics not available for 1955 through 1958.
§Death penalty abolished during this period.
Source: *Statistical Abstract of the United States*, 1955–1994.

that century, the number of non–Native Alaskans residing in Alaska was never particularly large. An estimate of the 1840 population placed the number at 730, less than 2 percent of the state's population.[1] While Russians tended to regard Native Alaskans as "savages," formal Russian policy never allowed enslavement, expropriation of property, or genocide. Native Alaskans were viewed as essential components used to exploit the region's resources.[2] To benefit trade and exploit resources, Russians sometimes forceably moved Aleut people to other areas of Alaska.[3]

Historical evidence suggests that during the early years of Russian presence, from 1741 to 1780, Native Alaskans resisted cultural and political domination with the same fervor that characterized the resistance of Native Americans throughout North America against European invaders.[4] Tlingits "consistently regarded Russians as enemies to be killed or avoided."[5] Contacts between Aleuts and Russians were more complex. At times, Aleuts were willing trading partners; on other occasions, Russians found them to be unreasonable. The 1769 log of a Russian sea captain offers a succinct appraisal of Aleut intentions toward Russians. After noting the brutality among Aleut people toward one another, the log continued: "[T]hey all join in hating the Russians, who they consider general invaders, and kill them whenever they can."[6] In the end, states one historian, the superiority of Russian technology and the distance between Aleut villages spelled their defeat. "But neither this defeat, nor the effectiveness of the Russian domination which followed it, should obscure the degree to which Aleuts resisted the invaders for the better part of thirty years."[7]

The clergy of the Russian Orthodox church maintained an active presence in Russian Alaska. They proselytized, educated, and acted as cultural and language interpreters between Native Alaskans and entrepreneurs and migrants. They built schools that served Native Alaskans, whites, and children of mixed ancestry. Marriages between Russian men and Native Alaskan women were considered legitimate by the church. Many Alaskan Russian Orthodox priests, being of mixed (Native Alaskan and Russian) ancestry, negotiated the language barriers that existed between Native Alaskans—with their numerous dialects—and white settlers and traders.[8] In the century between 1765 and the sale of Alaska to the United States in 1867, both Russians and Native Alaskans came to see themselves as intimately entwined—economically, spiritually, and by blood.

Native Alaskans

At the end of the nineteenth and the beginning of the twentieth century, the focus of social and economic activity in Alaska moved away from the fur-trading, coastal settlements established by Russians to Nome and remote inland gold-mining camps. Today, economic activity in Alaska remains almost totally limited to the exploitation of mineral and animal resources. Due to its climate and soil conditions, livestock grazing and large-scale farming are all but impossible.[9] In 1990, only 1,160 of 550,043 Alaskans defined their occupation as farming.[10] Severe winter weather also makes many forms of industrial development impossible.

The economic shift from fur trading to mining eliminated the economic significance of Native Alaskans. American interests did not need Native Alaskan labor and expertise to exploit mineral resources.

Even so, little violence was directed against Native Alaskans. Violence was likely abated by the sheer size of Alaska's landmass, its cold climate, and the relatively small size of inland Native Alaskan groups.[11] Nevertheless, the distribution of social status, economic resources, and political power never reflected the fact that Alaska's population remained predominately Native Alaskan until at least 1930 (see Table 7.2).

Similar to Southern states, Alaska's territorial legislature passed a statute (the Literacy Act of 1925) that required voters in territorial elections to be literate. The act, supported by nearly every newspaper in the state (*Anchorage Daily News, Anchorage Alaskan, Cordova Times,* and *Juneau Empire*), was intended to block efforts by William Paul (the first Native Alaskan elected to the territorial legislature) to make Native Alaskans a political force. A *Juneau Empire* editorial, reacting to a grandfather clause incorporated in the act, reasoned that "A White Man's Party Is Necessary."[12]

> Alaskan Natives were also forbidden by law from attending school with white children. The *Nelson Act* [1905] gave the responsibility to the territorial governor and local communities to fully fund the education of white children and children of "mixed blood with a civilized life," while the costs of educating Indian and Eskimo children remained a federal burden.[13]

Finally, Native Alaskans and whites in rural areas generally lived separate lives. In the settled areas of Anchorage, Fairbanks, Juneau, and Ketchikan, ethnic discrimination or Jim Crow was the rule of the day. Native Alaskans lived in distinct areas. Stores, hotels, restaurants, swimming pools, and movie theaters generally denied service to Native Alaskans or segregated their customers on the basis of race. Signs reading "No Natives," "We Do Not Cater to Native and Filipino Trade," or "No Dogs or Indians Allowed" were common sights.[14]

> Ketchikan was known as "Indian Town" because it was largely populated by non-white residents. Ketchikan was, in the 1930s, as racially divided as any small town in Georgia during the same period. Indians and Alaska Natives were barred from white schools, white churches, and many white businesses. Segregated seating areas were enforced in the movie theater. When a Native family was served in a restaurant, it was not

unusual for the proprietor to close the curtains so that white customers would not be discouraged from entering.[15]

Racial discrimination in public places was not formally defined as illegal until passage of the Alaska Equal Protection Act of 1945.[16] Since the mid-1940s, Native Alaskans have improved their political fortunes while the relative size of their population has decreased vis-à-vis Alaska's white population. Two 1996 estimates placed the proportion of Alaskan legislators claiming Native Alaskan ancestry at between 20 and 25 percent. By merging their political power with the Democratic party, Native Alaskans have expanded and protected their political, social, and subsistence rights.[17] With growing non–Native Alaskan, urban populations, however, it remains to be seen if Native Alaskans will retain an effective voice in state politics.

White Alaskans

Between 1890 and 1910, large numbers of whites came to Alaska from the lower U.S. states with the hope of making their fortune. Unlike the fervor that drove most whites to exterminate native populations and settle the lower Western frontier, newcomers to the Alaska Territory intended to make their fortune in the gold mines and return home. Thus, when the gold-mining industry took a severe downturn during the second decade of the twentieth century, the non–Native Alaskan population declined by 25 percent (see Table 7.2). Whites who stayed suffered long-term economic hardship because for five decades, the cash economy of Alaska was depressed. The class structure that did exist among Alaskans was based on few resources. Fifty people made up the state's white power structure. Weather was the great equalizer, and physical strength was of supreme importance.

With no potential of "striking it rich" in the gold mines, former prospectors and laborers sent north by employment agencies worked together in large syndicate-owned mines located in Nome, Tanana Valley, and Juneau. Others worked on the Kennecott Mine or Copper River railroads; still others (often Filipinos) worked in fish canneries. In general, white Alaskans bemoaned the effects that economic restructuring was having on their way of life: "The dreams of the lonely prospector [according to the author of the 1914 Alaskan Socialist party platform] are giving way to the ugly realities of wage slavery and job hunting."[18] Wage earners blamed the threat to wage labor on the immoral exploitation of Alaska's minerals, fish, and waterways by outside (non–Native Alaskan) economic interests. The "Alaska for Alaskans" campaign slogan of Progressive Republican James Wickersham, victorious candidate for Territorial Delegate to the United States Congress in 1914, testified to the popularity of this position among the electorate.[19]

The coming of World War II and the ensuing Cold War somewhat revived Alaska's economy. Investment in military bases, roads, and other projects brought into the state numerous military personnel and civilians.[20] By 1950, federal employees, who were mostly white, made up 53.7 percent of Alaska's work force.[21] Nevertheless, in 1958—the year preceding statehood—Alaska's economy was nearly defunct and salmon catches were at an all-time low. A former Alaska governor argued that the 1964 Anchorage earthquake, with the resulting influx of federal funds, was the only thing that saved the state from bankruptcy.[22]

For the most part Alaskans continued to blame their deplorable economic circumstances on a familiar enemy:

> [O]utside economic interests, particularly fishing and mining, . . . had plundered the territory's natural wealth and perpetrated a boom and bust economy for most of the twentieth century. As a territory Alaska had been denied the legislative control over its natural resources, particularly over commercial fisheries. . . . Statehooders perceived, accurately by most analyses, that Seattle-based fishing interests and other lobbies were effective in gaining the kind of federal regulation—or lack of regulation—they wanted.[23]

Two decades after statehood, the economic and demographic circumstances of Alaska shifted dramatically. State revenues grew from $599 million in fiscal year 1975 to $4.74 billion seven years later.[24] Alaska's white population numbered 39,892 in 1940, 176,315 in 1960, and 441,723 in 1990 (see Table 7.2). Large numbers of immigrants came from the oil-producing areas of the lower forty-eight states.[25] Moreover, Alaska's population became increasingly urban. Slightly over 67 percent of Alaska's 1990 population lived around the growing metropolitan centers of Anchorage, Fairbanks, and Juneau.[26]

TABLE 7.2
Alaska's White, Black, and Native Alaskan Populations

Year	Total	White	Black	Native Alaskan
1840	40,716	730 (1.57%*)	N/A	40,076† (98.43%*)
1880	33,426	430 (1.29%)	N/A	32,996† (98.71%)
1890	32,052	4,298 (20.9%*)	N/A	25,354† (79.1%*)
1900	63,592	33,888 (53.29%)	168 (.26%)	29,536† (46.45%)
1910	64,356	38,522 (59.86%)	209 (.33%)	25,625† (39.82%)
1920	55,036	28,251 (51.33%)	128 (.23%)	26,657† (48.44%)
1930	59,278	28,994 (48.91%)	136 (.23%)	30,148† (50.86%)
1940	72,524	39,892 (55.01%)	141 (.19%)	32,496† (44.81%)
1950	128,643	92,808 (72.14%)	N/A	35,835† (27.86%)
1960	226,167	176,315 (77.96%)	6,771 (2.99%)	43,081† (19.05%)
1970	300,382	239,409 (79.70%)	8,911 (2.97%)	52,062† (17.33%)
1980	402,000	323,900 (80.57%)	14,000 (3.67%)	64,100 (15.95%)
1990	550,043	441,723 (80.31%)	22,195 (4.04%)	86,125 (15.66%)

*Approximations only—missing data or error in initial computations.
†Includes persons designated as "other" in U.S. census.
Sources: Kynell, 1991: 30. U.S. Department of Commerce, 1970 and 1990.

Alaskan Justice

Alaska remained a federal territory longer than any other state. Fully ninety-two years passed between the Treaty of Cession in 1867 and statehood in 1959.[27] During the territorial period, the peoples of Alaska were governed by a combination of federal, territorial, and in-

. . . .

formal legal systems. Without access to law enforcement authorities in a vast untamed wilderness, an informal "miner's code" and several unique native justice systems governed the bulk of Alaska's population until the 1930s. Through these years, it is evident that Alaskans became increasingly resentful toward a federal system that dominated their lives from thousands of miles away. Former federal judge and Alaska's Delegate to the United States Congress James Wickersham argued that "the power of national bureaucracy had found a home in Alaska. He compared the federal control exercised over Alaskans . . . as more offensive than under the Czar."[28]

The Organic Act of 1884 provided the general framework under which Alaskans were governed until statehood in 1959. Under that act, all crimes remained, at least technically, federal offenses. A single appointed federal judge and four unpaid court commissioners were allotted to handle all criminal and civil law.[29] The Second Organic Act of 1912 allowed Alaskans to establish their own legislature and local courts; however, laws passed by that body could be vetoed by the federally appointed governor of Alaska or the United States Congress. Moreover, federal judges retained control over felony cases and all findings of lower courts could be appealed to them.

Many Alaskans considered the punishment dispensed by federal judges as excessive. Alaskans often viewed individuals accused of committing serious crimes as "neighbors gone wrong," victims of alcohol or the bush (cabin fever) rather than criminals.[30] Kynell found in fact that statehood, because it replaced federal judges with Alaskan judges, significantly affected court rulings:

> [G]un control laws remained far less stringent than Outside. . . . [Alaskan] state judges generally . . . [made] more use of probation, parole, and suspended sentences. Alaskan homicide sentences were somewhat lighter than in territorial days.[31]

Alaska's Executions

The entire history of Alaska under American law includes only twelve executions. None occurred after statehood. Only two other abolitionist states have carried out fewer executions (see Table 7.3). Evi-

TABLE 7.3
Total Executions in Abolitionist Jurisdictions, 1680–1989

State	Total Number of Executions	Blacks Executed
Wisconsin	1	0
North Dakota	8	1
Alaska	12	2
Michigan	13	1
Maine	21	3
Vermont	26	1
Iowa	45	7
Hawaii	49	0
Rhode Island	52	3
Minnesota	66	1
Washington, D.C.	118	80
West Virginia	155	77
Massachusetts	345	32

Source: Espy and Smykla (1987).

dence suggests that executing Native Alaskans or other minority persons did not violate the sentiments of early white Alaskans. Three of the eight persons executed between 1911 and 1957 were Native Alaskans. Two were African Americans. During this period, nearly 75 percent of known murderers were white, but white Alaskans generally received prison sentences for committing murders that drew death sentences for minorities.[32] Attorneys appointed to defend minority offenders were generally less than competent. The evidence that sent some minority offenders to the gallows was far from being beyond a reasonable doubt. Finally, more than one Native Alaskan who was unable to understand or speak English was tried, condemned, and executed without understanding the trial, witnesses, or the charges.[33]

The Abolition of Capital Punishment

Alaska's territorial legislature passed house bill 99 abolishing capital punishment in 1957, two years before statehood.[34] According to the

. . . .

memory of the junior cosponsor of HB 99, capital punishment was not a central issue for most legislators of the time.[35] Other information supports that observation. Not one official or unofficial document concerning HB 99 could be located in Juneau's state libraries and archives. During February, the month that Alaska's representatives debated and passed HB 99, only one capital punishment article was published in the *Anchorage Daily News*. That article reported only the length of the speech given by the bill's prime sponsor ("nearly an hour"), the argument of a single opponent (a nonlegislator), and the outcome of the vote, fourteen yeas, nine nays.[36]

Victor Fischer, a veteran of both Alaska houses, gave Warren Taylor, the bill's prime sponsor, the majority of the credit for ending capital punishment in Alaska.[37] As chair of the House Judiciary Committee, Representative Taylor was able to move the bill through that committee on a split vote (two yeas, two nays, and one abstention). During the day and a half debate preceding the full house vote on HB 99, Taylor gave—what Fischer called—the most psychologically moving and convincing speech he had ever heard.[38] Over sixty-five years old at the time, he attacked the morality of capital punishment. According to the *Daily News*, he quoted scripture and warned legislators about making "mistakes which can't be rectified."[39] Taylor also reasoned that "the cold-blooded way they [executions] are carried out makes you wonder if it isn't legal murder?"[40] Fischer recalled: "I served in the House for a number of years and in the Senate during the 1980s, but I never heard another speech like that."[41]

In a 1996 *Alaska Justice Forum* article Victor Fischer reasoned that fear of racial bias also played a role in abolishing capital punishment.[42] A public statement in 1985 by Senator Robert Ziegler (a former Democratic house member of Alaska's territorial legislature and a leader in the fight to repeal capital punishment) reinforced Fischer's perceptions and added yet another potential explanation for the passage of HB 99, which was lack of deterrence:

> If someone would show me that executing people would cause less murders I could be persuaded to change my mind, but nowhere yet has it been borne out statistically. . . . Most crimes are crimes of passion, plus I think minority groups would suffer most from the death penalty.[43]

. . . .

The bill eventually passed the Alaska senate by a considerable margin of twelve yeas to four nays.[44]

Efforts to Reestablish Capital Punishment

The 1973–1974 Legislature

The fact that seventeen years passed before a legislator attempted to resurrect the death penalty suggests that capital punishment was not a burning controversy during the early years of statehood. In 1974, a bill was introduced in the Alaska house calling for the execution of those convicted of first-degree murders in specific cases. After slight alteration, three of five House Judiciary Committee members reported the bill out with a "do pass."[45] With twenty-one yeas required for passage, the bill was narrowly defeated by a margin of twenty yeas, seventeen nays, and three excused.[46] After that defeat, capital punishment returned to its dormant state for another six years.

The 1981–1982 Legislature

Since the 1981–82 legislative session, a death penalty bill has been introduced in every Alaska legislature (see Table 7.4). With little notoriety, two bills (one in the house and one in the senate) were introduced during the 1981–82 legislative session. Both death penalty bills sought to authorize capital punishment for first-degree murder. Attached to the bill was a fiscal note, an official estimate of the financial expense of implementing the bill. According to that note:

> [T]he amount of state resources required to prosecute capital cases is unquantifiable at this time. It is bound, however, to be considerable, both at the trial and appellate levels. Recent experience in other states suggests that very protracted and expensive litigation may be necessary to implement this provision of the Act.[47]

Existing records indicate there was no further activity on either bill.

. . . .

TABLE 7.4
Legislative Attempts to Reinstate the Death Penalty in Alaska, 1981–1994

Session	House	Senate
1981–82	HB 458*	SB 73*
1983–84	HB 140*, HB 235†	SB 121*
1985–86	HB 163*	SB 119*
1987–88		SB 7*, SB 31* (CSSB 7)
1989–90		SB 17† (CSS 17)
1991–92		SB 13*
1993–94	HB 162*	SB 127*

*Died in committee.
†Passed by house or senate.
Source: Alaska House and Senate Records, Juneau.

The 1983–1984 Legislature

The first serious challenge to death penalty abolition occurred during Alaska's 1983–84 legislative session. During his successful campaign for governor, Bill Sheffield openly supported reestablishing capital punishment.[48] Three death bills were introduced, two in the house and one in the senate (see Table 7.4). The senate bill (SB 121) and one of the house bills (HB 140) simply sought the death penalty for first-degree murder. The remaining house bill (HB 235) would have queried state voters concerning their attitudes toward reestablishing the death penalty in Alaska. The outcome of the proposed referendum would have been solely advisory. A majority vote in favor of reestablishing capital punishment would not have altered the law. The intent of HB 235, according to its sponsor, was to inform legislators of public sentiment toward capital punishment; its intent was not to reestablish capital punishment. HB 235 received a good deal of attention from the 1983–84 legislature. It was reported out of the House Judiciary Committee on a split vote (two yeas and two nays) and was passed by the house.[49]

Preceding the house vote on HB 235, representatives debated the bill with only three representatives speaking in favor of the measure. Even the bill's primary sponsor shied away from directly supporting the death penalty. He argued that 91 percent of the "people" were demanding a vote on the issue.[50] On the other hand, seven representatives voiced outright displeasure toward the advisory vote and capital punishment. They contended that the ballot statement was unclear, misleading, and probably unconstitutional. One representative said: "If one hundred percent of my constituency were in favor of capital punishment[,] it still would not make me vote for capital punishment."[51] Opponents further reasoned that mistakes were sometimes made (between 1893 and 1962, seventy-four persons convicted of first-degree murder in the United States were later found to be innocent); that capital punishment was racist (the last six persons executed in Alaska were four Native Alaskans and two African Americans); that capital punishment did not deter murder; and that capital punishment was a simplistic answer to a complex problem. "The state should not get into the business of killing people."[52] When the debate ended, HB 235 was overwhelmingly passed by the house of representatives, with twenty-seven yeas, eleven nays, and two abstentions.[53] The advisory bill's success in the house was not duplicated in the senate. HB 235 died in the Senate's State Affairs and Judiciary committees.

According to official records, three public hearings on capital punishment were held during the 1983–84 legislative session. The Senate Judiciary Committee held a single public hearing, while the House Judiciary Committee held two. The longest of the three was the 1983 Senate Judiciary Committee hearing, where thirty-five persons either testified or submitted position papers. Twenty-two witnesses opposed the death penalty bill. Included in this group were seven attorneys, one of whom was also the area coordinator for the Unitarian Council; six private, non-affiliated citizens; two public defenders; two college professors; one physician; one Roman Catholic priest representing the Anchorage Archdiocese; one social worker; a representative of Amnesty International; and a representative of Alaska's ACLU. The rather strong contingent of lawyers testifying against reestablishing capital punishment moved the bill's sponsor to question the fairness of the hearing: "Where are they—the Joe Sixpacks—where are the people favoring capital punishment?" Thirteen testified in support of capital punishment. Seven were affiliated with the Moral Majority of Alaska.[54]

Those opposing capital punishment were rather consistent with their argument that people who commit murder do not consider deterrence (see Table 7.5). With decreasing frequency they also warned that the criminal justice system was biased and fallible, that killing people brutalized society, that capital punishment was uncivilized and expensive, that capital punishment violated human rights, and that capital punishment violated the U.S. and Alaska Constitutions.[55]

Supporters of the death penalty reasoned that there was "only a slight chance of an innocent person being executed. . . . We do not stop immunizations because some people are killed by vaccines."[56] Another pro–capital punishment witness argued that "beating, maiming and death—identical to [the crimes] committed—are necessary to teach lessons. . . . An eye for an eye. . . . Innocent persons are executed but risk is everywhere. The overall view of the Bible supports capital punishment. . . . Strong punishment will take away society's fear of crime. It has been proven to be a deterrent." Yet another person favoring capital punishment reasoned that society must be "either the killer or the killed."[57]

The *Anchorage Times* and *Daily News* both summarized the 1983 senate hearing on capital punishment in a similar fashion. Three out of four persons speaking opposed capital punishment. The Moral Majority of Alaska favored it while the Catholic church and Bishop Hurley of Anchorage were opposed. Ninety percent of those speaking were lawyers. There were also a couple of ministers and one private citizen. The executive director of the Moral Majority of Alaska reasoned that "capital punishment is definitely a means God set forth for society."[58] Senator Joe Josephson, a member of the Senate Judiciary Committee, admitted that most Alaskans would likely support capital punishment: "But my responsibility is to act on information and I think the public attitude would change if they had the opportunity to hear the testimony today."[59] Except for fewer witnesses, there was little difference between the Senate Judiciary Committee hearing and two House Judiciary Committee hearings that followed on February 11, 1984, and March 16, 1984.

Fiscal notes prepared by the prosecution division of the Department of Law, the Public Defender Agency, and the Adult Correctional Agency were extremely damaging to the cause of death penalty advocates during the 1983–84 legislative session. The House Judiciary

TABLE 7.5
Distribution of Arguments Offered for Opposing Capital Punishment*

Arguments	1983 Frequencies		1993 Frequencies	
1. Lack of deterrence/fails to make society safer	16	.2025	5	.1087
2. Unfairly applied	15	.1899	6	.1304
a. Capricious	(2)	(.0253)	(0)	
b. Racial bias	(8)	(.1013)	(4)	(.0870)
c. Class bias	(5)	(.0633)	(2)	(.0435)
3. Mistakes made/innocent executed	12	.1519	11	.2391
4. Brutalizes society/violence begets violence	9	.1139	3	.0652
5. Immoral/uncivilized/fails to respect life	9	.1139	8	.1739
6. Expensive	7	.0886	9	.1956
7. State does not have the right to take life/violates human rights	6	.0759	1	.0217
8. Unconstitutional	3	.0380	3	.0652
9. Bill(s) poorly drafted	2	.0253	0	
Totals	**79**	**.9999**	**46**	**.9998**

*Only those arguments mentioned by two or more witnesses are included in this table.
Sources: Senate Judiciary Hearing on SB 121, March 18, 1983, and Joint House/Senate Judiciary Hearing on HB 162 and SB 127, November 16, 1993.

Committee attached a fiscal note to HB 235 estimating that every death penalty case would cost Alaskans $200,000 to $250,000 in attorneys' fees for the prosecution's case alone.[60] A fiscal note prepared by the Public Defender Agency on HB 140 estimated that defending those accused of capital murder would cost the state taxpayers over $3.5 million in 1984 and over $4.4 million by 1988. Another fiscal note on HB 140 prepared by the Adult Correctional Agency estimated the cost of building a twenty-bed death row at $1,900,543, and the annual cost of operating death row at $1,008,723. Even Governor Sheffield no longer seemed interested in reestablishing the death penalty. Citing cost and lack of effectiveness as a deterrent, the governor said that he would be hesitant to sign a death penalty bill.[61]

The Adult Correctional Agency also submitted a "Position Paper on the Death Penalty," signed by the assistant commissioner for the Administration of Adult Correction. Citing cost, the possibility of executing an innocent person, and the ambiguity of deterrence, the agency's leadership expressed strong reservations about reestablishing capital punishment in Alaska: "The United States Supreme Court listened to a great deal of testimony on the issue of deterrence, but was unable to conclude from the evidence presented that there was a deterrent value to capital punishment."[62] The projected cost of implementing capital punishment weighed heavily on Alaska legislators. Meanwhile, a March 19, 1984, *Anchorage Times* article titled "Firing Squad, Lethal Injections Debated Next" relayed the cost estimates to the newspaper's readers.[63]

Varying sentiments toward capital punishment appeared in the Alaska press. A *Daily News* editorial cautioned members of the legislature that "the death penalty implicates every citizen in a cycle of violence that the state seeks to stop."[64] In a later editorial, a *Daily News* columnist praised a local judge for giving a murderer 396 years in prison and for speaking out against capital punishment as homicide by the state.[65] On the other hand, an editorial appearing in the March 7, 1983, edition of the *Juneau Empire* contended that some murders "suspend the rules of humanity" and deserve capital punishment.[66]

The 1985–1986 Legislature

On February 1, 1985, capital punishment bills were introduced in Alaska's house and senate. Neither bill was released from committee (see Table 7.5).[67] Legislative records indicate that no public committee hearings and no legislative or committee debates were held on either bill; however, the newly introduced capital punishment bills were discussed in the popular press. After reviewing the last execution in Alaska in 1950, a *Juneau Empire* (1985) article noted that "pressure . . . [was] building in the Legislature this year to reinstate capital punishment." The house bill's primary sponsor stated that a 1984 poll found that 84 percent of Americans favored capital punishment and that support cut across party lines: "I think if it gets to the floor it will pass either house." The article also stated that many members of the majority Democratic party strongly opposed capital punishment. According to the house majority leader, "It . . . [was] no more ethical for government to kill than for an individual to kill. Study after study indicates that it has little deterrent value." The new House Judiciary Committee chair was also opposed to capital punishment but promised to give the bill a "fair hearing."[68] The *Anchorage Times* reported that "Anchorage's district attorney, a Superior Court judge and two prominent defense attorneys [agreed] that capital punishment . . . probably doesn't reduce violent crimes."[69] One of these defense attorneys contended that support for capital punishment had more to do with personal political gain than protection of the public.

Nearing the end of 1985, a number of capital punishment advocates expressed their frustration with the legislature. The sponsor of the 1985 house bill, a former legislator and legislative candidate, organized a group called Alaskans for Justice. Its sole purpose was to gather enough signatures to place a death penalty initiative on the 1988 statewide ballot. One year later, members of Alaskans for Justice turned over the necessary number of signatures (21,317) to the Division of Election.[70] However, some signatures were disqualified and the initiative petition did not appear on the 1988 ballot.

The 1987–1988 Legislature

Alaska's senate provided the context for the 1987–88 legislative debate over the death penalty. Two death penalty bills were introduced in that chamber. The Senate Health, Education and Social Services (HESS) Committee combined the senate bills into a single piece of legislation (CSSB 7). CSSB 7 mandated an advisory vote of the people on the desirability of reestablishing the death penalty in Alaska.[71]

The Senate HESS Committee held two hearings on CSSB 7. During the first hearing, one witness spoke in favor and three witnesses spoke in opposition to the bill. During the second Senate HESS Committee hearing, twenty-one witnesses testified, fourteen in favor and seven in opposition to reinstating capital punishment. In response to those numbers, the chairperson of the Senate HESS Committee and cosponsor of the death penalty bill under consideration reasoned "that a tabulation of the evening's testimony came out two to one in favor of the bill. This is also the outcome of polls done statewide and nationwide."[72] Two statements made by witnesses favoring capital punishment suggest that some in their ranks were troubled by racial bias arguments. One reasoned that capital punishment was "not a matter of race but of people protecting themselves." Another "recommended that a clause be added so that prejudice does not influence a jury's decision and so that competent defense attorneys be selected."[73]

Three "fiscal notes" or estimates of projected expenses for implementing capital punishment were found in the Senate HESS Committee's file on capital punishment. The Department of Corrections, the Public Defender Agency, and the Office of Public Advocacy projected that the cost to their agencies of capital punishment for fiscal year 1992 would be $3.794 million. Nevertheless, a three yeas, one nay vote moved the bill on to the Senate Judiciary and Finance Committees.[74]

The Senate Judiciary Committee also held public hearings on the 1987–88 death penalty bill. There, nineteen witnesses testified. Ten persons (including the primary sponsor of the bill) testified in favor of capital punishment. Eight persons testified in opposition. The content of testimony differed little from that heard by the Senate HESS Committee.[75] After the hearing, the legislature took no further action on capital punishment.

The 1989–1990 Legislature

On January 9, 1989, the Republican senator from Soldotna, already the primary sponsor of 1985 and 1987 death penalty bills and the cosponsor of two others, launched another reinstatement effort. That bill, SB 17, brought Alaska closer to reestablishing capital punishment than any legislative action since 1983. SB 17 called for the execution of some persons convicted of first-degree murder. It also mandated an advisory vote on capital punishment. As with the previous proposals for advisory votes, its outcome would have had no legal bearing.[76] SB 17 was initially sent to the Senate Judiciary Committee, which, at that time, was headed by a strong supporter of capital punishment and a cosponsor of the bill. Given the makeup of the Senate Judiciary Committee and public support for capital punishment, lawmakers generally believed that capital punishment now had a good chance of becoming law. However, Governor Cowper—unlike his predecessor—was opposed to capital punishment.[77] Alaska's chief state prosecutor also expressed concern about capital punishment.

We don't have enough resources for the system now. We would do a less satisfactory job on 99.9 percent of what we do because we had this emotional issue out there. . . . The death penalty could actually work against conviction and punishment of some killers.[78]

Early in the 1989–90 legislative session, the *Daily News* also published a pro-death commentary from the sponsor of two previous Alaska capital punishment bills. This legislator stated he was "completely unpersuaded by this [racism] argument. Just about everyone I know in the criminal justice system agrees that we do have a fair and unbiased system."[79] Most articles and editorials appearing in the *Daily News*, however, opposed reinstatement. In response to the activity surrounding Ted Bundy's execution in Florida, a *Daily News* editorial concluded that "the same logic that killed Ted Bundy for his killings would also have us chopping off the hands of robbers, flogging adulterers in the town square and castrating sex offenders."[80] The March 8, 1990, *Daily News* article titled "Some Senators Won't Drop Death Penalty Bill" was less than complimentary concerning the numerous attempts by the Republican senator from Soldotna to reestablish capital punishment.[81]

The Senate Judiciary Committee held two statewide teleconference hearings in 1989. The hearings involved persons from Juneau, Fairbanks, Anchorage, Moose Pass, Sitka, Homer, Kotzebue, Soldotna, and Mat-Su. The total number of persons testifying at these hearings exceeded any Alaska death penalty hearing to date. At the first teleconference hearing forty-four persons testified. Nine witnesses favored and thirty-four witnesses opposed reestablishing capital punishment.[82] The *Daily News* reported that none of the persons testifying in favor of the death penalty bill indicated organizational affiliations. Organizational representation among persons opposed to capital punishment included Amnesty International, the Inuit Circumpolar Conference, the Coalition of Alaskans Against the Death Penalty, the Anti-Death Penalty Information Network, and Alaska's ACLU. Arguments presented by witnesses varied little from previous hearings.[83] The Senate Judiciary Committee chair, a strong death penalty advocate, conceded that testimony was heavily opposed to SB 17. She reasoned that Amnesty International and Alaska's ACLU had persuaded all their members to attend. She sarcastically commented to the death penalty bill's primary sponsor, "I'll bet you that 90 percent of them are abortionists."[84]

The second teleconference hearing involved seventy witnesses. Thirty-six spoke in opposition to the death penalty bill, while thirty-four spoke in favor. Arguments presented did not differ significantly from those voiced at past hearings; however, the hearing was far from typical. The morning session included telephone testimony from Stephen Layson and Ernest van den Haag, two well-known pro–death penalty academics—Layson an economist, and van den Haag a philosopher. Layson told the committee that each execution in the United States saved as many as fifteen lives. When questioned about the effect Alaskans could expect from reestablishing capital punishment, his statements were less optimistic. Layson reasoned that Alaska, given its small population and small number of murders, would only "deter four or five murders" with each execution. Moreover, Layson admitted that increasing the probability of arrest and conviction had greater deterrent effect than capital punishment. Professor van den Haag was not so reserved in his praise for capital punishment. He told the committee that "there is no proof for the absence of a deterrent effect. Consequently, we should continue to execute. It is better to execute a murderer needlessly than risk the life of an innocent person. If one innocent life is saved, it is worth the effort."[85] A front-page article appearing the next day in the *Daily News* reviewed the deterrence claims of Layson and van den Haag. After noting the caution exercised by Layson, the reporter remarked that van den Haag expressed no such reservations. In reference to executing an innocent person, a reporter wrote, "he [van den Haag] likened such a miscarriage to a construction error that causes a building to collapse, accidentally killing those inside."[86]

On February 16, 1989, the Senate Judiciary Committee listened to representatives from Alaska's Department of Corrections, the Public Defender Agency, the Office of Public Advocacy, and the prosecution division of the Department of Law discuss the financial burden that reestablishing capital punishment would have on their respective agencies. The only positive news for death penalty advocates came from the special assistant, Department of Corrections. He informed the committee that death-row cells could easily be incorporated into the newly constructed maximum security prison; therefore, the cost of housing and executing prisoners would be substantially lower than correctional officials had estimated in 1984. The projected cost of providing defense in capital cases remained high. According to a Public Defender Agency representative, ten persons would face the death penalty and it would cost $150,000 to defend each case. The most sobering news came from the Department of Law spokesperson. She stated that the fiscal note prepared by her agency was based on the assumption that only a portion of first-degree murder cases would be eligible for capital prosecution; however, SB 17 called for every first-degree murder case to be handled as a capital case. Thus, annual costs would be substantially higher than previously estimated. The Office of Public Advocacy representative referred to the fiscal notes of corrections, prosecution, and defense as "serious underestimations" of the cost associated with the imposition of the death penalty in Alaska.[87] It was noted that a New York study and California data placed the cost of each capital case at $1.7 to $1.8 million.

In an attempt to reduce projected expenses, the cosponsor of the 1989 legislation led a successful campaign to reduce the scope of his death penalty bill. Instead of having all first-degree murderers face the possibility of execution, the committee substitute bill gave prosecutors the discretion to select candidates for capital punishment.[88] The amended bill was reported out of the Senate Judiciary Committee. Four committee members signed the committee report with a "do pass" recommendation. One committee member signed the report with no recommendation.[89] Only the Senate Finance Committee stood between the 1989 death penalty bill and a vote of the full senate. The Senate Finance Committee held yet another public hearing on the bill.[90] The hearing was relatively brief. A total of nine witnesses testified—three in opposition and six in support of capital punishment. While many of the arguments were familiar components of Alaska's death penalty debate, the content of most arguments was far more sophisticated than what was delivered during the earlier Senate Judiciary Committee hearings. Persons arguing against capital punishment focused primarily on cost. Their arguments were saturated with figures and data from other states.

After the hearing, the issue of cost dominated Senate Finance Committee deliberations. Alaska's assistant attorney general told the committee that prosecuting capital cases was "very expensive" and constantly increasing. Her agency projected the cost of prosecution at $819,000 for the first year, $1.5 million for the second year, and $2.2 million for the third year.[91] She argued that capital punishment litigation would have essentially the same public safety effect as budget cuts: to take money away from law enforcement and thereby increase the rates of serious crime. Representatives of the Office of Public Advocacy and a past director of the Department of Corrections also referred to the cost of capital punishment as prohibitive. No agency representative spoke in support of SB 17.[92]

Alaska's death penalty debate took a short hiatus following the Senate Finance Committee hearing. By March of 1990, however, the death penalty bill introduced in 1989 once again took center stage. The latest fiscal notes, prepared by the state agencies that would be responsible for implementing capital punishment, estimated that it would cost Alaskans $5,862,000 in fiscal year 1994. The death penalty bill's primary sponsor countered by simply contending that the "fiscal notes" were too high. He reasoned that the projected cost for his bill should be zero, since the effective date for the death penalty component of the bill was more than a year away. It would only cost $2,200 to carry out the advisory election in the interim between passage and the effective date. Another member of the Senate Finance Committee wondered:

> how fiscal impact could be termed zero if capital punishment is set in statutes regardless of the outcome of the advisory vote. . . . [F]rom 1992 hence it would have a fiscal impact. . . . [F]iscal notes are supposed to project cost for five years.[93]

Legislators outside of the Senate Finance Committee were puzzled by the reasoning of the bill's sponsor. One of Alaska's most ardent supporters of capital punishment and a cosponsor of the bill in question, the Senate Judiciary Committee chair, called the senator from Soldotna's reasoning "absolutely irrational." She conceded that "for the bill to hold up to legal challenges, there must be enough money in the budget to give defendants a good defense and for the prosecution to thoroughly investigate each case."[94]

While the Senate Finance Committee ultimately reported out the 1989 death penalty bill to the Senate Rules Committee, support for SB 17 was far from overwhelming. Four fiscal notes attached to the bill estimated the economic cost of capital punishment through its first year (1992) at $2,690,300. Three senators signed with a "do pass," one senator signed with no recommendation, and two senators signed with "do not pass—the only thing that should be killed is this bill."[95]

During a brief debate that preceded the vote of the full senate, five senators argued against passage. One senator argued in favor of passage. Senators opposing the bill contended that Alaska was not soft on crime (with only Texas having a proportionately larger prison population), that capital punishment was too expensive, that deterrence was not supported by the existing evidence, and that twenty-one persons had been wrongly executed in the twentieth century. Another senator speaking in opposition told his fellow senators that he did not care what most Alaskans thought: "No person has the right to take a human life . . . a woman considering aborting or a jury."[96] On the other hand, the lone senator speaking in favor of the bill stated that "no one likes capital punishment," but the people want it.[97] The 1989–90 death penalty bill passed the senate with eleven yeas and nine nays.[98]

Optimism among death penalty advocates, however, was short-lived. Before receiving the bill, the Democratic cochair of the House Judiciary Committee reasoned that capital punishment would "have great difficulty getting the necessary support to pass the House in this late stage of the Session. . . . This isn't a burning issue of the day around here."[99] The House Judiciary Committee in fact failed to hold any capital punishment hearings and refused to release the bill from committee. The legislature was through with the death penalty for yet another session.

The 1991–1992 Legislature

Alaska's death penalty debate took a respite during the 1991–92 legislative session. However, the Republican senator from Soldotna, a sponsor of three of the previous four death penalty bills, was unable to remain completely silent on the issue. With little publicity, he introduced his fourth death penalty bill. This bill, however, sought only an advisory vote on whether or not Alaska legislators should reestablish capital punishment. The Senate Judiciary Committee approved the bill on a four to one vote.[100] The bill, however, died in the Senate Finance Committee.

Several factors suggested that the relative calm in Alaska's death penalty debate was to be short-lived. First, a number of high-profile murder cases in the state made regular appearances in the public press.[101] Second, a high-profile politician who strongly supported reestablishing capital punishment in Alaska was elected prosecuting attorney in Anchorage. Third, federal prosecutors, with the support of Anchorage's new prosecuting attorney, were actively seeking to apply federal death statutes in Alaska.[102] Finally, Wally Hickel was elected governor and promised to reinstate capital punishment.[103]

The 1993–1994 Legislature

Alaska's death penalty debate regained its intensity during the 1993–94 legislative session. Several death penalty articles, editorials, and letters were published in the *Daily News*. Although two death penalty bills were introduced in the legislature, the Republican senator from Soldotna, who was associated with nearly every legislative reinstatement effort from 1983 through the early 1990s, was absent from the debate. That role was assumed by a Republican representative from Anchorage, the primary sponsor of the 1993–94 house death penalty bill (HB 162). The senate bill (SB 127) was introduced by Senate Judiciary Committee members. The Republican chair of the Senate Judiciary Committee also took a relatively active role in the death penalty debate.

At the beginning of the 1993–94 legislative session hopes were high among Alaska's death penalty advocates that the death penalty would soon be a legal reality. Surveys suggested that 75 percent of Alaskans favored capital punishment for first-degree murderers. Anchorage's legislative assembly voted eight to one in support of capital punishment. The primary sponsor of HB 162 rejoiced: "It's an idea whose time has come. We haven't had a governor who would support it before."[104] The Senate Judiciary Committee chair exclaimed that "the Republicans are finally in charge of the legislature [Republicans were the majority party in the house and senate] and we're sick and tired of the failed social experiments of a bunch of liberals."[105]

By the end of the 1994 legislative session, the optimism of death penalty advocates had faded. Death penalty proponents would likely be denied a death penalty statute one more time. With the knowledge that capital punishment legislation was not moving, the chair of the Senate Judiciary Committee offered a substitute bill that removed everything from the senate bill except the part authorizing an advisory vote on capital punishment.[106] In the end, even the committee substitute bill was rejected. The 1994 senate bill was held in committee on the basis of a two yea, three nay vote.[107]

The house death penalty bill did not fare any better. Initially, it appeared that capital punishment would not make it out of the House Judiciary Committee, the bill's first legislative hurdle. That committee initially voted three to four against moving HB 162 to the House Finance Committee (the bill's second stop).[108] Perception of the bill's chances were far from optimistic, even among House Judiciary Committee members voting in favor of moving the death penalty bill out of the House Judiciary Committee. One such committee member reasoned that it was time to let another committee deal with it. In any event, because of its cost, he believed that it would die in the House Finance Committee.[109] Two Democrats and two Republicans voted against sending the bill to the House Finance Committee. Later, the absence of two Democratic committee members and vote changes by two Republicans allowed the House Judiciary Committee to move the bill on to the House Finance Committee.[110] Referring to the potential fate of the bill in the House Finance Committee, a *Daily News* reporter commented:

> [M]any of their [House Finance Committee members'] constituents strongly support capital punishment. But the estimated $5 million a year in additional legal fees that death penalty cases would cost the state is hard for lawmakers to swallow when the legislature is looking at cutting the state budget.[111]

The House Finance Committee held a brief public hearing on the bill and referred it to a finance subcommittee dominated by anti–death penalty legislators.[112] It died there.

. . . .

Between the introduction of Alaska's 1993–94 death penalty bills and their demise in committee, a number of events took place. First, the House and Senate Judiciary Committees held a joint public hearing on both death penalty bills.[113] For the most part, the distribution of issues discussed during the joint hearing was very similar to the distribution of issues discussed during the Senate Judiciary Committee hearing on capital punishment that took place a full decade earlier (see Table 7.5). However, the duration and sophistication of testimony concerning the financial expense of capital punishment increased significantly from previous years. In 1993, Alaska criminal justice agencies estimated the cost of capital punishment, five years after enactment, at $5 million.[114]

Expense was also the central focus of two additional public hearings on capital punishment.[115] Cost was likewise a major concern in the numerous capital punishment–related committee minutes and newspaper articles reviewed for this research. For example, the House Judiciary Committee chair, a Republican and former police chief, speculated that public support for capital punishment would go down if citizens knew the cost of capital punishment.[116] Late in the second legislative session, the primary sponsor of the 1993–94 house bill began his public hearing testimony on capital punishment by arguing that the estimated fiscal costs were too high.[117]

Records also suggest other changes were taking place in Alaska's death penalty debate. A *Daily News* article noted that death penalty opponents held a vigil to protest the house death penalty bill, an "Alaskans Against the Death Penalty" pamphlet was part of Senate and House Judiciary Committee files on capital punishment, and this group also had representatives debating and negotiating with legislators.[118] This organization negated the momentum death penalty supporters had gained at earlier legislative committee hearings. House Finance and Senate Judiciary Committee hearings held in 1994, in contrast to the 1993 joint House and Senate Judiciary Committee hearings and the 1989 Senate Judiciary Committee hearings, were dominated by persons and organizations opposed to capital punishment. Fourteen people testified at the final hearing on the 1993–94 house death penalty bill. Only one, the bill's primary sponsor, testified in favor of capital punishment.[119] A member of the House Judiciary

Committee lamented that public testimony on capital punishment had been "stacked with lawyers" and did not really reflect "current public opinion."[120]

Records suggest that the racial bias argument against capital punishment took on a uniquely Alaskan character during the 1993–94 legislative session. In a Senate Judiciary Committee meeting, one senator strongly argued that capital punishment would hurt his constituency, Native Alaskans.[121] During a Senate Judiciary Committee hearing and a House Finance Committee hearing on capital punishment, witnesses detailed past injustices inflicted on Native Alaskans along with the likely injustices that would befall Native Alaskans if capital punishment were reinstated.[122] During this period, the *Daily News* also published a major article that reviewed the racial characteristics of persons executed in Alaska. Two years later, the legislature remained unmoved. Republicans on the House Judiciary Committee opposed a reinstatement bill as well as a proposal for a citizen advisory vote on the issue. Republican opponents included a representative who was a former chief of police in Anchorage. He was joined by a former director of the Department of Corrections.[123]

Conclusion

A combination of numerous structural and situational factors account for the tenacity of death penalty abolition in Alaska. Data presented here do not support the notion that Alaska legislators have rejected capital punishment because of public opposition to executions, low murder rates, a peaceful history of ethnic relations, a lack of horrific murders, or an absence of moral entrepreneurs calling for capital punishment. Information gathered by this research suggests four structural factors that provide the requirements for death penalty abolition in Alaska:

1. A unique political and economic history;
2. Politically powerful minority populations;
3. A sparsely populated landmass; and
4. Limited state resources.

. . . .

Arguments (for example, racial and ethnic bias), in and of themselves, do not convince legislators to reject or accept capital punishment bills. Abolition in Alaska, as in other states, is a product of the interaction between the state's unique structural foundations and human agency— the activities and arguments of anti–death penalty advocates and legislators.[124]

Political and Economic History. Alaska was denied state status longer than any other state in the Union. As federal control moved into the twentieth century, many Alaskans came to view the laws imposed on them by the U.S. government, including capital punishment, as symbols of foreign political and economic domination.[125] The pro–death penalty testimony of the Anchorage district attorney in a 1993 death penalty hearing suggests he sensed that the anti–death penalty sentiment of many Alaskan politicians was at least partially reflective of their general animosity toward outside interference in Alaska's internal affairs. In an apparent attempt to sever that association the prosecutor from Anchorage equated passing a state death penalty bill with resisting federal domination of Alaska's legal system.

> The question is not whether or not there will be a death penalty in Alaska. There is [already a federal death penalty]. The question is do we want it decided by Alaska law, by Alaska judges, by Alaska juries; which is to say by the Alaska people . . . or do we leave it to the federal government—do we leave it to *our father* [italics added].[126]

The salience of the data concerning the execution of innocent persons and the statistics on racial and economic bias of capital punishment was potentially heightened by Alaska's foreign economic and political domination. Researchers working in the area of racial and ethnic studies suggest that individuals with personal experience of oppression are more likely to empathize with other oppressed persons.[127] Another study of death penalty abolition found evidence that a similar phenomenon played a role in death penalty debates in West Virginia, a state whose name is synonymous with outside economic domination.[128] More generally, Pepinsky found that two populations with a history of harsh treatment by foreign forces (Polish and Norwegian) were less likely to use harsh criminal justice practices against their own fellow citizens.[129]

Powerful Minority Populations.   While it is possible that racial bias arguments have moved some non–Native Alaskan legislators to reject capital punishment, death penalty abolition is more indebted to the presence of Native Alaskans in both of Alaska's legislative houses. A major factor that has differentiated the death penalty experiences of Native Alaskans from African Americans residing in other areas of the United States continues to be their access to the lawmaking machinery of the state. Unlike African Americans who were denied political rights well into the second half of the twentieth century, Native Alaskans have long been a political force in state politics. Their population size and geographical distribution guaranteed continuous Native Alaskan representation in both legislative houses. In 1996, "natives made up fifty percent of Alaska's rural population [and] twenty-five percent (five) of the Senators in Juneau (Alaska's State Capital) were Natives. Moreover, the Alaskan Federation of Natives maintains a political co-alition with Alaska's Democratic Party."[130] Consequently, Native Alaskans continue to command considerable political power. That power, which makes it possible to transfer group sentiments into law, is at least partially responsible for thirty-nine years of death penalty abolition. Native Alaskans and their elected representatives understand that the reestablishment of capital punishment would mean the execution of inordinate numbers of Native Alaskans. "Today Native peoples are more likely to be imprisoned than white Alaskans. If we had a death penalty, they would be more likely to be executed than white Alaskans."[131]

The potential for racial bias is, however, not the only reason Native Alaskans tend to renounce capital punishment. While Native Alaskans abhor the violence committed by fellow Native Alaskans, they do not seek blood revenge. The disastrous effect of alcohol on Alaskans is recognized as a determining factor in many of the heinous crimes committed by Native Alaskans: "Many Natives that commit heinous crimes were so intoxicated that they have little, if any, memory of what happened. . . . Natives view the possibility of Natives being executed by outsiders, regardless of circumstances, as reprehensible."[132]

. . . .

Sparsely Populated Landmass.   The fact that Alaska is sparsely populated facilitates death penalty abolition in Alaska. White Alaskans
tend to reside in urban areas while Native Alaskans tend to reside in
rural parts of the state. Rural areas—because of their proportionately
high numbers of Native Alaskans—continually elect Native Alaskan
legislators, who tend to support death penalty abolition. Moreover,
white and Native Alaskans generally operate in separate economies,
one capitalist and the other subsistence. Thus, Alaskans lack much of
the economic competition that drives most ethnic conflicts in other
parts of the world. However, as water, scenery, fish, and other nature
resources are transformed into the economic staples of tourism, ethnic
conflict and the demand for capital punishment among Alaskans will
likely increase.

Limited State Resources.   The state government of Alaska has limited financial resources and significant welfare-state responsibilities.
Thus, all proposed bills with fiscal impact must be reviewed and approved by the finance committees of the house and the senate, which
puts a double hurdle in the path of reestablishing the death penalty in
Alaska. As a consequence, cost was the most salient foe faced by Alaska's death penalty advocates from 1988 through 1994. The vice president of Alaskans Against the Death Penalty contended that cost played
the major role in the defeat of a 1995–96 Alaska death penalty bill.[133]
Regardless of the political capital to be made by reestablishing capital
punishment, the $4 to $5 million price tag—given the state's limited
resources—is beyond reach.

Because most Alaska politicians actively involved in attempts at reestablishing capital punishment are on the political and social fringes
of the Republican party, mainstream members of the party enjoy some
autonomy on the issue. When supporting capital punishment provided
political capital, it was supported. On the other hand, as it became
increasingly clear that capital punishment would negatively affect the
economic and political lives of mainstream Republicans, these legislators tacitly withdrew their political support. As long as capital punishment bills do not reach the floor of the house or senate and require a
public vote, many Republican legislators will not support death penalty legislation. A former Republican legislator and longtime sup-

porter of capital punishment blamed the failure of death penalty bills introduced during the 1990s on liberal Republicans.[134] However, if a capital punishment bill reaches the floor of the house or senate, it will likely pass. It is unlikely that many of Alaska's Republican legislators will publicly oppose capital punishment.

In summary, death penalty abolition remains under attack in Alaska. A serious attempt to reinstate took place in the 1995–96 legislature. Although unsuccessful, the tenacity of death penalty supporters in Alaska suggests that abolition will be tested in every legislature for the foreseeable future. If the oil industry in Alaska continues to attract immigrants from states with extensive capital punishment histories, if reapportionment continues to shift political power away from Alaska's rural and indigenous peoples to urban peoples residing in Anchorage, and if the Alaska legislature finds a politically acceptable way to fund capital punishment, the death penalty may soon become a reality.

Postscript

Anchorage attorney Averil Lerman recalled: "I became the self-appointed information officer of the Alaskans Against the Death Penalty (AADP) and an Alaska death penalty historian because people in Alaska don't consider death penalty problems in other states to be relevant to Alaska. Alaskans believe that they are different. I had to show them the racism in our own state's death penalty history."[135] Averil Lerman shows that history matters.

Colonialism and Capital Punishment

Race, Class, and Legal Symbolism in Hawaiian Executions, 1826–1990

Over roughly 150 years, from 1830 to 1980, Hawaii made the transition from an antediluvian kingdom to a modern state. During these years, Native Hawaiians saw the islands infiltrated by white or *haole* missionaries, American and European opportunists, immigrant laborers, and military personnel. During the immigration period, Hawaii underwent a political upheaval where white planters assumed control of the kingdom in 1887, declared a republic in 1893, and subsequently appealed to and received from the United States further protection as a territory in 1898. In 1954, Hawaiians finally witnessed the emergence of a territorial government elected by universal suffrage. Following the lead of Alaska's territorial legislature, among the first acts of Hawaii's new government was the abolition of capital punishment.[1] There is no mistaking the prominent role Native Hawaiians and Asian immigrants played in the drama of executions performed in Hawaii. From 1826 until 1947, Native Hawaiians, together with Chinese, Japanese, Koreans, and Filipinos, made up nearly all of those executed (see Table 8.1). Only three white males were among the eighty-two hanged after the commencement of "American-style executions" in 1826.[2] Following the arrival of immigrant workers in the 1860s, Asian agricultural laborers, primarily employed in the sugarcane industry, were most likely to be executed, as were those in ethnic groups with the most problematic labor relations with sugarcane planters.

TABLE 8.1
Known Executions in Hawaii, 1826–1947*

No.	Name	Year	Ethnicity	No.	Name	Year	Ethnicity
1	unknown	1826	Hawaiian	40	Shim	1906	Korean
2	unknown	1828	Hawaiian	41	Okamoto	1906	Japanese
3	unknown	unknown	Hawaiian	42	Higashi	1909	Japanese
4	unknown	unknown	Hawaiian	43	Yi	1909	Korean
5	unknown	unknown	Hawaiian	44	Kanagawa	1910	Japanese
6	unknown	unknown	Hawaiian	45	Lahom	1911	Filipino
7	unknown	unknown	Hawaiian	46	Nakamura	1912	Japanese
8	unknown	unknown	Hawaiian	47	Manigbus	1913	Filipino
9	unknown	unknown	Hawaiian	48	Bautista	1913	Filipino
10	unknown	unknown	Hawaiian	49	Rodirques	1913	Filipino
11	unknown	unknown	Hawaiian	50	Javellana	1914	Filipino
12	Kamanawe	1840	Hawaiian	51	Park	1915	Korean
13	Lonopauka	1840	Hawaiian	52	Hirano	1915	Filipino
14	Ahulika	1846	Hawaiian	53	Coronel	1915	Filipino
15	Kaomali	1846	Hawaiian	54	Golaste	1915	Filipino
16	Ayou	1856	Hawaiian	55	Yee	1917	Korean
17	unknown	1857	Hawaiian	56	Verver	1917	Filipino
18	Kahaliko	1867	Hawaiian	57	Florencia	1917	Filipino
19	Hooleawa	1867	Hawaiian	58	Garcia	1917	Filipino
20	Angee	1867	Chinese	59	Doyoylonga	1917	Filipino
21	Tin	1869	Chinese	60	Bonella	1917	Filipino
22	Kuhelea	1873	Hawaiian	61	Ichioka	1921	Japanese
23	Kaaukai	1875	Hawaiian	62	Ruiz	1923	Filipino
24	unknown	1881	unknown	63	Austero	1927	Filipino
25	Poloa	1881	Hawaiian	64	Reyes	1927	Filipino
26	Ahapa	1889	Chinese	65	Rivera	1927	Portuguese
27	Akana	1889	Chinese	66	Lacambra	1927	Filipino
28	Woo	1889	Chinese	67	Fukunaga	1929	Japanese
29	Noa	1897	Hawaiian	68	Kacel	1929	Filipino
30	Paakaula	1897	Hawaiian	69	Calibo	1932	Filipino
31	Tsunikici	1898	Japanese	70	Tabiolo	1933	Filipino
32	Kapea	1898	Hawaiian	71	Encio	1933	Filipino
33	Yoshida	1898	Japanese	72	Mahoe	1937	Hawaiian
34	Gisaburo	1902	Japanese	73	Quinionis	1940	Filipino
35	Miranda	1904	Puerto Rican	74	Flores	1941	Filipino
36	Colon	1906	Portuguese	75	Gargarin	1941	Filipino
37	Kang	1906	Chinese	76	Leonski	1942	unknown
38	O'Connell	1906	Irish	77	Gargus	1943	unknown
39	Woo	1906	Korean	78	Domingo	1944	Filipino

. . . .

No.	Name	Year	Ethnicity	No.	Name	Year	Ethnicity
\multicolumn{8}{l}{Known Executions in Hawaii, 1826–1947 (continued)}						

No.	Name	Year	Ethnicity	No.	Name	Year	Ethnicity
79	Perry	1945	unknown	81	Thomas	1945	black
80	Pearson	1945	black	82	Mickles	1947	black

*The combination of Koseki (1978), Espy and Smykla (1987), and Theroux (1991) gives a grand total of 82 recorded executions for Hawaii for the period of 1826 to 1947.

Race and Class in Hawaii

The decline of the Native Hawaiian population throughout the second half of the nineteenth century and, almost simultaneously, the increasing demand for labor in the burgeoning sugar industry brought large numbers of nonwhites and non–Native Hawaiians to the islands. Francis Conroy (1953) outlined the circumstances:

> The reciprocity treaty negotiated between the United States and Hawaii in 1876 removed the U.S. tariff on Hawaiian sugar and opened to Hawaiian planters the prospect of immense expansion with an assured market. The problem of labor supply was magnified accordingly.[3]

With the introduction of contract immigrant labor, not only were new racial and ethnic groups being introduced to the islands, but new classes of labor were created in the developing economic base. Sugarcane workers and their families brought their native cultures and assumed the position of ready-made minority groups. Over time, Japanese immigrants became the majority of the islands' population. Historical records indicate that white plantation owners viewed contract workers from China, Korea, Japan, and the Philippines as necessary and well-disciplined supplements to the dwindling native labor force, while Hawaiians adjudged other Pacific Rim peoples as acceptable racial supplements to their indigenous gene pool.[4]

Explaining the overrepresentation of lower-class Asians on the scaffold in Hawaii requires separating the intertwining strands of race prejudice and class antagonism. In addition, nowhere else did the U.S. military, particularly the navy, have such a profound bearing on economic conditions and race relations. Following the coup that toppled the Native Hawaiian monarchy in 1893, the mainstream media were dominated by white Republicans until 1954.[5] Thus, the generally accepted sources for gaining an understanding of the community reflect the white perspective almost exclusively. While oral history projects have illuminated the lives of Chinese, Japanese, Korean, and Filipino immigrants in some respects, with specific efforts directed at race and ethnic politics and labor relations, research on the character of the criminal justice system and the sociopolitical impact of executions has yet to be carried out.

The position of the ethnic enclaves, and in this case the community of immigrant workers as they existed within the sugarcane industry and their social status throughout Hawaii, present a compelling case for viewing the islands from an internal colonialism model.[6] Hawaii fits the criteria of the classic colony as Blumer and Duster understood it. Colonizers "wanted something clear, visible, and tangible from the colony," in this case sugarcane.[7] Second, colonial elites required cheap labor and brought immigrants from Asia and Portugal to satisfy this need. Hawaii represents a geographical unit that made use of the death penalty while under territorial status, and subsequently abolished capital punishment when universal suffrage became a reality under political home rule. It is not surprising that the chances of reinstatement of capital punishment are almost nil.[8]

Pre–1893 Hawaii and the Influence of Missionaries

Hawaii has a history of executions extending far into the nineteenth century, when the islands were a sovereign kingdom.[9] Executions for a variety of crimes including murder, rape, and treason were carried out. In addition, Native Hawaiian traditions made little distinction between children and adults in regard to penalties for such offenses. A chief, and later the king, was the senior executive and judicial officer in the Native Hawaiian kingdom. Law by decree was common and taboos or *kapus* were often imposed upon acts that the royal head had banned in order to maintain the existing social order. His subjects were his property to do with as he saw fit. All the land of the islands was the personal property of the king and its governance bore certain important similarities to the feudal system of medieval Europe. Distribution was contingent on favor at court and Native Hawaiians lived with the constant reminder that their bodies and their land were bound to royal power and custom.

Although whites had been known in the islands since Captain Cook's visit in 1776, outside influences had little impact on Native Hawaiians until the arrival of Congregational missionaries in the early 1820s. The missionaries, largely from New England, brought with them a contempt for royal power and a singular disdain for capital punishment. Their influence among the Native Hawaiian ruling class was considerable, causing what Goonatilake called a "reversal of values and cultural colonialism" that utterly transformed Hawaii.[10] Missionaries helped to reduce the use of cruel punishments and significantly abbreviated the incidence of death decrees made by the monarchs and nobility. Yet by the late 1860s, the influence of European and American entrepreneurs who frequented the islands in growing numbers had minimized the impact of the missionaries.

Immigration Period, 1850–1917

From the arrival of missionaries in the 1820s until the revolution of 1893, Hawaii was ruled by a feudal monarchy. Because the missionaries who arrived in the first half of the nineteenth century deplored the use of capital punishment, the courts, set in place in the islands from the 1840s through the 1860s, only infrequently handed down sentences of death, but when they did, Espy and Smykla have shown that these sanctions were reserved for Native Hawaiians.[11]

The dire need for workers in the sugarcane fields and the immigration of foreign labor were major elements in the use of capital punishment as a device of social control and a symbol of white rule in the islands. While the need for labor among sugarcane planters had increased dramatically, the Native Hawaiian population had significantly decreased due to smallpox and venereal disease. There existed a clear necessity to import cheap labor from Asia and the growing numbers of Chinese who emigrated to the West seeking work seemed promising.

Beginning in the early 1870s, the Chinese had arrived in large numbers to take jobs in the sugarcane fields and were followed by successive waves of Japanese and Filipinos who arrived in the islands over the next fifty years.

By the 1890s, immigrant populations in the islands outnumbered both Native Hawaiians and whites, who had banded together to make efficient use of Asian labor. Both Native Hawaiians and whites faced a serious dilemma. Without immigrant labor the profits of the sugarcane business could not be fully exploited. Importation of large groups of Asians who were the least expensive to obtain and maintain seemed to be the answer. However, those workers threatened to outnumber and dominate the small island republic where white settlers were relatively few and the Native Hawaiian population was steadily decreasing.[12] The importation of foreign labor also threatened the sugarcane business directly because profits were vulnerable to labor militancy and strikes. The government and the planters employed a threefold strategy to blunt the effect of the foreign influx:

1. The constitution of 1887 withdrew naturalization for Asians and enhanced what one planter called the "exalted destiny of the white man and his power to control and govern both men and elements."[13] Simply put, "residents of American or European parentage could vote. Orientals could not."[14] Persons born in the islands were also included in the franchise, but providing proof of citizenship was nearly impossible for the poor and few had access to the resources to sue for their rights. Not only were Asians barred from voting, but more importantly, they were excluded from juries.

2. Planters made a concerted effort to diversify labor importation so that no one ethnic group would become dominant.[15] Despite the fact the Chinese workers tended to be docile and cheap, planters feared that labor militancy would erode their power over the sugarcane workers and consequently practiced a divide-and-conquer tactic, pitting one ethnic group against the other. Portuguese, Japanese, and later Filipino workers took their places. Contract labor in most cases accepted lower wages before they arrived in the islands but often demanded raises for subsequent

periods, ushering in the introduction of a new group when labor militancy eroded profits.[16]

3. Whites kept a hold of key legislative, executive, and judicial posts, a hegemony much like that described by Genovese involving whites over slaves in the antebellum American South.[17]

Systemic Intent and the Anti-Chinese Campaign

Six Chinese men mounted the scaffold for murder in Hawaii between 1867 and 1897. All were convicted by juries comprised mostly of whites and Native Hawaiians. At trial, none of the six presented a criminal defense that would have encouraged historians to believe any of them were not guilty. Individually, their public, state-sanctioned deaths can be interpreted as the necessary closure to a succession of tragic events that demanded intervention by the kingdom's justice system. When a criminal justice system selects only minorities for its ultimate sanctions, however, the symbolic meaning becomes undeniably clear—as reassurance that the interests of the dominant race are secure and its power firm. In addition, it serves to warn the subservient members of a community that the prevailing order is in place and that the greatest force will be used to maintain the system. Capital punishment is akin to lynching; they both reaffirm the dominant racial or economic discourses and terrorize the minority survivors.

The first Chinese immigrant laborers arrived in Hawaii in 1850, the result of a declaration by the Native Hawaiian monarchy that reacted to the need for a larger agricultural labor force to exploit the potential profits in sugarcane.[18] Imported Chinese in 1853 made up only 1 percent of the population but increased to 22 percent by 1896, at a time when the number of Native Hawaiians was decreasing due to disease, childlessness, and intermarriage with whites.[19] The social and political disintegration that occurred in China during the nineteenth century forced large numbers of Chinese from their mainland homes to the Pacific Rim. They were known as "coolie" labor in Hawaii. Despite the fact that whites brought many diseases to the islands with their arrival in the 1820s, "in the eyes of the Hawaiian, the introduction of leprosy was due solely to the Chinese [and] was called *mai pake* or

'Chinaman's disease.'"[20] Imported Chinese laborers were also blamed for the appearance of non-native insects, the practice of gambling, which was common in China, and the use of opium, which had supposedly spread from Chinese sugarcane workers to Native Hawaiians.[21] In 1866, the French Consul, Jules Dudoit, was murdered by his Chinese cook.[22] This crime and the murder of an elderly Native Hawaiian in 1867 by a Chinese worker began an anti-Chinese campaign in the press headed by the editor of the *Pacific Commercial Advertiser*, Henry M. Whitney. Since sugarcane planters desperately needed immigrant labor, their efforts in 1869 to bring more laborers to the islands caused great concern among Native Hawaiians, whose population had declined roughly 50 percent between 1823 and 1866.[23]

The issues of interracial sexuality and intermarriage also emerged. The scarcity of Chinese women, who were rarely brought to Hawaii with labor gangs, was cited as a problem that supposedly fostered violent, frustrated, solitary Chinese males. Many in the anti-Chinese movement felt that the presence of more Chinese women would reduce sex crimes against Native Hawaiian females. The problem of unattached nonwhite males in the islands was frequently cited as a serious problem, yet no evidence exists showing that unmarried Chinese were proportionately more numerous as a criminal class.

There is evidence that many in the Native Hawaiian and white communities watched the growing anti-Chinese movement in California and applauded it, but feared that the exclusion of Chinese from the mainland would increase their presence in the islands.[24] However, the Reciprocity Treaty of 1876 between the United States and Hawaii, which lifted the tariff on imported sugar and promised enormous profits for sugarcane planters, probably improved the public attitude toward imported Chinese labor and lessened the panic brought about by the expulsion of Asian labor by the United States in 1882 by the Chinese Exclusion Act. Profits in sugarcane did not protect the Chinese community from arson. This type of ethnic cleansing consumed the Chinese section of Honolulu in 1886 and again in 1900. English-language newspapers hailed the conflagrations as welcome purges of disease and as an "ultimate blessing."[25] Evidently, Chinese lives were held in low esteem.

. . . .

The Arrival of the Japanese and the Growth of Labor Militancy

The horror of plague and smallpox epidemics diminished following the burning of Chinatown in 1900, and although the numbers of Native Hawaiians continued to decline, the issue of the native population passed from the public mind with the coup by the white oligarchy in 1893 and annexation by the United States in 1898. At that time, the increasing importation of Japanese workers had serious consequences for sugarcane planters. Conditions were little better than indentured servitude and were described as the "Pacific version of debt peonage."[26] For those workers who could escape the sugarcane fields, many returned to their home countries, thus creating a demand for more laborers to fill their places. Workers from Japan tended to be the least pliable and most militant group to immigrate. Between 1890 and 1906, Japanese workers struck sugarcane planters nearly one hundred separate times, twenty-nine of those strikes coming in the seven years between 1890 and 1897.[27]

Hawaii's annexation in 1898, which curtailed Chinese immigration, and the Gentlemen's Agreement of 1907, which effectively cut off labor supplies from Japan, increased the bargaining power of those workers already in the fields. The free labor market forced sugarcane planters to adapt and change their expectations of workers. Because the Japanese were prohibited from moving to the mainland, they considered their futures tied to life in Hawaii and increased their demands for higher wages and better living conditions. The Japanese made up 65 percent of the work force, compared to 9 percent Chinese, 5 percent Korean, and only 0.5 percent Filipino.[28] The tension built between management and labor until the summer of 1909, when spontaneous walkouts on several of the sugarcane plantations launched a work stoppage throughout the territory. Through organizations based in the Japanese community, workers demanded higher wages, an end to racial differentials in pay, and improved living conditions.[29] The Great Strike of 1909 ended in August of that year with workers achieving few material victories over the planter elite. The labor militancy of the Japanese and their increasing presence on the scaffold testifies to the use of the death penalty as a symbolic as well as practical weapon against an oppressed ethnic working class. Consequently, between 1889 and 1910, a period of unprecedented labor militancy, nearly half (six of fourteen) of those executed were Japanese (see Table 8.1). The strike, however, succeeded in focusing attention on labor militancy and sugarcane planters looked to the Philippines for a new group that promised to be less militant and more pliable.

The Filipinos

Filipinos were the logical choice as a continuing source of sugarcane labor following two decades of upheaval among Japanese workers. After the Spanish-American War in 1898 and the appropriation of the Philippine Islands from Spain, Filipinos were technically American citizens and could be imported without the usual complications of bringing in workers from foreign countries. Almost immediately following the defeat of Spain in 1898 and through 1906, Filipinos were in open revolt throughout the Philippines, engaging American troops in pitched battles as well as guerilla actions. Thousands of immigrant laborers were sent to Hawaii, where many would remain, working in sugarcane fields, in sugar mills, and in domestic situations. While it is not clear how many Filipinos died as a result of atrocities perpetrated by Americans during that war, it is apparent that American servicemen held Filipinos in very low esteem, referring to them as "animals" and describing in letters sent home to relatives how they tortured these people.[30] It is fair to say that military personnel reflected the views of the American government, including President Theodore Roosevelt, who commonly referred to the Filipinos as "Malay bandits" and "Chinese half-breeds."[31] The most telling statement by the military regarding the mistreatment of Filipinos was made by General Frederick Funston, who was quoted describing them as a collection of "liars and thieves" needing "the gallows more than the ballot box."[32]

In the wake of a brutal guerilla war, the United States Congress enacted the 1909 Payne-Aldrich Tariff limiting the amount of sugar and tobacco that the United States could import from the Philippines.

This made for a decade of further economic hardship, and over the next two decades motivated approximately 30,000 Filipino agricultural workers to seek relief through contract labor in Hawaii. The immigrants submitted themselves to a labor system ruled by whites and in a territory dominated by a military they had recently fought.[33] The American government purposely treated Filipinos in a manner similar to the way in which they treated Native Americans. Policy formulations for newly acquired territories followed a Native American typology that amounted to holding "racially and culturally distinct peoples . . . without the promise of citizenship or statehood, permanently excluded from the American political community and deprived of equal rights."[34] According to General Jacob H. Smith, military commanders reflected a "kill and burn" mentality in the Philippine War (1898 to 1906), much like the Vietnam version of search and destroy, but with the added dimension of killing Filipinos on sight as one would "shoot niggers somewhat in a sporting manner."[35]

The attitude of Americans did not improve when Filipinos arrived in Hawaii. Depriving Filipinos of basic civil rights meant disciplining them when they demanded better treatment. Discipline was also necessary in order to realize the full exploitation of profits in sugarcane. Filipinos were disallowed free access to the nation that had designated them citizens, were denied work arbitrarily because of their racial classification, and were the targets of racially based legal sanctions to help curb the possibility of intermarriage.

> The fact that most of the Filipinos who are here [Hawaii and the West Coast] are young men, that almost no young Filipino women are in this country, represents a serious situation. There is little home or family life for the Filipino immigrants.[36]

Bogardus not only commented on the problematic social life of Filipino men in Hawaii, but exposed the paranoia that infected whites in a society that did not stigmatize interracial unions. Filipinos represented a growing group of males who had to be controlled, who were competing for wives and partners. It is not surprising that Filipinos constituted the largest single group to be executed by white Hawaiian governments after 1893 (see Table 8.1).

The Ascendance of White Supremacy:
The Triggering Events

At the turn of the nineteeth century, Americans presumably adhered to the ideal of "one man one vote." Yet, as Smith recognized, nonwhites in Hawaii made up a segment of the population that could not exercise their full entitlements as citizens. This state of reduced civic participation for nonwhites followed the provisions of the constitutions of 1887 and 1893, documents that effectively denied nonwhites the vote. Smith referred to this exclusion as a function of "ascriptive citizenship," effectively denying universal suffrage in the case of nonwhites and relegating them to second- or third-class status.[37]

The uneasy relationship between a multiracial community and white-controlled justice system was strained further by the presence of the military in Hawaii. In particular, the U.S. Navy set the tone for the conduct of the U.S. military in Hawaii in the 1893 revolution when the USS *Boston* naval forces supported the white planters, led by Sanford Dole.[38] Hawaii was also affected by a large army and navy presence that created serious tensions between white military personnel and nonwhite islanders and servicemen.[39] The actions of military personnel reflected the attitude of the United States in general and the sentiments of most federal officials regarding the newest American citizens added to the nation in 1898. The military maintained a keen interest in the islands because of their excellent natural anchorage at Pearl Harbor, their large carrying capacity for troops, and their central location in the Pacific Ocean.[40] The islands were always viewed as a vital regrouping location for commercial and military vessels and did function as a springboard for U.S. military deployment in the Pacific. Hawaii was used strategically to observe and repel aggression from the Japanese, our most viable competitors in the hemisphere and, ironically, the most numerous ethnic group in the islands. Following 1898, U.S. military presence in the islands was always palpable, and despite the existence of the Honolulu Police Department, the U.S. Navy Shore Patrol have always kept a high profile. In Honolulu and around naval facilities, locals regarded naval police as brutes to be avoided.[41]

The Organic Act of 1900 was used to invoke military rule and martial law (Executive Order no. 9066) in Hawaii following the bombing of Pearl Harbor in 1941. In *Duncan v. Kahanamoku*,[42] the United States Supreme Court found that military commanders and courts had exceeded their rightful authority in maintaining and enforcing martial law over Hawaiian civilians. Put simply, the security of a vital base was in danger of compromise and a state of war existed. The military assumed that because the populace of the islands was overwhelmingly Asian and featured a significant minority of ethnic Japanese, they were less than loyal. The high court specifically addressed the position of military authorities on race and stated in a candor uncommon for the time that "extraordinary measures in Hawaii, however necessary, are not supportable on the mistaken premise that Hawaiian inhabitants are less entitled to Constitutional protection than others."[43] Overall, military rule between December 1941 and August 1945 led to relatively harsh sentences, and draconian measures were implemented under the rubric of national security.[44] In addition, military authorities saw fit to freeze rents, wages, and prices; censor newspapers, books, and radio broadcasts; and impose licensing regulations on the sale and purchase of commodities, such as cloth and eggs. All firearms were ordered confiscated and impounded. Most important, the military tribunals were specifically given the power to hand down summary sentences of death.[45] During World War II, three blacks and one Filipino were executed. At that time, martial law and military tribunals in Hawaii were not unlike those imposed by civil authorities in prior decades.

Guarding the Race

Now and then triggering events arose that tore the veneer from everyday life in the colony, pitting the classes and castes against each other and making race the undeniable focus. The kidnap and murder of Gill Jamieson by Myles Fukunaga in the fall of 1928 was one of those triggering events. Following the abduction of the ten-year-old white boy, suspicion immediately focused on the Japanese community. What was described as a "lynch mob" atmosphere pervaded Oahu.[46] Fukunaga was eventually caught passing marked bills from a ransom he had extorted from the Jamiesons. An examination of Fukunaga's mental state revealed that the penury and psychological privation he had experienced as a child had seriously affected him.[47] It became apparent to investigators that Fukunaga had perpetrated the kidnapping in order to pay the rent due on his parents' house and murdered Gill Jamieson in revenge for the Hawaiian Trust Company's threats to evict his family. Fukunaga had imitated the 1924 Leopold-Loeb Chicago kidnap and murder in an attempt to emulate American criminals. This finding appeared to many in the community as evidence of serious mental defect. Despite the evidence that Fukunaga was insane, a brief trial concluded with a sentence of death.

The Japanese community responded by protesting the sentence and citing the fact that white offenders who had murdered two separate Japanese victims faced no death sentence. One of those offenders was David Buick, who had robbed and murdered a Japanese taxi driver.[48] Found guilty of second-degree murder, Buick served five years and left Hawaii.[49] In stark contrast, Fukunaga's appeals were denied and Governor Lawrence Judd refused to intercede. Many in the Japanese community saw this as a clear injustice and evidence of a double standard based on race.

Before tempers had cooled following the Jamieson kidnap and murder, the 1931 *Massie* case exposed and intensified the problem of race in the islands. It also demonstrated the overwhelming influence of the military as an arbiter of racial social intercourse.[50] The "assault" of Mrs. Thalia Massie, granddaughter of inventor Alexander Graham Bell and wife of Kentucky-born naval officer Lt. Thomas Hedges Massie, was supposedly perpetrated by a group of "Hawaiian boys." News of the assault reverberated throughout the islands.[51] Poor handling of the case by local authorities laid bare racial tensions and non-white dissatisfaction with the local system of justice in general and the fear and loathing of the U.S. Navy in particular.

These tensions were further exacerbated by the naval commander of the Fourteenth Naval District, Admiral Yates Stirling, Jr., who publicly commented that the perpetrators of the assault should be lynched and that whites should "string them up in trees."[52] Not only did the military community feel that lynch law was appropriate, but the local tourist industry did as well, sensing a need to placate the fears of potential tourists. The swift sword of justice seemed to be necessary, particularly after *Time* magazine published a devastating exposé on the *Massie* case

. . . .

proclaiming that Hawaii had become an unsafe venue because the "yellow men's lust for white women had broken bonds" in the islands.[53] All five of the defendants were released after their trial ended in a hung jury. Military personnel rioted in the streets of Honolulu and the Pacific Fleet was ordered to avoid Honolulu in subsequent maneuvers for fear of additional violence between citizens and navy men.[54] Following the trial, Mrs. Massie's husband and mother kidnapped and murdered one of the defendants, Joseph Kahahawai. After a lengthy trial, with Clarence Darrow representing the defendants, they were found guilty of manslaughter. The presiding judge passed a sentence of one hour, time served. The following week, the convicted killers left the islands on a luxury liner bound for California in a furor of national publicity.[55]

The Post-War Experience and the Rise of Ethnic Politics

The *Fukunaga* and *Massie* cases effectively exposed the simmering racial tensions that enveloped the islands and clearly demonstrated that the criminal justice process was seriously flawed by elitism and racism. Both of these cases came into public view during a period when the punishment of nonwhite offenders was frequent and decisive. Yet the intercession of a world war and the impending social and political changes that would dramatically alter Hawaii came to the surface with the litigation and disposition of the *Majors-Palakiko* case.[56] Majors and Palakiko were two prison escapees of Native Hawaiian ancestry who were charged with the rape and murder of a prominent business woman, Mrs. Therese Wilder. On its surface the crime contained the same racial and class elements that energized white outrage in the *Fukunaga* and *Massie* cases. All the attributes of the white power structure mobilized to deal out severe punishment, and the newspapers played their part in describing the crime in detail to their readers.[57] Local political leaders referred to the perpetrators as "heinous, dastardly fiends." The Board of Supervisors of Honolulu County posted a reward of $1,500 and appointed a special crime committee chaired by the same judge who presided in the *Massie* case, the Honorable Alva E. Steadman.

There was evidence that the community was "aroused"[58] and the newspapers, armed with quotes from Honolulu Mayor Wilson and others, seemed to show that the murder of a prominent local widow was the latest in a series of crimes that amounted to a "crime wave" that had overwhelmed the islands since the end of the war.[59] All newspaper coverage took the position that the killers should be promptly caught, tried, and hanged. If such a crime had occurred in the decades before the world war, it would have been a foregone conclusion that trial and execution were inseparable, but the charges brought against Palakiko and Majors gave no indication of premeditation, nor did Mrs. Wilder's murder indicate that "extreme cruelty" was applied. Without these conditions murder in the first degree was inappropriate and the death penalty not applicable. However, public pressure, mostly applied by whites who knew the victim or were prominent in the community, prevailed on the prosecutor to reinstate first-degree murder charges and obtain two convictions and sentences of death.

The case went through a number of appeals and stays until Governor Samuel Wilder King, a relative of the victim, commuted the death sentences in 1954 and Governor Burns paroled the two in 1962.[60] The *Palakiko-Majors* case was pivotal in one key respect: it exposed the embarrassing fact that the old order supporting racism and bigotry remained and that change was overdue. The changes in Hawaii connected with the decline of sugarcane revenues during the Great Depression, the economic development associated with World War II, and the social changes that followed (desegregation of the armed forces and the Cold War) convinced many that the conduct of the criminal justice system was not in line with the rest of the country.

Universal Suffrage and the Abolition of the Death Penalty

The high media profile of the *Palakiko-Majors* case coincided with a movement by ethnic nonwhite voters in general and the Japanese Nisei (Japanese who were American citizens by birth) in particular, over-turning the control of the white-dominated Republican party in Hawaii.[61] Following the bloodless revolution of 1887, a new constitution provided explicitly that only those males of "Hawaiian, American, or European birth or descent" who were property owners, literate, and duly registered could vote.[62] By 1930, little had changed in regard to the vote in Hawaii. Seventy-five percent of the voting electorate was Hawaiian or white. As late as 1932, those eligible to vote participated in elections at an exceptional rate of 80 percent and effectively dominated the territory's political system.[63] The 1950s was a decade of serious political and psychological achievement for Hawaiians of all ethnic backgrounds. Nonwhites obtained universal suffrage in 1954. Statehood was adopted in 1959. During this period, a global trend in decolonization was sweeping across Asia and Africa.

After World War II, social conditions had changed significantly in Hawaii and a new group of native-born ethnics assumed their place in the islands' power structure. Haas put it pointedly when he commented that the "rise of multi-racial trade unions, oriented as they were toward Democratic party politics, spelled ultimate defeat for the Republican Party."[64] Indeed, a victorious political coalition of Chinese, Filipinos, and Japanese wedded "political disfranchisement to ethnic solidarity at the polls" and provided for repeal of the territorial death penalty statute.[65] The outrage toward unequal justice which many in the ethnic communities felt and which capital punishment had come to symbolize was apparently justified when considering Wittermans's and Castberg's breakdowns of crime and population.[66] Whites and Native Hawaiians, who were traditionally aligned with the Republican party, had apparently the highest propensity to commit both major and minor offenses (see Table 8.2).[67]

The treatment of nonwhite Hawaiian citizens, particularly the treatment of ethnic Japanese by the military government, and the outrage surrounding the *Majors-Palakiko* case, cannot be overestimated in the polarizing effect they had on Japanese Nisei voters and on the legislative agenda of nonwhite Democrats elected after 1954.

Economic Considerations, Reinstatement, and the Continuing Symbolism of Capital Punishment

In Hawaii the narrative of capital punishment does not end with its abolition in 1957. The death penalty retains a continuing presence on the political landscape, having been proposed in both the Hawaii house and senate sixteen times since 1971.[68] Advocates of reinstatement appeared on the political scene in 1968. In August of that year, members of the Bill of Rights Committee suggested that the question of capital punishment should be submitted directly to the voters in response to surveys that had demonstrated wide public support for capital punishment.[69] Violent crimes, other than homicide, did increase dramatically from 1959 to 1990, especially after 1969 (see Table 8.2). Certainly violent crime was a serious concern for the travel industry, and the movement for harsher penalties, including capital punishment, was in part related to Hawaii's dependency on tourism. Their concern was expressed in national publications: "Hawaiians realize that their economic growth depends on making tourists feel secure. Impromptu citizens groups have lobbied for greater police protection and harsher sentences for criminals."[70]

Even so, the movement for reinstatement of capital punishment, as recorded in the local newspapers, never mentioned the effect of violent crime on tourism revenues. Instead, legislators supporting capital punishment cited a litany of other reasons for their advocacy:

1. To deter life-sentenced inmates from repeating their crimes in jail;[71]
2. To address the fear of organized crime;[72]
3. To counter the "world-wide wave" of terrorist kidnapping;[73]
4. To condemn offenders who kill while committing other felonies;[74]
5. To condemn killers of prison guards, policemen, and other justice officials;[75]
6. To provide a general deterrent to crime;[76]
7. To prevent murder-for-hire schemes;[77]
8. To punish repeat murder offenders;[78] and
9. Finally, as a mandatory punishment for drug traffickers.[79]

The concerns of the Honolulu community about crime were not directly related to personal security, but were rooted, as they always had been, in the economic life of the islands. Tourism and travel had taken over as Hawaii's major industry. Tourist revenues had been in-

TABLE 8.2
Data on Crime in Hawaii, 1959 and 1966

	Percentage of major and minor offenses in 1959 (Wittermans 1964)	Percentage of population in 1959 (Wittermans 1964)	Percentage of major and minor offenses in 1966 (Castberg 1966)	Percentage of population in 1966 (Castberg 1966)
Japanese	15.4	54.0	6.1	32.2
Caucasian	23.1	20.0	32.0	23.6
Hawaiian	23.5	6.1	29.7	16.2
Chinese	3.0	13.3	3.4	6.0
Filipino	2.6	1.2	14.9	10.8

Sources: Wittermans, 1964. Castberg, 1966.

creasing since 1950 and had grown 15 percent each of the years between 1965 and 1980; however, revenues took a serious downturn in the 1980s and continued to decline in the 1990s.[80] During this period of unprecedented economic change, Hawaii had also realized a serious increase in most violent crime. Between 1959 and 1972, rates of rape soared nearly five times, robbery climbed six times, and assaults increased almost seven-fold.[81] The exception to the general increase in crime was first-degree murder. Murder rates fluctuated from a low of 2.0 per 100,000 in 1963 to a high of 9.0 per 100,000 in 1974. Overall, the mean murder rate during the 31-year period (between 1959 and 1990) was 4.14 per 100,000, only 0.64 higher than the 1959 rate of 3.5 per 100,000 (see Table 8.3).[82] Clearly, proponents of reinstatement could not claim that homicides had increased so dramatically that a radical change in state law was merited.

Since 1992, murders have decreased in Hawaii as they have in the rest of the nation, and the character of most homicides in Hawaii demonstrates that tourists are not usually at risk. In 88 percent of murder cases recorded between 1992 and 1997, offenders and victims were related by blood or marriage, or were connected through domestic, workplace, or social situations that would not affect tourists.[83] If capital murder did not pose a particular problem for Hawaii, why would proponents of executions so adamantly and consistently propose reinstatement? Clearly, the symbolic value of having capital punishment as a

TABLE 8.3
Violent Crime in Honolulu, 1959–1990
Total Violent Crime Breakdown (Rates per 100,000)

Year	Total Offenses	Murders/ Manslaughter	Forcible Rapes	Robberies	Felony Assaults
1959	6,704	17 (3.5)	19 (3.9)	108 (22.1)	39 (8.0)
1960	6,380	12 (2.4)	18 (3.6)	68 (13.6)	32 (6.4)
1961	7,685	12 (2.4)	21 (4.2)	68 (13.6)	47 (9.4)
1962	8,857	19 (3.4)	15 (2.7)	118 (21.3)	97 (17.5)
1963	8,761	11 (2.0)	18 (3.3)	78 (14.1)	98 (17.8)
1964	10,340	13 (2.3)	15 (2.7)	95 (16.9)	359 (63.9)
1965	12,522	18 (3.1)	6 (1.0)	130 (22.6)	282 (49.1)
1966	13,826	18 (3.1)	30 (5.2)	151 (26.1)	306 (52.8)
1967	15,217	17 (2.8)	33 (5.5)	144 (23.9)	315 (52.3)
1968	19,804	20 (3.2)	52 (8.2)	167 (26.3)	338 (53.3)
1969	21,224	23 (3.6)	82 (12.7)	272 (42.1)	183 (28.3)
1970	21,148	25 (4.0)	85 (13.5)	473 (75.0)	251 (39.8)
1971	24,530	31 (4.8)	124 (19.1)	715 (110.4)	381 (58.8)
1972	20,782	44 (6.6)	149 (22.4)	428 (64.4)	366 (55.1)
1973	35,225	36 (5.3)	150 (22.1)	663 (97.8)	287 (42.3)
1974	43,753	62 (9.0)	189 (27.4)	981 (142.1)	328 (47.5)
1975	50,232	58 (8.2)	169 (24.0)	1,050 (148.9)	319 (45.2)
1976	45,766	40 (5.6)	164 (22.8)	1,112 (154.8)	380 (52.9)
1977	46,984	46 (6.4)	176 (24.4)	1,081 (149.7)	357 (49.4)
1978	51,892	38 (5.2)	187 (25.8)	1,473 (203.1)	346 (47.7)
1979	52,926	48 (6.5)	223 (30.4)	1,568 (213.5)	357 (48.6)
1980	57,718	65 (8.5)	264 (34.6)	1,729 (226.9)	398 (52.2)
1981	49,548	40 (4.8)	265 (34.7)	1,320 (148.4)	340 (59.7)
1982	50,600	25 (3.1)	269 (34.4)	1,457 (156.9)	400 (61.3)
1983	46,228	45 (5.6)	249 (29.4)	1,243 (130.0)	599 (87.1)
1984	44,560	25 (3.3)	255 (30.2)	1,117 (115.9)	533 (82.5)
1985	42,048	36 (4.1)	248 (29.4)	965 (99.4)	552 (86.5)
1986	46,455	46 (4.8)	241 (31.0)	1,052 (106.3)	737 (103.1)
1987	48,949	36 (4.8)	322 (36.3)	985 (98.0)	915 (124.2)
1988	49,469	28 (4.0)	283 (32.5)	833 (84.1)	1,042 (136.5)
1989	52,909	43 (4.8)	412 (44.6)	815 (83.2)	1,027 (137.6)
1990	51,028	34 (4.0)	278 (32.5)	889 (91.4)	1,211 (153.0)

Source: *Uniform Crime Reports*, 1959–1990.

general response to violent crime carried an important meaning, even if the particular crime it punished was not a significant threat to tourists. Voters and the tourist industry could be assured that something decisive was being done by government about crime. A real effort was being undertaken to remedy the problem plaguing the tourist industry, the single enterprise that was the economic livelihood of the state. Hawaii's condition of dependency, whether on sugarcane or tourism, still remains a key element in determining the motivations for punishments.

Conclusions

The conduct of the criminal justice system in the life of a colony is of unparalleled importance in judging the quality of life, even after colonial status has changed politically. It is best characterized by Fanon's image:

> The colonial world is a world cut in two. The dividing line, the frontiers are shown by barracks and police stations. In colonies it is the policeman and the soldier who are the official, instituted go-betweens, the spokesmen of the settler and his rule of oppression. . . . [T]he policemen and the soldier by their immediate presence and the frequent and direct action maintain contact with the native and advise him by means of rifle butts and napalm not to budge. It is obvious here that the agents of government speak the language of pure force.[84]

The presence of racism and the efforts by whites to institute a regime of white supremacy in Hawaii are not the only reasons for the eventual political backlash against the use of capital punishment and its eventual abolition by a multiracial electorate. Separating, restraining, and terrorizing minority groups was a primary function of the death penalty in Hawaii, but it was also seen as an instrument of discipline for an immigrant labor force in the immensely profitable production of sugarcane. Hence, the shifting focus of death sentences follows exactly the succession of immigrant groups that entered Hawaii from 1870 to 1915, from the Chinese to the Japanese, and eventually to the Filipinos, specifically those persons recruited for labor gangs in the sugarcane fields. The practice and symbolic nature of capital punishment were clearly critical components of racial and class struggles in Hawaii. They conveyed the message to immigrant peoples that an economically dominant white/Hawaiian hierarchy was in place. Part of the "property of whiteness" was the guarantee of a fair hearing in Hawaiian courts and a near universal rule that exempted whites from death sentences. On the other hand, resistance by nonwhites to the established judicial, racial, and economic orders would be repaid with the noose. Later, the symbolic elements attached to the reinstatement of capital punishment promised to reassure tourists that crime would not be tolerated, thereby helping to maintain the tourist industry.

The ascendancy of a white, planter class over a series of nonwhite ethnic groups is best explained theoretically by the "internal colonialism" theory, which clearly demonstrates that within a given society a dominant ethnic group and/or economic class can institute and maintain an exploitative relationship with subordinate ethnic groups.[85] Historical evidence demonstrates that the influx of immigrant laborers and the attempts by capitalists to subordinate workers, mainly nonwhite Asians and other Pacific Rim peoples, had a significant impact on the process and outcome of judicial proceedings. Ultimately, J. Edgar Hoover's remark that the death penalty is a "warning" has a striking relevancy when applied to Hawaii.[86] After studying Hawaii's history of executions, it seems clear at whom such a warning was directed and what it meant.

Postscript

Sister Joan Chatfield noted that the issue of capital punishment frequently comes before the state legislature and that "[e]ach time the legislation was brought up by someone who was not native to Hawaii, who was not connected with the local community, and who was a relatively new legislator who came in from another state and who was motivated by political self interest."[87] Even after the worst mass murder in Hawaii history in 1999, in which seven people were killed, both

Peter Carlisle, the present prosecuting attorney from Honolulu, and his predecessor, Keith Kaneshiro, publicly oppose capital punishment. Mr. Kaneshiro was quoted as saying: "Hawaiians fear that the death penalty would be given disproportionately to racial minorities and the poor."[88] The powerful legacy of the oppression of minority people lives on.

Death Penalty Abolition, Reinstatement, and Abolition in Iowa

Historical and Cultural Background

At its origins in 1838, the Iowa Territory inherited the Michigan territorial law that punished murder with public hanging.[1] The first Iowa territorial governor, Robert Lucas, opposed capital punishment, as did Iowa Unitarians and Quakers.[2] In 1846, the chief justice of the Iowa Territorial Supreme Court, Charles Mason, opposed the death penalty. As he reasoned, the innocent might be executed, capital punishment is not a deterrent to murder, and Jesus Christ preached forgiveness.[3]

Iowa achieved statehood in 1846. There were sixteen votes on the death penalty in the Iowa legislature between 1851 and 1878. In 1872, the *Des Moines Register* launched a campaign against capital punishment, arguing it was both "uncivilized and impossible to enforce."[4] That year the death penalty was abolished by a margin of fifty-four to twenty-one in the Iowa house and thirty-one to fourteen in the Iowa senate.[5] After a "dramatic lynching" in 1874, many newspapers and the public blamed the incident on abolition.[6] There was an unusual 1875 lynching of a man by a mob of women. The man had been accused of attempted rape. Thereafter, the balance seemed tipped in favor of reinstatement.[7] Prior to the reinstatement of the death penalty in 1878, there were actually several instances of mobs taking the law into their own hands.[8] Indeed, there were "215 known lynchings . . . and approximately 450 attempted lynchings" in Iowa.[9] In only two instances were prosecutions of the perpetrators even mentioned by law enforcement authorities, and none of the perpetrators were apprehended for the murders. In a frontier environment of remote wilderness and few accessible areas, lynch mobs had the tacit approval of authorities who lacked the personnel and resources to maintain order.[10]

The movement toward reinstatement of capital punishment was also furthered by a "national depression and a real crime wave" that generated more support for renewed executions in Iowa.[11] In 1878, capital punishment in Iowa was reinstated by a vote of sixty-one to thirty-two in the house and thirty to sixteen in the senate. "Lynchings, murders, and public opinion were mainly responsible for bringing capital punishment back to Iowa."[12] Acton noted that "in both 1876 and 1878, citizens petitioned the legislature for restoration. Moreover, in 1877, voters actually elected some legislators committed to bringing back the death penalty."[13] The *Ottumwa Democrat* heralded the restoration of the death penalty as bringing an end to lynchings and as a means of curtailing the perceived crime wave. "The good people of the state will breathe easier and fewer of them will have their skulls split open this year," the *Democrat* proclaimed.[14] Thereupon, Iowa became the first American state and the first jurisdiction in the English-speaking world to abolish and then restore the death penalty.[15]

Iowa's Relevant Cultural Characteristics

Since achieving statehood in 1846, Iowa has executed forty-one prisoners.[16] Bowers mentions only ten states with fewer executions. Prior to statehood, four individuals were executed in the territory.[17] Since the 1950s, Iowa has executed only one person.[18] In the 1950s, its execution rate was 0.4 per 100,000—last among death penalty states. Thus, Iowans have little collective memory of using the death penalty, making it much easier to be ambivalent—and even hostile—to restoration efforts. Iowa's legislature originally abolished the death penalty in 1872 under pressure from two Des Moines newspapers, the *Register* and the *Leader*. The *Register* was instrumental in the second abolition effort, and the newspaper's opposition continues today.[19]

Clearly the 1960s was a special period in U.S. history, when there was "a push for democratization of American society and [an] emphasis on moral politics."[20] These political characteristics were reflected in the governor's race of 1964 when Harold Hughes pressured the state legislature to abolish capital punishment. (These political characteristics resurfaced in 1994.) The 1964 race involved a candidate for governor who was widely admired by the voters and lionized by the *Register*. The newspaper's influence has been both cultural and political.

Iowans are among the least mobile in the nation, with 77 percent born in the state.[21] The pattern is now quite clear: People are less likely to execute those fellow citizens who have lived in the same community for a long time, who are well known to them, and who are racially similar. Iowa is ranked thirty-fifth among the states in its minority population, with approximately 2 percent nonwhite,[22] and its murder rate ranks forty-eighth among all states, much lower than the national average.[23] Articles in the *Register* show that in the 1960s and 1990s homicides tended to be the result of conflicts in domestic relationships.

The impending execution date of convicted murderer Leon Tice in 1965 again motivated Governor Harold Hughes to take a stand against the death penalty. In 1963, Hughes had been unsuccessful in preventing the execution of federal prisoner Leo Figura, the last person to be executed in Iowa.[24] The murder of young Anna Marie Emry in Iowa triggered an unsuccessful reinstatement effort in 1994. The puzzle is that in the neighboring state of Kansas the gruesome murder of a young girl triggered a death penalty law in spite of the state's similarity to Iowa: low murder rates, a low minority population, as well as a long abolitionist tradition.[25]

Minor Crime and Domestic Homicide in the 1960s

The *Register* reported many incidents of minor crime during the thirteen-month period from August 1964 to August 1965. For example, articles about these crimes included one titled "Steal 2 Topcoats, Suit at Cleaners," in which it was reported that a "sharp instrument had been used to 'pick' a rear door lock."[26] Another article reported a woman being "bilked out of $40 by a man posing as an FBI agent."[27] The *Register* placed several minor crimes involving youth on the front page. "Arrest Girls at Beer Party" was the report of "three Des Moines girls told to report to a discussion class for youthful offenders after they were noticed in a crowd on the street."[28] An article titled "Arrest 2 Boys in Prowlings" focused on the investigation of a nine-year-old and a fourteen-year-old held by police for "house prowling" and "cashing one $10 check obtained from a mailbox."[29] Young persons involved in minor crimes were also the subject of an article titled "Jail 4 Youths for Annoying," involving individuals arrested for "loafing and annoying passersby" at a main intersection of downtown Des Moines.[30]

Today, minor crimes such as these might seem innocent and even comedic. One of the most notorious tales of minor crime from 1964 to 1965 concerned "college kids [who] got out of hand."[31] The riot in Arnold's Park "resulted in more than 50 arrests and left a sordid trail of debris and damage."[32] The seven hundred rioters chanted "We want beer! We want booze!"[33] Injuries were minor with bruised hands and heads and large-size hangovers. The police chief was struck on the head by a rock.[34] The *Register*'s emphasis on minor crime in the 1960s implied that Iowa was a safe place to live and that the crimes that did occur were not serious or life-threatening and that crime in Iowa did not require the death penalty.

The *Register* articles on domestic homicide were more distressing. Children were sometimes targets of parental or caregiver violence. A mother and her male companion were charged with manslaughter in the death of a baby.[35] A fourteen-year-old boy was held in the "fatal shooting of his father."[36] In this case, the boy admitted the shooting and was charged by police. The *Register* reported instances of spousal or partner murder: "Mrs. Lucille Stumpf was pronounced dead at Broadlawns Polk Hospital" from a gunshot wound, and her husband was admitted in "critical condition with face and shoulder wounds."[37] A woman shot her boyfriend in her home after he had "threatened to beat her."[38] However, the *Register*'s representation of this domestic crime implied that it did not affect the public at large and thus there would be no reason for restoring the death penalty for murderers such as these.

If domestic homicides robbed citizens of a sense of security in their homes, stranger homicides took away any feeling of personal safety in public spaces. The *Register* printed multiple articles, typical of the journalistic style found in the 1990s but unusual in the 1960s, on the murder of Janice Snow.[39] Janice Snow had been found stabbed four-teen times.[40] Such stranger homicides in the 1960s in Iowa were repre-sented by the *Register* as rare occurrences. They were anomalies—cer-tainly nothing that would give most citizens cause for alarm—and certainly not a triggering event for the death penalty. Martha Coco, director of the Iowa Field Services Department, lists the number of Iowa homicides in 1965 at thirty-six;[41] however, the *Register* printed only twenty-eight articles on homicide, and 32 percent of those cov-ered domestic homicides. Clearly, the *Register* did not consider this volume of murder significant enough to call for reinstatement of the death penalty in 1965. In fact, the *Register's* editors were enthusiasti-cally on the side of abolition.

The 1964 Gubernatorial Election

The two major party candidates in the 1964 election for governor were Democratic incumbent Governor Harold Hughes and Republi-can state Attorney General Evan Hultman.[42] The issues they wrestled with included daylight saving time, methods of paying for improve-ments to the state highway system, whether to offer wholesale dis-counts to state liquor stores, the state's highway speed limits, a right-to-work law, and the death penalty.[43] Each gubernatorial candidate wanted the backing of law enforcement agencies. Speaking at two dif-ferent times to the Iowa State Policeman's Association, each candidate voiced his opinion on the issue of state-sponsored executions.[44] Gover-nor Hughes reported to the association that he intended to renew his plea for legislative repeal of Iowa's death penalty. Attorney General Hultman told the police officers that capital punishment was a deter-rent to major crime and described any movement to abolish the death penalty as "a sign of softness."[45]

The 1964 election year was the best year for the Democratic party in Iowa history: "Democrats won all statehouse races and at least five of the state's seven congressional seats."[46] Governor Harold Hughes proved to be the greatest vote getter with an early estimate of a 350,000 margin over Hultman.[47] "Democrats won complete control of both houses."[48] The average age of those holding these positions was thirty-five. Harold Hughes was "young as politicians go" at forty-two.[49] Chief *Register* political writer George Mills noted that "almost without exception, all of these [state] offices have been in Republican hands without interruption since 1939."[50] Now Democrats controlled the house by one hundred and one to twenty-four and the senate by a narrower margin of thirty-four to twenty-five.[51] When Iowa's legislature changed from Republican to Democratic control in the 1964 election, it signaled a change in the political environment. Iowa's governor and legislature differed from the previous Republican administration by emphasizing fairness and the humane treatment of all its citizens. This difference in political leadership would lead to the abolition of the death penalty in 1965.

Governor Hughes could be aptly characterized by his populist views. He appealed to farmers and "kept in touch with his roots throughout his entire political career."[52] The man was largely above political partisanship. These qualities were apparent in his policy not to terminate state employees when the Democrats took control of the statehouse offices.[53] By the fall of 1964, Hughes had become a national political figure. He delivered the seconding speech for President Lyndon Baines Johnson at the Democratic National Convention.[54] A *Register* editorial reported that Hughes's career was on the rise and his decision whether or not to seek the U.S. Senate seat held by Republican Jack Miller of Sioux City was of utmost importance to the Iowa Democratic party. "Few Democrats [were] likely to venture a candidacy for a major state office" until Hughes made his own career decision.[55] As it turned out, Hughes made a successful bid for the U.S. Senate seat.

Hughes's views on state withholding tax and the right-to-work law were appealing to farmers and blue-collar workers. He wanted to take advantage of available revenues so that the middle class (such as farmers) would not be forced to bear the brunt of financing state government, and he did not favor a right-to-work law.[56] Hughes felt that unions were collective bargaining agents for the average working person, and if "union shops" were prohibited, unions would be effectively cut out of the negotiations for better wages and improved working conditions, leaving employees open for exploitation by employers.[57]

The *Register* was clearly behind Governor Hughes's efforts to abolish the death penalty in Iowa. First, an editorial on January 10, 1965, reflected a sense of urgency regarding the 1965 legislature and Hughes's election platform: "There will be more than normal interest in Governor Hughes's recommendations to the Legislature this year. He undoubtedly will propose a number of long-range measures for reform and reorganization."[58] Later, editorials portrayed Hughes as a champion of those individuals who might have been treated unfairly in the state's criminal justice system. When Hughes commuted the death sentence of convicted murderer Leon Tice of Council Bluffs, the paper reported that "jurors in first-degree murder cases may have no information on the background of the accused unless the information happens to be admissible as bearing on the question of guilt or innocence."[59] Hughes "considered Tice's crime 'ghastly,'" but added: "I believe that no one can read the whole story of the defendant's life . . . without reaching the conclusion that the society itself bears some stern responsibility in the tragic events for which the defendant stands convicted."[60] Hughes was undoubtedly sensitized to this issue by the 1963 execution of a federal prisoner in Iowa that he had attempted to prevent.[61]

Death Penalty Legislation

Many of those in the 1965 Iowa house were newly elected and had little experience with negotiation. The *Register* described "two-thirds of the Senate [as being] experienced legislative hands, while about two-thirds of the Representatives are newcomers."[62] "The crucial battles of the 1965 legislative session were fought in the Senate" due to the five to one ratio of Democrats to Republicans in the house, compared to the only slight majority of Democrats to Republicans in the senate. In the senate, thirty votes were required to pass a bill. The Iowa senate leader Andrew Frommelt of Dubuque had the arduous task of keeping "control over the slim Democratic majority so he can fulfill the promises made in the party's platform."[63] Even if the Democrats had had five cross-over votes, it would have been "disastrous [on] partisan issues."[64]

The legislature took up the capital punishment bill early in the 1965 session. On January 27, a bill (house file 8) to abolish the death penalty

. . . .

was ready for action by the House Judiciary Committee.[65] HF 8 was "an act to abolish the death penalty as a punishment for certain crimes and to substitute imprisonment for life or a term of years."[66] There was no committee recommendation either for or against passage although Governor Hughes recommended passage of the bill.[67]

When the Iowa house took up the death penalty bill in early February, debate centered on amendments to the bill.[68] One amendment would have allowed the death penalty "for such crimes as murder of a guard or some other person by a lifer trying to escape." That was defeated sixty-seven to forty-eight.[69] Also defeated (eighty-three to twenty-seven) was "an amendment to permit capital punishment for murders involving rape, robbery, or burglary and kidnapping for ransom."[70] Iowa's dominant newspaper strongly advocated abolition of capital punishment. The *Register*'s editors believed that due to "the position taken by the governor and the Democrats in their party platform that the time is now ripe for action," noting that according to an Iowa poll, "57 per cent of the public opposes the death penalty."[71] The house passed the death penalty abolition bill on February 5, 1965, by an "overwhelming" eighty-nine to twenty-nine vote.[72] There were eighty-one Democrats and eight Republicans supporting HF 8, and fifteen Democrats and fourteen Republicans opposing abolition of the death penalty.[73]

The vote for abolishing the death penalty was decisive. Thirteen days later, on February 18, the senate concurred by a thirty-five to twenty vote margin. Yea votes included those of twenty-nine Democrats and six Republicans, while four Democrats and sixteen Republicans voted nay.[74] Thus, partisanship was obviously an important factor in the vote. The Iowa senate's action followed a two-and-a-half-hour debate.[75] Governor Harold Hughes called the measure, which took effect on July 4, 1965, a "great step" and said that Iowa was thus a "more humane and wholesome society."[76] He stated: "I believe [abolition] is good for Iowa and clearly in the interests of more effective and realistic correctional procedures."[77]

During the legislative debate on the death penalty, the *Register* took the side of abolition. The newspaper declared that the "time is ripe for action" and that the legislature had an "unprecedented opportunity because of the position taken by the Governor, and the Democrats in their party platform, to make Iowa law more humane, [and] less brutalizing."[78] When the house voted to abolish the Iowa death penalty, a *Register* editorial had urged the senate to take the next step to pass the abolition bill.[79] A *Register* editor announced that the "Iowa Legislature took action favored by a majority of Iowans" and that the "vigorous campaigning against capital punishment by church groups and other organizations" was partly responsible for the bill's passage.[80] Churches would play an even more important role in the 1995 vote on the death penalty.

Iowa's Reaction to the Southern Civil Rights Movement

During the months prior to the vote on the death penalty, the *Register* devoted considerable space to the depiction of inhuman treatment of African Americans in the South. The *Register* covered the murders of Northern college students who went to Mississippi to assist with voter registration drives during Freedom Summer in 1964. The newspaper also devoted space to photographs of African Americans being beaten or abused by law enforcement officials. The *Register*'s advocacy of the repeal of the death penalty in Iowa was consistent with its intense negative coverage of the South from 1964 to 1965. By abolishing the death penalty, Iowans would be showing mercy and respect for all life in contrast to the actions of white Southerners and in contrast to the frequent executions in the South.

Each day Iowans could see on television the brutality of Southerners toward African Americans. The *Register* focused on the actions by Southern law enforcement authorities toward those promoting civil rights for African Americans. Segregationist Sheriff Jim Clark of Selma, Alabama, and his posse were frequent subjects of *Register* articles. Selma, Alabama, was likened to "an underdeveloped country, short on industry and industrial skills, short on leadership and education."[81] Southern white leaders were portrayed in the manner of Tom Anderson, "one of the leaders of the national council of the John Birch Society," who blamed "Washington for all the woes of the human race."[82]

The *Register* covered the brutality of Southern law enforcement officials. Those in charge of protecting individuals from crime were usually responsible for the criminal actions against African American civilians. Certainly, Sheriff Jim Clark required no assistance in creating the portrait of a Southern white racist who was enamored with his control over the powerless. Clark, in a squad car, led African American children on a two-and-a-half-mile forced run "out of Selma into the countryside after they had demonstrated in front of the courthouse for the right to register to vote."[83] The children were made to form lines and run on a road leading out of Selma. Deputies beat with sticks any escaping child. Finally, the youngsters were able to run into the farm fields out of the "reach of the Sheriff and his deputies."[84] Sheriff Clark "locked hundreds of them up in three weeks."[85] "A three-judge federal court ordered Sheriff Clark to cease using members of the county posse," which included those on horseback.[86] Clark had regularly used the posse, composed of civilians, in dealing with peaceful courthouse demonstrators.[87]

In addition, Iowans carefully scrutinized the actions of the KKK. The vilification of the South included an editorial by the *Register* that called upon Congress and the House Committee on Un-American Activities to study KKK activities. During the mid-1940s, the same question had "come up to the Committee and was side-stepped by a 5 to 1 vote to 'defer until a future time.'"[88] The bodies of three slain civil rights workers were recovered in Mississippi in August 1964.[89] Federal charges singled out the men who had "plotted to intercept the three civil rights workers and 'assault, shoot, and kill them.'"[90] However, it was not until March 27, 1965, and the murder of Mrs. Viola Liuzzo, that "virtually assured an immediate investigation by Congress of the Ku Klux Klan."[91] Due to an increasing climate of Southern violence, "a responsible investigation of the Klan is just as warranted as a responsible investigation of a foreign-led subversion," according to an editorial.[92] The *Register* ran articles nearly every day on the violence occurring in Selma during the spring months of 1965. For example, a headline read "Whites Beat 3 Ministers After March," where "three white ministers who came here [to Selma] to participate in civil rights marches were attacked by five white men as they walked two blocks from city hall."[93] "A Negro leader told a federal judge of wholesale terror when state troopers and mounted possemen using clubs and tear gas routed a right-to-vote march."[94] The Reverend James Reeb's beating death occurred prior to meetings, marches, and demonstrations in Selma over denied civil rights.[95]

The *Register* showed the sharp differences between the cruelty of white Southerners and the peaceful demonstrations of the Reverend Dr. Martin Luther King, Jr. Dr. King was credited by the *Register* as having "spiritual dynamite . . . in the form of public songs and prayers, walks on the sidewalk and quietly ordering meals in restaurants, willingness to suffer rather than to inflict suffering."[96] Dr. King was also praised by Iowa's leading newspaper for being wise and for a nonviolent reaction to Alabama authorities who nationwide were being criticized for their suppression of the peaceful voter registration protests.[97]

Northern states were quick to judge the actions by Alabama authorities. The civil rights movement galvanized the 1960s by producing "a heightened sense of moral awareness."[98] Carrying "considerable moral weight," the Iowa house passed a resolution that "expressed its shock" at the actions of Alabama authorities.[99] Selma was viewed as a prime example of "deep lawlessness, providing a lurid background to the opening of the president's campaign against crime."[100] Through daily coverage of Southern white violence and the poverty-stricken conditions of Southern blacks, the *Register* set Iowans apart from their neighbors in Dixie—just as was true earlier in Minnesota, where the Duluth lynchings were roundly vilified by the press and lawmakers (see Chapter 5).

Reinstatement Efforts in the 1990s

During the 1990s, Iowa had a Republican governor with a legislature split between the Republicans who controlled the house and the Democrats who controlled the senate. The same structural foundations from the 1960s were present in the 1990s: a low crime rate including a low murder rate, few minorities, and low population mobility. Surprisingly, triggering events such as a child's murder, which might have focused legislators' attentions on death penalty restoration, did not prove powerful enough to propel reinstatement. Due to the Republicans' control of the governor's office and the Iowa house, mainline Protestant churches had to form a solid alliance in order to keep capital punishment from being reinstated.

Articles on minor crimes, so frequent in the 1960s, were all but forgotten in the 1990s. Crimes of violence were used to create sensationalized news stories. Yet in the 1990s, Iowa remained a safe state in which to live. In 1995, Iowa tied with South Dakota as the state with the lowest murder rate in the country, second only to North Dakota. With a murder rate of 1.8 per 100,000, this figure was "65 percent less than the West North Central Region rate of 5.1."[101] This geographic area is comprised of Kansas, Minnesota, Missouri, Nebraska, North Dakota, and South Dakota. "The U.S. murder rate was 8.2 murders per 100,000 population, making Iowa's rate for this particular violent crime 78 percent less than the national rate."[102]

By the 1990s, levels of domestic violence had increased since the 1960s. Although the percentage of articles focusing on domestic conflicts had decreased, a review of the *Register* suggests that Iowans were more likely to kill their loved ones during the thirteen months of September 1994 to September 1995 than during the period reviewed in August 1964 to August 1965. Of the 247 articles on Iowa homicides from 1994 to 1995, forty-seven (19 percent) focused on acts of domestic lethal violence. From 1964 to 1965, the proportion of Iowans murdered by a family member or intimate acquaintance as represented in the newspaper was 31 percent (nine of twenty-eight) from 1964 to 1965. In the thirteen-month period from 1964 to 1965, the number of articles per murder was 0.78 (twenty-eight murder articles for thirty-six murders).[103] The number of articles per murder rose dramatically to 3.86 from 1994 to 1995 (247 murder articles for 64 murders).[104] In other words, for each murder that occurred in Iowa from 1994 to 1995, there were almost four articles. Clearly the awareness of Iowans about violent crime had increased from the mid-1960s due to a dramatic change in coverage by the *Register*.

The murder of Anna Marie Emry was almost a triggering event for the restoration of Iowa's death penalty. Anna Emry was nine years old when an acquaintance of the family abducted, raped, sodomized, and stabbed her to death. The child's parents, Peggy and Tony, working-class Iowans, mounted a petition drive to restore the Iowa death penalty. Petitions with over 65,000 signatures were presented to Governor Branstad on the capitol steps, with journalists from across the state covering the event.[105] This child's murder became a rallying point for death penalty reinstatement efforts.

On the other hand, *Register* headlines portrayed Iowa and its capital as a safe place to live. Des Moines saw crime diminish in 1994 with drops in incidents of aggravated assault, burglary, counterfeiting, and forgery.[106] The metropolitan area also saw a drop in homicides. At the same time, "Iowa, mirroring the national trend, has cut its violent crime rate by boosting its incarceration rate."[107] But the *Register* made its readers aware of minority homicides. Some sensationalistic journalism involving African American or Asian crime might have led to the restoration of capital punishment in 1995 if there had been a large minority population in Iowa and a high level of violent crime, but neither of these characteristics were present.

The 1994 Gubernatorial Election

Crime was at the center of the Iowa gubernatorial race. Being tough on violent criminals was the primary focus of debate during the 1994 Iowa gubernatorial election and it played a key role in the legislative debate on the restoration of the death penalty. The two major party candidates for governor were Democratic Attorney General Bonnie Campbell and incumbent Republican Governor Terry Branstad. Even before the election and the beginning of the 1995 legislative session, chief *Register* political commentator David Yepsen predicted the death penalty would be "a hot issue. Recent homicides around the state and Governor Terry Branstad's renewed push for the penalty are propelling the question."[108] Although Yepsen did not believe that the issue would carry Branstad to victory, Yepsen did believe that Branstad's support of the death penalty would give him an edge with "the blue-collar, Joe Six-Pack, Bubba voter who used to be for the Democrats."[109] Rural Iowa voters who would otherwise support a Democratic candidate had a difficult time believing that liberal Bonnie Campbell, an opponent of capital punishment, would be hard on criminals if elected. Substantial publicity centered on the young murder victim, Anna Marie Emry, and this did not bode well for Campbell. Even with an endorsement in a *Register* editorial, this was not to be Campbell's election.[110]

Incumbent Governor Branstad made the most of the Emry family politically. Branstad met with Peggy and Tony Emry and conveyed his desire to reinstate capital punishment, making anyone convicted of first-degree murder eligible for lethal injection.[111] Bonnie Campbell also expressed her grief and shared her sympathies with the Emrys, but still would not support the restoration efforts. The Emrys resented Campbell's lack of support for restoration, but at the same time they expressed their desire that "Anna's name not be used for political gain."[112] The Branstad campaign violated the Emrys' wishes when:

> Governor Terry Branstad's campaign briefly aired [paid political spots] about the death penalty that invoked the name of Anna Marie Emry. The commercial followed by two days a personal plea by Tony and Peggy Emry . . . for no politician [to] use the death of their daughter for political gain this election year.[113]

The Emrys demonstrated ambivalence about the death penalty by not allowing the death penalty law to be named after their daughter and not allowing the governor to use their daughter's murder in his campaign.

The limited actions of the Emrys on behalf of the restoration efforts can be contrasted with the Schmidts of Kansas, whose daughter was murdered in 1993. The Schmidt family went before the Kansas house of representatives to plead for the passage of the death penalty bill. Stephanie Schmidt's father, Gene, also founded a nonprofit organization, "Speak Out for Stephanie," which lobbies for tougher criminal laws.[114] In addition to these activities, the Schmidt family appeared on national television talk shows hosted by Maury Povich and Larry King to promote the restoration of capital punishment. Kansas reinstated capital punishment in 1994. On the other hand, Tony Emry stated that he and his wife had shunned all requests for television interviews and offers of book and movie contracts based on the events surrounding Anna Marie's murder: "I do not know what Anna Marie's feelings about the death penalty would be and it would be unfair of me to decide that for her."[115] In their sensitivity for their daughter's memory, Tony and Peggy Emry negated what might have been a triggering event in the restoration efforts of the Iowa death penalty.

The candidates spent considerable time comparing the expenses of capital punishment with life in prison. Bonnie Campbell's calculations on the cost of locking up a person for life were compared with the figures Branstad's campaign publicized if appeals were reduced during the postconviction process.[116] Similarly, during the legislative debate in the Iowa houses, a key issue was the effect the death penalty might have on the state budget. Seeing the actual budget in the *Register* served as a point of opposition for some of those who might otherwise have been capital punishment proponents.

Bonnie Campbell charged that "Branstad's tough talk on crime this election year is at odds with the record he has compiled during his three terms as governor."[117] In the end, her credibility was damaged when the facts she provided regarding Iowa conviction rates and sentencing were found to be inaccurate. Campbell's campaign staff had misrepresented the nature of life in prison, minimizing the severity of Iowa's toughness in sentencing murderers.[118] Governor Terry Branstad said his "decisive victory over Democrat Bonnie Campbell signals a more conservative era in Iowa politics that will propel his agenda through the Legislature next year."[119] After the election, GOP control of the Iowa house grew from sixty-four to thirty-six (over a previous fifty-one to forty-nine), while the Democrats remained in control of the senate with a margin of twenty-seven to twenty-three.[120] Everything seemed in place for reinstatement of capital punishment: a Republican governor, a Republican house, and angry murder victims' families lobbying for this legislation. In addition, the *Register*, while still adamantly opposed to capital punishment, published nearly four articles on every murder in the state, surely stirring up public concern.

Although the *Register* endorsed Bonnie Campbell for governor, the combination of appearing soft on crime while opposing capital punishment undoubtedly factored into her losing the election. Despite the fact that Branstad's support for the death penalty helped win him the election, when it came time to lobby for the law before the legislature, he did not follow through. Iowans seem to want a governor who talks tough on crime, but they are ambivalent enough about capital punishment that they will accept a politician who only symbolically endorses such legislation.

Governor Terry Branstad was a stark contrast to his 1965 counterpart. In an interview at the governor's office, Branstad listed his reasons for favoring the death penalty: "Christianity, deterrence, and retribution."[121] As a Roman Catholic, he found "no problem reconciling" his "religious views with [his] political life. Murder is obviously a violation of civil law" and must not be "tolerated in the state of Iowa." Branstad stated that the death penalty is "morally right, for the safety of the citizens of Iowa and for the retribution of the victims and their families." On the other hand, he was quite aware that the Roman Catholic church hierarchy, the "Bishops in New York, were against the death penalty and had just recently written a public statement" to that effect.[122]

When asked about the legislative process, the governor said that the leadership in the house supported the bill as it went through debate and was voted upon. The Emrys helped with their presence and, "I met with them and expressed my condolences. They were strong supporters of that bill. The grandmother, too. I had quite a few discussions with the Emrys."[123] Branstad predicted that Iowa would eventually have a death penalty: "There was no support in the Senate and with the strong organized opposition that it [the capital punishment bill] received from churches, it just wasn't going to happen this session, but it will be passed within the next 10 years."[124]

While Branstad supported the capital punishment bill, the *Register* outspokenly opposed the restoration of capital punishment.[125] Former Republican Governor Norman Erbe remarked to *Register* reporter David Yepsen that the death penalty does not serve any deterrent, although during his term as the state's attorney general he "had no second thoughts about allowing the executions to proceed" since it was his job to enforce the law.[126] During the house vote, it was fairly clear that the death penalty reinstatement bill, house file 2, would clear the chamber with a comfortable margin. On Thursday, February 23, 1995, the bill was reported out to the Iowa senate by a highly partisan fifty-four to forty-four vote.[127] One Democrat and fifty-three Republicans voted for reinstatement, while thirty-three Democrats and eleven Republicans opposed such action.[128]

. . . .

Reactions by church leaders were immediate, as a letter from the pastor of Des Moines's Fellowship Baptist Church illustrates: "Of the many supporters of the death penalty, none is more alarming than those who profess Christianity [which several legislators did during the house debates] alleging that their [position] is somehow superior because they believe in the inerrancy of the scripture."[129] A state representative quoted in the *Register* also denounced the death penalty by stressing Iowa's great difference from the South: "Look at the South. You don't think that race doesn't have anything to do with people in jail in the South?"[130]

The final blow to HF 2 were the amendments that senators kept tagging onto it.[131] Following the Iowa senate's vote by a wide margin of thirty-nine to eleven to reject the capital punishment bill, a six-hour debate took place[132] during which no one from the governor's office came forward to lobby in favor of the bill's passage through the senate.[133] Voting for HF 2 were one Democrat and ten Republicans; voting against the bill were twenty-six Democrats and thirteen Republicans.[134]

In the end, Republican Representative David Milage of Bettendorf, a "strong supporter of the penalty," told a *Register* reporter, "I think the great lobbying efforts by churches against the bill and no organized lobbying by those in support" led to the defeat of capital punishment.[135] Just as churches had flexed their organizational muscle against capital punishment in the 1965 session, the ten Protestant denominations making up an alliance did so again in the 1990s. Jim Ryan, director of Iowa Ecumenical Ministries, noted that "Ecumenical Ministries works because it is conservative and organizers worked through their own church structures." The Ecumenical Ministries alliance was centered around the different denominations, "local pastors and lay people."[136] "Methodists did radio spots opposing the bill, the Church had to make a witness. We had to be sensitive to the feelings of the families [of murder victims;] I think we were successful in that," Ryan said.[137] When questioned about the Ecumenical Ministries' coalition with other non-Protestant groups, Ryan said, "[w]e had a press conference with the [Roman Catholic] Bishops" in order to create a stronger network of Catholics and Protestants.

Evidence of the organizational strength of the death penalty opposi-

. . . .

tion was also reflected in the testimony of those who participated in the Iowa house's public hearing on February 4, 1995. Of the eighty-seven private citizens registered prior to the meeting, only eight supported executions. Representatives of the following organizations participated in this meeting in opposition to the death penalty: Iowans Against the Death Penalty, the Des Moines Chapter of the NAACP, the Iowa Peace Network, the Iowa Coalition Against Sexual Assault, the Iowa Attorney General's Office, and the Des Moines Chapter of the National Lawyers Guild. Of those at this public hearing, 30 percent registered their affiliation with organized religious groups. These groups included the Des Moines Valley Friends (Quakers), the United Methodist Church, and the Fellowship Baptist Church.[138]

Former Governor Harold Hughes lobbied against the death penalty thirty years after the 1965 legislature abolished the law. Hughes wrote the *Register* restating his opposition to the death penalty prior to the March 2, 1995, senate vote. Though ill and just released from the hospital, Hughes felt strongly enough about the senate vote to write a lengthy editorial that called for rejection of the law "which discriminates against the luckless, the poor, and minorities."[139] "I am one of those people for deeply religious reasons, [who] believes in the absolute sanctity of human life. 'Thou Shalt Not Kill' is the shortest of the Ten Commandments, uncomplicated by qualifications or exceptions."[140]

Summary

Distinct themes are present in the nineteenth- and twentieth-century debates on capital punishment. Iowa's legislature restored the death penalty only six years after the 1872 abolition.[141] Abolition of capital punishment was being blamed for frequent lynchings throughout the state and a perceived crime wave.[142] With some legislators being elected solely on the platform of restoration, a bill was passed in 1878 reinstating capital punishment. Rural Iowa newspapers lauded the legislature for restoration.[143] During the 1960s, the *Register*'s emphasis on minor crime demonstrated to the public that Iowa was a safe place to live and that crime was not serious or life-threatening. Meanwhile, the domestic homicides of the 1960s were portrayed as not affecting the public at large and thus there was no reason to have a death penalty. Stranger homicides were represented by the *Register* as being relatively rare occurrences. The 1964 Iowa gubernatorial election had incumbent Democratic Governor Harold Hughes and Republican Evan Hultman vying for votes over the issues of state highway improvements, state liquor sales, highway speed limits, and the future of capital punishment. After Harold Hughes was reelected, he advocated the abolition of the death penalty and was backed wholeheartedly by the *Register*. The successful repeal of Iowa's death penalty in 1965 was a result of Harold Hughes's charismatic leadership of the Democrats, Democratic control in both houses, and the enthusiastic support of the *Register*. In reaction to the Southern civil rights movement, the Iowa legislature passed a bill chastising Alabama for its treatment of African Americans. Iowa's reaction to the brutality of Southern whites was to abolish the death penalty—so common in the South—signaling respect for all human life.

Although during the 1990s the *Register* reported on violent crimes, minor crimes went all but ignored. Even so, Iowa was still a safe place to live, tying with South Dakota for the next to lowest murder rate in the nation.[144] As portrayed in the *Register*, the threat of homicides was only present if one lived with a violent individual. The 1994 Iowa gubernatorial election between incumbent Republican Governor Terry Branstad and Democrat Bonnie Campbell focused on the death penalty. After his reelection, Governor Branstad displayed a definite lack of commitment to the death penalty by failing to send any lobbyists to the Iowa legislature during the 1995 capital punishment debates. The 1995 defeat of the capital punishment bill was a consequence of the *Register*'s claims of a safe living environment, the lack of lobbying efforts on the part of Branstad's office, the legislature's apparent ambivalence about the bill, and church solidarity against the issue.

Relevant demographic characteristics include the fact that from the 1960s through the 1990s, Iowa had a low rate of resident mobility. As Hagan and Berk et al. found, it is critical for death penalty abolitionists to have the backing of the press,[145] and the *Register* has been a firm opponent of capital punishment for over one hundred years. Differences in the triggering events help explain why Kansas has a death penalty and Iowa does not. In 1994, Stephanie Schmidt, a young college woman, was abducted, assaulted, and murdered in Kansas.[146] The Schmidt family reacted by creating a pro–death penalty lobbying organization in her name, appearing on national television talk shows, and lobbying for capital punishment before the Kansas legislature. By contrast, the Emry family reacted to their daughter Anna's murder by placing limits on the use of her name for political gain during the 1994 campaigns. The Emrys did collect signatures on a resolution favoring restoration of the death penalty, yet they refused contracts for books and movies that dealt with the case. Kansas and Iowa share demographic, cultural, and political characteristics including widespread opposition to capital punishment by the churches; and yet the differing reactions of the murder victims' families triggered events that help explain the restoration of the death penalty in Kansas and its continued abolition in Iowa.

Postscript

The last major effort to reinstate capital punishment came in 1997, when the Iowa senate soundly defeated a bill by a vote of thirty-nine to eleven.[147] Since 1998, Democratic Governor Tom Vilsack has strongly opposed capital punishment.[148]

The Life and Death of the Death Penalty in West Virginia

A defining characteristic of West Virginia has long been its dire economic situation. In much of the state there is little level land and thus only minimal agricultural activity, leaving the local economy largely dependent upon the coal industry.[1] After World War II, consumers switched from coal to other fuels, "[a]nd ever since the Great Depression, West Virginia has been a virtual synonym for the grinding poverty of Appalachia."[2] The use of cheap foreign-produced coal and the collapse of the American steel industry further aggravated the state's economic problems. By 1983, West Virginia's unemployment jumped to 21 percent, the highest rate in the nation. In addition to these problems, flooding in 1985 ravaged the state, causing $550 million in damage.[3] According to the 1990 census figures, only three states had a greater percentage of citizens living below the poverty level. The state's median family income was exceeded by all but two states.

In Europe during the nineteenth century and earlier, the more depressed the economic situation the more capital punishment became the keystone of government control.[4] Similar patterns existed in the United States from the eighteenth to the twentieth century.[5] Given these historical patterns, it is especially curious that West Virginia, with its recurrent economic problems, should have abolished the death penalty.

Most U.S. states whose legislatures have abolished capital punishment boast long traditions of abolition—Michigan, Wisconsin, Iowa, Maine, North Dakota, and Minnesota. Hawaii and Alaska legally rejected capital punishment more recently, but both states rarely carried out executions prior to abolition.[6] As noted earlier in this book, Zimring and Hawkins argue that a "history of frequent executions . . .

serves as a kind of precedent, reassuring political actors that their own participation is neither inhumane nor immoral . . . on grounds that, historically, executions do not violate local community morality."[7] West Virginia is an exception to these patterns. At the beginning of the twentieth century, individuals could be executed in West Virginia for first-degree murder, treason, kidnap, or rape.[8] Before capital punishment was abolished in 1965, 155 prisoners were executed in West Virginia.[9] That number far exceeds all other U.S. states whose legislatures have abolished capital punishment.[10]

Prior to 1920, approximately 70 percent of those executed in West Virginia were blacks (see Table 10.1). The percentage is similar in other Southern states during this period.[11] However, blacks made up a smaller proportion of the population in West Virginia than in any other Southern state.[12] Thus, before 1920, the likelihood of blacks being executed was as high—or higher—in West Virginia than in other Southern states.

In addition to West Virginia's enduring economic crisis and history of executions, it should be added that elements of West Virginia's population are well-known for their religious fundamentalism and anti-intellectual opposition to modern school textbooks.[13] This is hardly the cultural environment from which one would expect progressive legal reforms. In short, West Virginia's economic circumstances, execution history, and tendency toward anti-intellectualism provide unlikely foundations for death penalty abolition.

On the other hand, West Virginia's non-mobile population and small and decreasing black population fit the typical model of an abolitionist state.[14] The 1990 census listed only six states with higher percentages of their populations born in state. In 1870, 4 percent of the population was black, declining to an all-time low of 3.1 percent in 1990. West Virginia's total population has remained relatively unchanged for over one hundred years, varying between 1.7 and 2 million.

Additionally, for several decades, West Virginia's overall crime rate has remained the lowest in the nation.[15] In an interview the state's assistant director of corrections observed that states with little migration, racial homogeneity, and low violent crime rates exhibit a sense of community conducive to death penalty abolition. "West Virginia lacks

TABLE 10.1		
Number Executed in West Virginia by Race, 1760–1959		
Year	White	Black*
1760–1849	4	22
1850–99	13	17
1900–19	8	19
1920–59	45	19

*Eight observations are missing.
Source: M. W. Espy and J. O. Smykla, *The Espy File.*

a significant black population. It's you and me and Bobby Joe, with no identifiable crime element."

Original Abolition

There were relatively few legislative attempts to abolish capital punishment in West Virginia before 1965. In 1955, an abolitionist bill passed the West Virginia house of delegates on a fifty-four to forty-four vote.[16] In 1957, 1959, and 1963, similar bills (HB 128, HB 16, and HB 12, respectively) were introduced in the house. All three house bills died in committee. In 1965, West Virginia abolished capital punishment. On February 12 of that year, the house passed house bill 517, a bill substituting life without the possibility of parole for capital punishment. In cases where juries recommended mercy, capital offenders became eligible for parole after serving ten years.[17] HB 517 was cosponsored by delegates Jesse Barker of Kanawha County and Robert Holliday of Fayette County. Robert Holliday was a newspaper publisher, a cosponsor of the 1963 abolitionist bill, and a vigorous public proponent of death penalty abolition. The bill was passed and forwarded to the West Virginia senate with no floor debate.[18] Legislative records show that the initial house vote on HB 517 was eighty-two in favor and fourteen opposed.[19]

Initial senate discussion of HB 517 centered on West Virginia's image, deterrence, and morality. The bill's primary senate proponent, Paul Kaufman, argued that sickness and poverty cause murder; therefore, those guilty of such crimes deserved treatment rather than death.

. . . .

Earlier, he contended that the "[u]ltimate final passage [of abolition] would bring a great moral uplift in West Virginia. . . . It would be a great step toward providing the nation and the world with a different image of this state. . . . [It] would be an improved image of enlightenment."[20] Another senator argued: "The essence is, you're taking away a human life [and] I have no right to take away that which I did not give."[21] On February 25, after amending HB 517 to allow parole for all capital offenders, the senate voted twenty to eleven to abolish capital punishment.[22] West Virginia's house was unwilling to go along with the senate's liberal parole amendment and a combined senate/house committee was appointed to work out the differences between the house and senate versions.[23]

During the month-long struggle over the precise shape death penalty abolition would take in West Virginia, Robert Holliday reminded his colleagues that the poor and ignorant are the only ones executed.[24] Three days later, immediately preceding the floor vote on the senate's amended version of HB 517, he said: "Let's take our place and show that we believe in life and that we are better than the murderer and that we are a civilized people here in West Virginia."[25]

The first house and senate compromise on HB 517 allowed persons sentenced to life "without mercy" to become eligible for parole after serving twenty-five years. Persons sentenced to life "with mercy" would be eligible for parole after serving ten years.[26] Both legislative houses rejected the compromise legislation.[27] A second compromise bill was successful, calling for life without the possibility of parole for persons convicted of capital crimes "without mercy" (the original house bill). The house passed the second compromise bill on a sixty-three to thirty-seven vote.[28] On March 12, 1965, the senate voted by the slim margin of eighteen to sixteen in favor of the second compromise bill.[29]

In the end, fifteen Democratic senators supported abolition and twelve were opposed, while three Republicans voted for abolition, with four against.[30] After reporting the vote, the *Charleston Gazette* argued: "The sensitivity the majority of legislators have demonstrated by prohibiting a barbarity reflects a most desirable image change" for the state, and Governor Smith signed the bill abolishing the death penalty on March 18, 1965.[31] At the signing he reasoned that the new law would allow those who are rehabilitated to be released by way of executive pardons and that West Virginia joined other states that were not afraid of progress.[32]

The press remained divided throughout the 1965 capital punishment debate. The *Gazette* favored abolition, noting that the typical candidate for execution was "illiterate and impoverished."[33] Another *Gazette* editorial argued: "Apparently, in this age of rehabilitation and enlightenment more and more individuals, judges, public officials, jailers and prosecutors consider capital punishment to be cruel and unusual punishment, unworthy of a civilized society."[34] Later, a *Gazette* article quoted the former state penitentiary warden, Orel Skeen: "The person with money or influential friends just doesn't get sentenced to death. The sentence is largely reserved for the poor, the ignorant, or for members of minority groups."[35] On the other hand, the *Charleston Daily Mail* editorials opposed abolition.[36]

In an interview Robert Holliday noted: "We are civilized and not backwoods people. Further, people in the state recognize the power of monied people over coal mines and the class bias of capital punishment." Don Marsh, a former *Gazette* editor who was credited by Delegate Holliday with writing the article that initiated the 1965 death penalty debate, asserted that the *Gazette* wields a pervasive humanistic influence on West Virginia's political processes. Historically, "Kanawha county through the *Gazette* has fostered humanism. To be for it [the death penalty] as a politician is to bring down the *Gazette* on you."

Reinstatement Efforts

Capital punishment bills were introduced in the senate in 1969 and annually from 1971 to 1988. Of the twenty-four death penalty statutes introduced during this period, only two passed the senate—a 1971 bill, twenty-one to twelve,[37] and a 1972 bill, nineteen to twelve.[38] Every year since 1973, at least one death penalty bill has been introduced in the West Virginia house. Of the fifty-two house bills introduced between 1973 and year-end 1988, only the one in 1979 passed, sixty-two to thirty-eight.[39] The three bills approved in their house of origin died in the judiciary committee of West Virginia's other legislative body.

. . . .

The proposed legislation produced many debates reflecting both the changing problems in each historical period, as well as continuing structural conditions.

The Early Post-Abolition Period, 1970–1974

Events that would move some legislators to call for reinstating capital punishment were not long in coming. Following the 1970 murder of an inmate at the State Penitentiary at Moundsville, Governor Arch A. Moore, a three-term Republican governor, voiced his support for re-establishing capital punishment.[40] Altering its 1965 position, a *Mail* editorial voiced strong opposition to reinstatement.[41] Demands for re-instatement became increasingly heated after the 1972 killing of a prison guard by a Moundsville inmate. The state's director of corrections changed his mind and announced his support for reestablishing the death penalty.[42] Likewise, prison guards publicly requested reinstatement.[43] The senate responded as it had in 1971 by passing a death penalty bill and forwarding it to the house.[44]

The following year (1973) Governor Moore joined the state's attorney general in support of a limited capital punishment bill. Three such measures were introduced during the 1973 legislative session. Governor Moore argued that prison violence among those already sentenced to life in prison for an earlier murder necessitated the punishment.[45] The *Gazette* countered that reinstating capital punishment would hurt the image of the state: "[W]e think the State of West Virginia, trying so desperately to improve its image in the eyes of the nation, would be taking a dreadful backward step if it were to return to the sanctioning of legal killing."[46] Later in the legislative session, a riot at Moundsville's state prison involving the killing of an inmate and five guards taken hostage invigorated death penalty demands from prison guards, legislators, and the governor.[47]

At least one death penalty bill was introduced in each legislative session between 1974 and 1977. A 1976 *Mail* article titled "Death Penalty Bill Tops Law Maker List" attests to the continued prominence of the issue among West Virginia legislators. Conditions remained unaltered in 1978.[48] The sentiments of those favoring the passage of a capital punishment bill were no doubt strengthened by the killing of three highway patrol officers during the preceding year. Nevertheless, the house minority leader reasoned, "I'm not convinced they'll get it out of committee. Of course, if it gets to the floor it will pass."[49] House Judiciary Committee Chair Roger Tompkins, credited with preventing the 1977 death penalty bill from leaving his committee, reported that although his uncle had been murdered, he remained opposed to the death penalty.[50] Indeed, even with the recent state trooper killings, the Senate Judiciary Committee chair also remained opposed.[51]

In this early post–abolition period, killings associated with Moundsville's state prison became a more significant legislative death penalty issue than the state's overall crime rate, a trend that continued for nearly two decades. The operation and power of the House and Senate Judiciary Committees also became clear during this period. The *Mail* noted that the real question was "whether a few lawmakers will bottle up the issue in committee so it can't get to the floor where the full membership can vote."[52]

The Issue Heats Up, 1979–1980

After the sensational murder of a hostage in Pineville, West Virginia, many felt a death penalty bill would pass both houses, and Democratic Governor Rockefeller said he would sign a bill with the "right restrictions."[53] A delegate opposed to capital punishment was quoted as conceding that the Pineville episode "drove the final nail in the coffin carrying the death penalty to victory."[54] A clear majority (58 percent) of West Virginia's citizens favored reinstatement of the death penalty.[55] Of thirty-one senators contacted, nineteen supported capital punishment while seven were opposed.[56] Both the *Gazette* and the *Mail* printed the observations of a former Moundsville warden, noting, as he had in a 1965 *Gazette* article, that all eleven men executed while he was warden were poor and therefore could not afford the best lawyers.[57] Robert Holliday, absent from the legislature from 1972 through 1980, likewise reasoned that the death penalty was used primarily against blacks and poor people.[58]

. . . .

In 1979, the House Judiciary Committee held public hearings on capital punishment. Testifying at these hearings, the house speaker voiced opposition based on racially discriminatory application.[59] Following the public hearing, House Judiciary Committee members held a "marathon" session to decide the fate of that year's death penalty bill, HB 787. Delegate Charlotte Lane, a Republican committee member from Kanawha County, offered numerous amendments, all of which failed. One of her motions required that the governor throw the switch on the electric chair, another stipulated public executions, and still another required the trial court judge and prosecutor to be present at executions.[60] These amendments obviously attempted to use sarcasm as a weapon. Nevertheless, the House Judiciary Committee reported out HB 787 with a recommendation to pass.

Sarcastic attacks on the death penalty continued during floor debates on HB 787. One proposed amendment to the death penalty bill would have required the televising of all executions.[61] House Majority Leader and former House Judiciary Committee Chair Roger Tompkins held house members "spellbound" during his emotional attack on the death penalty. He observed it was the poor, illiterate, and inarticulate who were typically executed. He equated the act of voting in favor of the capital punishment bill with pushing "the button that will send 2,000 volts through the body of a human."[62] He continued: "I am pleading for life and charity." The only African American member of West Virginia's house of delegates noted widespread racial discrimination in granting commutations and lamented the fact that the "death penalty has been the special privilege of the poor and blacks."[63] Another delegate described the individuals executed as "those that cannot afford a fine defense, the illiterate and inarticulate—minority, of the 94 persons executed in West Virginia 43 percent were blacks. Blacks make up 6 percent of West Virginia's population."[64]

This opposition notwithstanding, the house speaker predicted capital punishment would fly through the house, that the Senate Judiciary Committee would report it out, that the senate would pass it, and that Governor Rockefeller would sign it.[65] Everything seemed to be in place. The first house vote on capital punishment since 1965 was scheduled to take place.[66] As noted above, HB 787 indeed passed the house, sixty-two to thirty-eight.[67] While the senate appeared to be in favor, the press reported correctly that a majority of Senate Judiciary Committee members were opposed; thus the bill died in committee.[68]

Judiciary Committee Stalemate, 1980–1983

In November 1979, months after that year's legislative session had adjourned, a state trooper was killed in a prison break involving fifteen inmates.[69] A delegate rationalizing his intentions to introduce a capital punishment bill in the upcoming 1980 legislative session noted that escapees already serving life have nothing to lose by murdering.[70] After holding public hearings, the Senate Judiciary Committee voted eleven to seven against sending a death penalty bill to the floor.[71] The committee also voted eight to five in favor of killing a bill calling for a popular referendum on capital punishment.[72] There was some discussion among death penalty advocates in the legislature about circumventing the Senate Judiciary Committee. In West Virginia a two-thirds vote of the senate or house membership is required to remove a bill from committee and place it on the floor for consideration. Senators favoring capital punishment did not have an appetite for undermining the committee system.[73] At this time, frustration with the structure and power of legislative committees surfaced in the *Mail*. An editorial, referring to the senate judiciary chair, asked: "Who elected Sen. Palumbo king?"[74]

In 1981, the House and Senate Judiciary Committees held a joint public hearing on capital punishment. Preceding the hearing, a Senate Judiciary Committee member expressed doubt about whether the death penalty could be implemented without racial and economic bias: "I don't think it can ever be administered lawfully as a fair law."[75] At the hearings, the state's Moral Majority leader spoke on behalf of that year's death penalty bill while a representative of the Quakers spoke in opposition. An African American lawyer representing the state bar association called the death penalty "racial and economic injustice."[76] Following the hearing, the Senate Judiciary Committee blocked the bill by the closest of margins with a tie vote of seven to seven.[77]

In 1982, a West Virginia state court ruled that conditions at the

State Penitentiary at Moundsville constituted cruel and unusual punishment. Inadequate medical care and the size of cells were considered the most serious problems.[78] Death penalty bills were introduced in both houses but debates were limited and no formal action was taken on any bill. Late in 1982, the *Mail* reminisced: "At least three times in the past decade, one legislative chamber has passed a reinstatement bill only to see it die in committee in another chamber."[79]

More Trouble at the Prison, 1984–1988

In 1984, a survey reported that 72.4 percent of West Virginia citizens favored reestablishing the death penalty.[80] One year later, a *Mail* survey found that a majority of the state's legislators were also in favor of restoring capital punishment.[81] The house speaker voiced support for capital punishment while the senate president "wasn't sure of how he would vote on a death penalty bill but said he likely wouldn't oppose it."[82] The *Gazette* published an editorial deriding the new Senate Judiciary Committee chair for allowing opinion polls to alter his sentiments toward capital punishment.[83] The editorial was in reaction to published statements attributed to the first-term chair by a *Mail* staff writer. According to these alleged statements, the Senate Judiciary Committee was going to report a death penalty bill to the senate floor within two weeks. The committee chair was quoted as saying, "People all over the state want it and I think it's an idea whose time has come."[84] With that said, the bill never cleared committee.

After a hiatus in 1984 and 1985, the Senate Judiciary Committee resumed a near annual event, a public hearing on restoring capital punishment. Due to the large number of people wishing to testify, the 1985 hearings were conducted over two days, February 21 and March 19. On the first day of testimony, four senators spoke in favor of reinstating the death penalty. The titles of two newspaper articles best sum up the unexpected outcome of West Virginia's 1985 death penalty debate: "Judiciary Panel Rejects Death Penalty"[85] and "Death Penalty Bill Dies in Judiciary."[86]

On January 2, 1986, the press reported a riot at Moundsville.[87] Three prisoners were killed in the incident.[88] In a 1988 interview the editor of the *Gazette* referred to West Virginia prisons as the worst in the United States. In another interview a longtime state senator, interested in prison reform, declared West Virginia's prison system to be troubled by simplistic management, racism, and coercion. The 1986 senate death penalty bill was a product of the "Report of Senate Select Committee on the West Virginia Penitentiary." The Senate Select Committee was charged with examining and recommending solutions to the problems at Moundsville.[89] The committee concluded, in accordance with the prison guards at Moundsville, that the death penalty was required to control those serving life sentences.

The State Prosecuting Attorney's Association voted unanimously to support the 1986 reinstatement effort.[90] Representatives of most of the state's major religious denominations remained opposed, however, referring to the application of the death penalty as racially and economically biased.[91] A *Gazette* headline, "Capital Punishment Proponents Face off at Hearings," described the 1986 Senate Judiciary Committee hearings on capital punishment. Robert Holliday, at this point a state senator, reasoned that because the poor and minorities were those most likely to be executed, "West Virginia stood at one of its proudest moments when it abolished the death penalty in 1965."[92] An Amnesty International representative cited additional evidence of racism—that executions were more likely when the victim was white rather than black.[93] The 1986 legislative debate on capital punishment ended without the issue being voted on by either the House or Senate Judiciary Committees.

Reflecting on the killing of six prisoners that had taken place in the state prison over the past twelve months, a January 6, 1987, *Gazette* editorial asked whether "West Virginia can't follow humane principles common in Europe, but must be more like Turkey, South Africa, Iran and Communist nations that conduct executions?"[94] A January 9, 1987, *Mail* editorial noted the expense of executions in Virginia to be $1 million or more.[95] The cost of capital punishment, together with its questionable moral and deterrent value, made it obvious that West Virginians should find another answer to the violence at Moundsville. The editorial writer reasoned that building more prison space would be less costly and more humane. The 1987 debate ended with the annual ritual of a Senate Judiciary Committee public hearing on capital punishment. After the 1987 hearing, the committee chair reasoned that he would not put the death penalty issue on his committee's agenda unless there was some activity on capital punishment in the house. There was not.

Conclusion

The Origins and Maintenance of Abolition Economics

Adamson, Galliher et al., and Rusche and Kirchheimer suggest that the effect that an economic environment has on legislative action is not determined by the general wealth or poverty of a people;[96] rather, it is the degree to which the economic elite perceive the underclass as a threat that determines the nature of law. In short, it is the amount of separation between the poorest and the wealthiest citizens that tends to determine the level of legal harshness in a given society. In more highly stratified societies the degree of threat has been found to be highly correlated with greater numbers of police as well as homicides caused by police and arrest rates.[97]

By contrast, economic and social homogeneity in West Virginia is conducive to less brutal criminal sanctions and death penalty abolition. Poverty affects the collective psyche of West Virginians. Political and social elites tend to blame the pervasive economic hardships faced by the state on "economic outsiders" who colonized and exploited the people and resources of West Virginia for private gain. As was the case in Alaska and Hawaii, executions are not popular among people who have "colonized" views of their social histories. Among West Virginians, the perceived threat to the community is external, not internal. Low levels of violent crime, population stability, and homogeneity no doubt facilitate and perpetuate such thinking. The senate sponsor of many death penalty bills bemoaned the liberal, pro–labor union ideology of the state legislature. The chief counsel to the House Judiciary Committee agreed that "politicians cannot run on the [death penalty] issue. People in this state have a distrust of authority and are suspicious of being screwed by someone for they feel colonized in that power has been historically used against them."

Race

Some evidence also suggests that individuals who are members of exploited groups are more likely to empathize with past and current hardships of other socially disadvantaged groups.[98] The most typical arguments for abolition in West Virginia's newspapers and legislative debates are that executions make a society look uncivilized and that capital punishment discriminates against the poor and minorities. To reinforce these claims legislators and journalists have only to look at West Virginia's execution history. Table 10.1 indicates that during the state's early years, the vast majority of those executed were black—all the more abhorrent given the very small black population in West Virginia. Widespread poverty may well make West Virginia's legislators more sensitive to the problems of racial minorities. The low crime rates and low percentage of African Americans in the state combine to produce a situation where they are collectively perceived, not as a threat, but as an example of the liability of poverty. In short, the widespread poverty in the state produces an awareness of the discriminatory nature of the criminal law and a rejection of the death penalty.

The Mass Media

The success of death penalty abolition in West Virginia, as in Michigan and Iowa, cannot be understood without reference to the state's major newspapers.[99] The effects of racism and poverty on the administration of capital punishment are frequent topics in West Virginia's newspapers. Editorial writers have never tired of pointing out that death penalty abolition bolsters the image of West Virginia as a truly civilized place in spite of its poverty. The *Gazette* is the state's strongest supporter of death penalty abolition among the media. The *Gazette* has been appropriately described as the state capital's leading newspaper and as a "progressive and sometimes crusading force."[100] As the data indicate, this powerful newspaper has always been adamantly opposed to capital punishment. At one point in time, the editor and publisher of the *Gazette*—while serving in the house of delegates—personally led the opposition against efforts to restore the death penalty. This powerful newspaper was a force in the abolition of the death penalty and, more recently, a force in its maintenance. In the words of the chief counsel to the House Judiciary Committee, "politicians fear the *Gazette*—by far the best newspaper in the state."

Committee Structure

To understand long-term death penalty abolition in West Virginia, it is also necessary to consider the legislative committee system operating in both the senate and house of delegates—a system built strictly on political patronage rather than seniority as in many U.S. states. Committee chairmanships in the house and senate are powerful patronage positions with something approaching veto power over legislative activities. Chairs of the House and Senate Judiciary Committees have used their power to effectively block consideration of nearly all death penalty bills discussed here, often contravening the sentiments of most lawmakers. The strong committee system is so ingrained in West Virginia politics that senators and delegates are not willing to spend the political capital necessary to attempt to override committee leadership. Moreover, West Virginia has no provision for a citizen initiative or statewide referendum. Thus, neither legislators nor citizens can circumvent the power of congressional leadership. In Oregon, by contrast, citizens have voted on the issue of capital punishment seven times during the twentieth century, with differing results.[101]

Bureaucratic Conservatism

The experiences in West Virginia and other abolitionist states also reflect the fact that bureaucrats typically support the status quo no matter what that status quo represents. Shils contends that laws "become traditions once they have been made [and] remain on the statute books for many years."[102] Politicians and other leaders of government are generally oriented toward the past and are strong supporters of tradition. Whatever the idiosyncratic origins of death penalty abolition in a given state, once executions are abolished, those in positions of political and organizational power tend to give it their support. The leadership in West Virginia's Democratic and Republican parties are unwilling to cede to the other a monopoly on the moral premise that capital punishment contradicts the sanctity of human life.

The State Penitentiary at Moundsville

During the latter decades of the twentieth century, the death penalty debate in West Virginia was largely defined by the violence at the State Penitentiary at Moundsville. Factors generating that violence were not difficult to uncover: only 50 percent of the prison guards at Moundsville had graduated from elementary school, numerous cells had no lighting, prisoners in solitary confinement were given no blankets, and inmates were typically idle.[103] Thus, for thirty-five years public concern with murder and capital punishment primarily stemmed from West Virginia's grossly underfunded state prison system.[104] Absent this violence, West Virginia's capital punishment debate would have involved far fewer reinstatement bills. On the other hand, the fact that violence remained largely contained behind prison walls probably lessened the fervor of death penalty advocates.

In accordance with the problems associated with the State Penitentiary at Moundsville, West Virginia opened a new prison in early 1995 at a cost of $61.8 million—a major sum for such a poor state.[105] All of the prisoners at Moundsville were transferred to the new facility by April 1995. The new institution is equipped with extensive electronic security controls, as well as a hospital, classrooms, gymnasium, chapel, and library. Having taken steps to control prison escapes and violence, it is understandable that by year-end 1999 no death penalty bill had been passed in West Virginia.

The Symbolic Value of Death Penalty Abolition

The symbolic value of death penalty abolition in West Virginia may be far greater than in an economically developed state, such as Michigan. West Virginia lacks the characteristics or social traits often associated with "success" in an advanced capitalist society. West Virginia does not possess the structural and geographical resources necessary to achieve economic strength. In world system terms, West Virginia is a peripheral state embedded in a core industrial nation. Moreover,

West Virginia is a small, sparsely populated state with little chance of affecting national politics. Under these circumstances a "civilized" self-image and state prestige assume considerable symbolic significance. Abolitionists in West Virginia are committed to maintaining death penalty abolition as well as improving the overall prestige of their state.

Postscript

The editor of the *Gazette* noted: "In our state there was a recent scandal involving the head of the state police crime lab headed by Fred Zain. For years he testified that the prosecution was always correct according to his scientific results. . . . [W]hen DNA became routinely available it was found in case after case that he had routinely provided incorrect information. Later it was discovered that the lab didn't even have the capacity of running the tests he described, and that he had lied to get convictions." Zain was fired in West Virginia and then hired by Texas, where he continued the same practices. "Ultimately he was indicted in West Virginia and in Texas for perjury. This is the perfect argument against the death penalty."[106]

CHAPTER

11

Summary and Conclusions

Organization, Race, Religion, and the Death Penalty in the Nation's Capital

Many of the patterns found in the nine states whose legislatures have abolished capital punishment make a return appearance in Washington, D.C. The residents of this city, including its African American majority, are disenfranchised U.S. citizens.[1] Southern U.S. senators, race, and religion played major roles in recent death penalty debates in the nation's capital. In 1992, a member of the congressional staff of U.S. Senator Richard Shelby of Alabama was murdered in D.C. Shortly thereafter, Senator Shelby called for a referendum[2] to reinstate capital punishment in D.C. The referendum, which was attached to that year's appropriations bill,[3] allowed for the execution of juveniles as young as sixteen. It did not preclude from execution the mentally retarded, nor did it provide for mandatory appellate review of death sentences. It even allowed the execution of D.C. citizens to be contracted out to other states.[4]

A political coalition involving religious leaders, community activists, and civil libertarians organized the resistance to reestablishment. Some residents undoubtedly knew the history of the use of the death penalty in D.C., where 80 of the 118 executed had been black.[5] In any case, the Southern Christian Leadership Conference convened a multifaith council of the most influential clergy in D.C.[6] Noontime rallies, block parties, door-to-door canvassing, motorcades, and city-wide days of worship provided reliable public information. This coalition was supported by the ACLU and Amnesty International, and it received financial contributions from various religious denominations.

The religious community provided a hub around which the civil libertarian and community activist programs revolved. The referendum lost, rejected by 68 percent of D.C. voters. A majority of the voters who rejected the referendum were African Americans.[7] The measure passed narrowly in white residential precincts where voter turnout was heavy.

In 1997, U.S. Senator Kay Bailey Hutchinson of Texas decided that Washington, D.C., needed capital punishment.[8] In response to Senator Hutchinson's initiative in Congress, it was clear that some factors had changed since 1992. Marion Barry, who was the mayor throughout this period, was five years later greatly compromised politically. In 1992, Barry had been an adamant opponent of the death penalty. In 1997, however, with a Republican Congress in place and with no other alternative to acquire needed funding for road repairs than to accept Congress's demands for capital punishment, Mayor Barry introduced death penalty legislation to the D.C. Council.[9] The council's lone Republican representative also introduced legislation to reinstate the death penalty. As in 1992, the religious community was galvanized against Senator Hutchinson, the mayor, and the city council member. The coalition was able to form a committee of community leadership to strongly lobby the D.C. Council and dominate public hearings on the matter.[10] Again, block parties, motorcades, and public forums were used in the same way as in 1992. Many of the characteristics found in abolitionist states were evident here, including the attention to organizing resistance to death penalty initiatives, assistance from religious and civil rights groups, as well as views of capital punishment as racist and consistent with the politics of the Deep South. In the end, the D.C. Council failed to reinstate the death penalty.

Making Sense of Death Penalty Abolition in the United States: Empirical Findings

We began this study in 1985, aspiring to make a difference in death penalty politics. We hoped that by studying abolitionist states we could provide some insight into furthering the abolition of the death penalty throughout the United States. The case studies presented here answer some significant questions surrounding state-sanctioned killing. Additionally, data presented here provide theoretical insight into the sociological study of punishment and lawmaking. Finally, these data offer practical information to anti–death penalty activists. We will start our analysis by revisiting the questions that provided the organization for the research discussed in Chapter 1.

What Is the Relationship Between the History of Executions, Murder Rates, and the Death Penalty?

The relationship between capital punishment and other violence in a particular political unit or state is not as straightforward, inevitable, or evolutionary as some suggest.[11] The history of state-sanctioned violence among abolitionist states differs little from the histories of the states that continue to execute significant numbers of their citizens. During the nineteenth and twentieth centuries, as Southern states were employing violence to control and exploit blacks, the Northern Central states were involved in the ethnic cleansing of Native Americans from their territories. To accomplish their respective tasks Southern and Northern states allowed, facilitated, and at times carried out numerous killings in the form of war, execution, and lynching. The primary factor that separated the violent cultural histories of Southern and Northern states was economic motivation. Violence in the North was motivated by pure and simple genocide, making way for incoming European settlers. Violence in the South was motivated by the need to politically control and exploit black labor, maintaining the sharecropper system. The task of Northern states ended with the near-total annihilation of Native Americans. Given the continued economic and political disenfranchisement of numerous African Americans, the task of the Southern states continues. Thus, death penalty abolition in the Northern Central states of Michigan, Wisconsin, Minnesota, North Dakota, and Iowa cannot be explained by the cultural evolution of "civilized" Enlightenment ideals. One wonders what the laws of those states would be today if politically and economically viable Native American populations had survived into the twenty-first century.

Zimring and Hawkins contend that "the boundaries that separate most of the twelve states that have executed [the most] from those that have not [executed anyone] appear to be the product of differences in governmental tradition, exemplified by a prior history of extensive executions."[12] In short, the history of the use of capital punishment gives rise to cultural traditions either supportive or nonsupportive of executions. While it is clear that cultural tradition or sensibilities are related to the decision to execute, death penalty abolition is not so easily explained. As Table 11.1 demonstrates, the move toward abolition does not fit well into a moral evolution model. Abolitionist states vary widely in their historical use of capital punishment. West Virginia, for example, has officially executed 155 persons. During the 1950s, five years before its legislature abolished capital punishment, West Virginia ranked seventeenth among executing U.S. states, hardly a cultural tradition of abolition (see Table 11.2). Thus, a combination of economic factors, demographic shifts, and cultural traditions more realistically fit the data.

Low murder rates offer yet another explanation for the abolition of capital punishment in the United States. At first glance this explanation appears plausible. For example, between 1945 and 1954, the average murder rate among seven abolitionist states ranged from a high of 1.6 per 100,000 (Iowa) to a low of 1.0 per 100,000 (Rhode Island). Closer scrutiny mediates against the notion that murder rates play a determining role in death penalty debates across the nation. For example, between 1945 and 1955, the states of West Virginia (not yet an abolitionist state) and Michigan had relatively high murder rates of 5.3 and 4.4 per 100,000, respectively. Moreover, Alaska's high murder rates did not stop legislators there from abolishing capital punishment in 1957. Alaska entered the Union in 1959 as an abolitionist state with an average murder rate that ranked eleventh among U.S. states.[13] Since 1970, murder rates in abolitionist states reflect the maximum possible variation. North Dakota, Iowa, and Maine tend to have some of the lowest murder rates in the nation, while the nation's leaders typically include Alaska, Michigan (see Table 11.3), as well as Washington, D.C.

While the history of violence, executions, and murder rates has a limited impact on death penalty abolition, heinous acts against children, women, and the elderly generally have considerable influence on capital punishment legislation. Political leaders, the public, and the press are understandably outraged by the occurrence of particularly

. . . .

TABLE 11.1
Year of Final Abolition Among Abolitionist States

State	Year
Michigan	1847
Wisconsin	1853
Maine	1887
Minnesota	1911
North Dakota	1915
Hawaii	1957
Alaska	1957
Iowa	1965
West Virginia	1965

Source: *Capital Punishment*, 1998.

TABLE 11.2
Total Executions in Abolitionist States

State	Total
Wisconsin	1
North Dakota	8
Alaska	12
Michigan	13
Maine	21
Iowa	45
Hawaii	49
Minnesota	66
West Virginia	155

Source: Espy and Smykla, 1987.

brutal homicides. Nevertheless, states with comparatively few homicides should have little reason to reinstate the death penalty. In practice, however, brutal homicides in any abolitionist state, no matter how rare or how common, become potential triggering events or opportunities to reinforce the notion that capital punishment is required to maintain social control. Such an event, no doubt, was responsible for South Dakota reestablishing capital punishment in 1939. Opponents of capital punishment cannot say that there exists an acceptable number of homicides—no matter how low the murder rates may be. As a

TABLE 11.3
Homicide Rates Among Abolitionist States, 1970–1999

State	1970	1980	1990	1999
Alaska	12.2	9.7	7.5	8.6
Michigan	8.9	10.2	10.4	7.0
West Virginia	6.2	7.1	5.7	4.4
Hawaii	4.0	8.5	4.0	3.7
Wisconsin	2.0	2.9	4.6	3.4
Minnesota	2.0	2.6	2.7	2.8
Iowa	1.9	2.2	1.9	1.5
Maine	1.5	2.8	2.4	2.2
North Dakota	0.5	1.2	0.8	1.6

Source: *Uniform Crime Reports*, 1970–1999.

consequence, every abolitionist state has a legal provision that allows the incarceration of offenders judged to be the most dangerous for actual life without any possibility of parole.

Is Economic Crisis Related to Death Penalty Abolition?

Rusche and Kirchheimer demonstrated that over several centuries capital punishment was used most widely during economic downturns when there was a surplus of labor and when those executed had no economic value.[14] On the other hand, during periods of economic boom when labor was in demand, workers could not be sacrificed on the gallows. Table 11.4 demonstrates that recent unemployment rates among abolitionist states are not consistent enough to support Rusche and Kirchheimer's reasoning. In the United States some abolitionist jurisdictions have chronic problems with their economies, such as Alaska, Michigan, West Virginia, and Washington, D.C., while others do not. In themselves, economic factors do little to explain death penalty abolition in the United States.

Three factors work against the instrumental use of capital punishment to negotiate cyclical downturns in the economies of the states studied here. First, the populations of Maine, North Dakota, Wisconsin, Minnesota, Iowa, and West Virginia are relatively small, homogeneous, and rural—all factors that mediate against executions. Sec-

TABLE 11.4
Unemployment per 100,000 in Abolitionist States, 1975–1999

State	1975	1980	1985	1990	1995	1999
Michigan	12.5	12.4	9.9	7.1	5.3	3.8
West Virginia	8.6	9.4	13.0	8.3	7.9	6.6
Alaska	6.7	9.7	9.7	6.9	7.3	6.4
Maine	10.3	7.8	5.4	5.1	5.7	4.1
Wisconsin	6.9	7.2	7.2	4.4	4.8	3.0
Minnesota	5.9	5.9	6.0	4.8	3.7	2.8
Iowa	4.2	5.8	8.0	4.2	3.5	2.5
North Dakota	3.7	5.0	5.9	3.9	3.3	3.4
Hawaii	8.2	4.9	5.6	2.8	5.9	5.6
U.S. Average	**8.3**	**7.0**	**7.2**	**5.6**	**5.6**	**4.2**

Source: *Statistical Abstract of the United States,* 1975–1999.

ond, Alaska and Hawaii have politically powerful minority populations that actively resist the reinstatement of capital punishment. Third, cultural traditions limit the severity of criminal punishments. Public officials in abolitionist states are not free to proceed at will: "Security considerations and the instrumental use of punishment are always in tension with cultural and psychic forces which place clear limits upon the types and extent of punishment which will be acceptable."[15]

What Is the Relationship Between Public Opinion and Death Penalty Abolition?

Zimring and Hawkins argue that death penalty abolition is always secured against the will of the people.[16] Moreover, they contend that after abolition, popular sentiment against death penalty abolition declines until "after several years" when anti–death penalty sentiments dominate. Among the states studied here, it is impossible to specify accurately the state of public opinion at the time of abolition. All available evidence suggests that the majority of citizens living in abolitionist states at the end of the twentieth century would verbally support the notion of reinstating capital punishment. Zimring and Hawkins's conclusion that popular support for abolition inevitably increases with the passage of a few years is inconsistent with opinion polls showing

. . . .

that attitudes concerning capital punishment differ little, if at all, between the residents of abolitionist and death penalty states. For example, after more than 150 years of abolition, most in Michigan still appear ready to reinstate capital punishment.

Evidence gathered here, however, suggests that Zimring and Hawkins might well be correct in their assumption of growing popular support for abolition. If public opinion polls in abolitionist states accurately reflect support for the death penalty, it is reasonable to assume that significant numbers of politicians would use capital punishment as their ticket to political success. However, numerous interviews during the course of this study concluded that "you cannot win on capital punishment in this state." How can this be true? There are two interconnected answers for this apparent contradiction. First, residents in abolitionist states have an opinion on capital punishment, but that opinion has little to do with their everyday lives. Under these circumstances, people vote for legislators and governors based on economic and other interests rather than on a candidate's death penalty position (for example, as in Wisconsin, North Dakota, and Minnesota). Second, those in abolitionist states tend to be abstractly supportive but practically opposed to the death penalty. In recent years, pro–death penalty legislators in Maine and Michigan, for example, have attempted to reestablish capital punishment by way of a referendum. Both efforts failed to get the necessary number of signatures to put the issue on the ballot. The work of Lifton and Mitchell suggests that the unwillingness to sign a petition reflects the tendency among advocates to separate the principle of execution from actual killing.[17] Signing a petition brings such persons closer to the reality of capital punishment. From a distance it is easier to maintain the luxury of advocacy without considering the consequences of that advocacy. Signing the petition puts citizens closer to the execution chamber.

What Roles Do Economic, Political, and Social Elites Tend to Play in Abolition Debates?

As one might expect, economic elites were not among the death penalty activists located in any abolitionist state. Economic elites were not involved in the death penalty politics of the states examined here.

These data suggest that economic elites either viewed capital punishment as a nonissue, or viewed death penalty abolition as desirable. In Michigan, for example, death penalty abolition provides economic elites with considerable social and political capital. Elites directly involved in the death penalty debates of abolitionist states tended to come from the ranks of politics, religion, human rights, and law. Groups supporting death penalty abolition tend to be well informed and well organized. Persons favoring reestablishment, for the most part, lacked formal training and political organization.

Among politicians, Republicans tended to favor capital punishment while Democrats tended to favor abolition. The position of the Republican party was of considerable significance. In some instances, the Republican party has been divided on capital punishment, thereby neutralizing its influence in reinstatement debates. In some states, the Republican party has provided prominent and outspoken death penalty opponents. In general, the Democratic party leadership in abolitionist states has publicly opposed the reinstatement of capital punishment, which, together with division among the Republicans, has given abolitionist forces greater political power. Moreover, bipartisan leadership tends to neutralize public opinion toward legislators.

Republican leadership in abolitionist states is powerless in West Virginia, Hawaii, and Washington, D.C., and is deeply divided in Iowa, Maine, Michigan, North Dakota, and Wisconsin. Yet triggering events, for example, a heinous murder, present situations where legislators are called on to take a stand for or against executions. Positions on capital punishment inevitably become public, and the cost of opposition to capital punishment depends on the strength of pro–death penalty sentiments in the community and the ability of organized political groups to punish politicians for taking an abolitionist stance.

Representatives from nearly every organized religion are found at most legislative hearings on reestablishing capital punishment. Fundamentalist Protestants tend to provide the religious support for reestablishing the death penalty. Representatives of other mainstream religious organizations are solidly behind death penalty abolition. The role that religious elites play in exposing issues of racism and class bias to the general public and political elites cannot be overstated. Religious influence on discourses concerning appropriate criminal sanctions is anything but new: "[F]rom the medieval period onwards, Western legal systems have increasingly separated themselves from religious authorities and conceptions, but something of that earlier, religious culture still remains, and from the Middle Ages right up to the present, religious beliefs have been an important force in shaping the practice and evolution of punishment."[18] The moral leadership that Pope John Paul assumed in Missouri and Massachusetts cannot be ignored (see Appendix). Sister Helen Prejean, author of *Dead Man Walking*, had a similar effect on a recent legislative effort to reestablish capital punishment in Alaska. Of course, the effectiveness of religious opposition to capital punishment varies. In executing states, Protestant and Roman Catholic leaders often feel some difficulty in expressing their opposition to capital punishment. Their assertiveness tends to vary with the support of Republican party officials for capital punishment and the views of the local news outlets. While institutionalized racism has spread throughout America, there appears to be significant regional differences in the freedom to discuss it openly.

Law enforcement, prison, and court personnel comprise the third major group of elites actively involved in abolitionist politics. Their presence in death penalty debates tends to reflect their proximity to the issue. It is their lives that would be most impacted if capital punishment were reestablished. Anti–death penalty advocates from this group tend to focus on exposing the mental and physical pain of criminal sanctions. Garland accurately describes the message these critics often deliver. They "attempt to work on the sensibilities of the public (or at least upon the governing elite) [by trying] . . . to make visible the brutality and suffering which is hidden in . . . [jails, court process, and death chambers] to bring violence out from behind the scenes, thus allowing it to impinge upon public consciousness and disturb the public conscience."[19]

While anti–death penalty forces in abolitionist states tend to be articulate and well organized, advocates of reinstatement were limited as much by their own statements and lack of organization as by abolitionist rhetoric. The strength of abolitionist forces in most non-executing states forces politicians in those jurisdictions to consider seriously the personal and professional consequences of actively supporting capital punishment. As a result, few mainstream politicians openly pursue reinstatement. Those that ignore their party and openly challenge death penalty abolition tend to be inhumane in their speech and therefore easily vilified in the press. Senator Laffin of Maine reacted to these circumstances by openly boasting that he did not care what his colleagues or the press thought of him. He seemed oblivious to the fact that the sentiments of his colleagues and the press were instrumental in defeating his efforts to reinstate capital punishment in Maine.

What Is the Relationship Between the Mass Media and Death Penalty Abolition?

The press is an interpreter of all murders, racism, and executions, providing a lens through which people can know about crime in their community. The editorial position of the *Los Angeles Times* has been of great significance in the success of bills in the California state legislature.[20] Moreover, Hagan found the position of the press was important across all types of legislative activity, as well as across a myriad of times and places.[21] Newspapers also play pivotal roles in local death penalty debates. Absent the *Des Moines Register* and the *Charleston Gazette*, Iowa and West Virginia would likely be death penalty states. Newspapers have also been significant contributors to death penalty abolition in other states.

For example, since Michigan became the first American state to abolish capital punishment for murder in 1847, its press has been nearly unified in characterizing the death penalty as racist in practice and Southern in ethos. Newspaper articles routinely discuss the racial makeup of death row prisoners in the South, where African Americans are highly overrepresented. At times, Southern death penalty advocates have been characterized in Michigan newspapers as crude and zealous. A Detroit newspaper reported that a capital punishment advocate in the Michigan legislature was educated at fundamentalist Bob Jones University in South Carolina, and that other supporters, including a senator and prosecutor, began their public careers as opponents of school busing to achieve racial balance.

In Maine, Alaska, Hawaii, and West Virginia the early histories of local executions are frequently recalled in the press as prime examples of how capital punishment is used against racial minorities: Native

Hawaiians, Native Alaskans, and African Americans. In North Dakota the potential of racial bias in death penalty administration was also emphasized. Capital punishment was abolished in Wisconsin early in the state's history, and it has not gone unnoticed in the press that those sentenced to death prior to statehood in the early nineteenth century were often Native Americans. During the 1990s, the racism inherent in the administration of the death penalty was noted, including the fact that many death sentences imposed in the South may have been the result of discrimination based on the race of the victim.

Is Population Diversity Associated with the Death Penalty?

Contrary to the claims that abolition can be expected in states with the least mobile populations,[22] our case studies include all variety of mobility patterns, from the extreme stability of Iowa and West Virginia to the great mobility found in Alaska and Hawaii (see Table 11.5). On the other hand, the nine case studies discussed support our assertion that executions and population diversity are strongly associated. The tendency to execute racial and ethnic minorities characterizes the execution histories of the abolitionist states. When Maine, Alaska, Hawaii, North Dakota, Minnesota, Wisconsin, West Virginia, and Michigan performed executions, racial and ethnic minorities were the victims of choice. These case studies demonstrate a close association between death penalty abolition and demographic shifts. The observation of one historian is exemplary: "[O]pposition to capital punishment became widespread after Wisconsin achieved separate territorial status in 1836. The nature of capital crimes with the region, too, began to change. No longer did military personnel or Indians figure so largely in them; ordinary white citizens, too, got involved."[23] In other words, the urge to execute dissipated as the relative size of minority populations declined. Michigan, Alaska, and Hawaii appear to be exceptions to the relationship between size of minority populations and executions (see Table 11.6). However, the comparatively large size of Michigan's minority population is a somewhat recent phenomenon. When Michigan abolished capital punishment in 1847, less than 1 percent of its population was black.[24] On the other hand, race and ethnicity played a different role in Alaska and Hawaii. Similar to recent

TABLE 11.5
Percentage of Population Born in State of Residence, 1990

State	Percentage	Rank
Iowa	77.6	3d
West Virginia	77.3	6th
Wisconsin	76.4	7th
Michigan	74.9	9th
Minnesota	73.6	11th
North Dakota	73.2	12th
Maine	68.5	21st
Hawaii	56.1	34th
Alaska	34.0	48th

Source: The census of 1990.

events in Washington, D.C., the large and politically powerful minority populations of Alaska and Hawaii exercised their political interests in 1957 and abolished the death penalty.

Making Theoretical Sense out of Death Penalty Abolition in the United States

Economic circumstances, demographics, ideology, and human struggle coalesced to bring about and maintain death penalty abolition in nine U.S. states. The exact influence these factors exerted on abolitionist processes varied by state. Referring to the Badger state: "Wisconsin had a twin heritage in its opposition to . . . [executions]. New York, whence came many of the first settlers, abolished public hanging in 1835. . . . Michigan, of which Wisconsin had been a part, forbid capital punishment in 1847."[25] The histories, ideas, and efforts of people affect lawmaking:

> Cultural struggle, exposé journalism, and moral criticism—the traditional tools of the penal reformer—do have some measure of effectiveness in bringing about . . . change. Penal forms are embedded within objective social structures and cultural frameworks. Political initiative, moral argument, the cultivation of sensibilities, and cultural education all play a part in shaping the details and regimes of society's . . . [punish-

TABLE 11.6
Percentage of Minorities in Abolitionist States, 1970–2000

State	1970	1980	1990	2000
Hawaii	61	67	67	75.8
Alaska	21	23	25	30.6
Michigan	13	15	17	19.8
Wisconsin	4	6	8	11.1
West Virginia	4	4	4	5.0
North Dakota	3	4	5	7.7
Minnesota	2	3	6	10.5
Maine	1	1	2	3.0
Iowa	1	3	3	6.1

Source: *Statistical Abstract of the United States,* 1970–2000.

ment policies]. Even if we cannot see the immediate possibility of changing society's infrastructure of class relations or its exclusory institutions, its administrative rationality, and its moral pluralism, we can still look to the influence of moral and cultural struggles ... [to alter punishment policy]. Social institutions may be more flexible than structuralist sociology allows.[26]

For death penalty abolition to become the law of the nation, political, religious, and social activists must continue to expose the horrors of executions. Moreover, the relationship between race, ethnicity, and capital punishment must be kept in the public eye.

EPILOGUE   **Abolition in the Courts**

Three additional U.S. states, Massachusetts, Rhode Island, and Vermont, do not currently have valid death penalty statutes. Death statutes in those states were—unlike the nine states previously discussed—the result of court rather than legislative action. As could be expected, the social processes surrounding judicial decisions differ from the dynamics of legislative action, although the cultural characteristics of these three states bear similarities to some of the nine abolitionist states.

The Death Penalty Struggle in Massachusetts

As early as 1804, Massachusetts governors began lobbying against capital punishment.[1] Executions were seldom performed, and from 1835 through 1849, only one black man and an Irish immigrant were executed. Abolition bills were considered by the state legislature in 1836, 1837, 1848, and 1851. A house report on capital punishment in 1836 seems amazingly contemporary. Here it was argued that capital punishment was contrary to Christian morality and the commandment "Thou shalt not kill."[2] It was also noted that capital punishment "provides no sufficient safeguards for minorities."[3] The claim was also made that the death penalty, slavery, mutilation, and torture were "contrary to the spirit of the constitution" of Massachusetts.[4]

In 1927, the infamous executions of two Italian immigrants, Nicola Sacco and Bartolomeo Vanzetti, were carried out.[5] Perhaps it was with these two cases in mind and the earlier claims of unconstitutionality that in 1975 the Massachusetts Supreme Judicial Court, which is composed of lifetime appointees, ruled that the state's death penalty law was unconstitutional under the provisions of the Massachusetts State Constitution. The court reaffirmed its decision in 1980 when the district attorney of Boston sought a declaratory judgment that a 1979 capital punishment law conformed to the state constitution. In 1984, another capital punishment law was passed by the legislature and signed by the governor, only to be found unconstitutional—the third time within a decade.[6]

In 1997, efforts to reestablish capital punishment in Massachusetts were reinvigorated by the sexual assault and murder of a ten-year-old Cambridge boy. The following year, state legislators responded to the crime but by the narrowest of margins defeated reinstatement when, at the eleventh hour, one legislator changed his support to a no vote. Reestablishing capital punishment became the centerpiece of Republican Paul Cellucci's campaign for governor. Cellucci's effort was successful. He defeated an anti-death Democratic candidate for governor and Republican members of the legislature immediately wrote a bill that would have made sixteen crimes executable offenses, including the killing of a police officer or a child under fourteen years of age. The stage was set for a close legislative vote on capital punishment. The *Boston Globe* editorialized that life without the possibility of parole was a satisfactory punishment for murder. The ACLU reminded citizens and legislators of recent death penalty cases in Illinois where innocent people were nearly executed. Nevertheless, polls suggested that a clear majority of Massachusetts residents favored reestablishment. The governor stated that capital punishment was worthwhile if it saved only a single life: "It is one way that society can send a clear and unmistakable message that we're not going to tolerate deadly, horrific violence in our state."[7]

The equation, however, began to shift with Pope John Paul's January 1999 visit to the United States. Here, John Paul's message to "resist the culture of death and to choose to stand steadfastly on the side of life" moved Missouri Governor Mel Carnahan to commute a death sentence and the nation's Roman Catholic bishops to take a stand strongly favoring the abolition of capital punishment. The bishops released a Good Friday message declaring "a day when we recall our Savior's own execution" and calling on "all people of goodwill, and especially Catholics, to work to end the death penalty."[8] Following his testimony before a Massachusetts legislative hearing on capital punishment, Cardinal Bernard Law of Boston told reporters that "the teachings of the church are very clear. . . . For a well-informed Catholic to support capital punishment, it would be morally wrong. And if one knowingly rejects the teachings of the Church it is wrong, morally evil, and a sin." Public opinion polls, however, suggested that Roman Catholics were no less in favor of the death penalty than others.[9] Governor Cellucci responded to Cardinal Law by noting: "I mean, that's his opinion. There's an awful lot of Catholics in Massachusetts and an awful lot of them support the death penalty." In the end, the 1999 death penalty bill was rejected by a majority of Massachusetts legislators.[10]

Death Penalty Debates in Rhode Island and Vermont

Rhode Island was a pioneer in death penalty reforms, having first abolished public executions in 1833 and capital punishment in 1852.[11] The immediate cause for abolition was the infamous 1845 execution of John Gordon, an Irish immigrant, for the murder of Amasa Sprague, a wealthy Protestant businessman infamous in the Rhode Island community for his exploitation of immigrant Irish workers. The trial, conviction, and execution took place at a time in Rhode Island's history when Protestant-Catholic relations were terribly strained by widespread anti-Irish bigotry.[12] Massive Irish Catholic immigration was altering the political balance of power in what was fast becoming a predominantly Roman Catholic state. There was deep suspicion in the Catholic community that John Gordon was an innocent victim who was convicted on the basis of questionable circumstantial evidence and anti-Irish and anti-Catholic prejudice. Even though there were obvious errors in the trial and contempt for the Irish was expressed in court by both the prosecution and defense attorneys, Gordon was convicted and sentenced to death. After his execution, a massive crowd of Irish Catholics lined the streets and followed the coffin to the burial grounds in Providence.

After the 1852 abolition bill had been passed, the only provision retained for executions was in the case of murder by a prisoner serving a life sentence.[13] In 1973, after 121 years, the Rhode Island legislature

. . . .

passed a new law providing for death for *any* prisoner who should commit murder in the state. As of this writing, however, the state has not even attempted to construct the gas chamber that was specified as the method of execution in the 1973 statute.

The Rhode Island Supreme Court ruled in 1979 that the newly enacted death penalty law was unconstitutional. That same year, the Rhode Island legislature passed a law providing for life in prison without the possibility of parole for those convicted of first-degree murder, apparently drawing much of the support away from capital punishment. Death penalty abolition in Rhode Island has also been assisted by the state's diminutive geographical size and relatively small population (fewer than one million residents) where people seem to know their neighbors. Moreover, this is a homogeneous state with a larger proportion of Roman Catholics than any other state in the nation, approximately 66 percent.[14] In this very Catholic state the execution of John Gordon is frequently mentioned by death penalty opponents. This emphasis of ethnic discrimination serves a similar function to the history of racial bias in application of capital punishment in the nine abolitionist states.

Vermont's constitutional convention of 1777 represented the very essence of progressive thought and "suspended property requirements for voting and office holding, abolished slavery and the imprisonment of debtors, . . . subjected all judges to annual election or legislative recall, granted access to all government meetings and records, . . . and allowed complete liberty of conscience in religion."[15] In 1843, the Vermont legislature passed a law requiring that after sentencing, "the execution of a capital offender was ordered to be stayed [until] fifteen months after conviction" and not until after this delay would the governor be obliged to order the execution.[16] The delay was not sufficient for Governor William Slade, for he ignored the law and refused to issue the order for execution at the required time. Even in the face of these delays, the state legislature did not attempt to impeach the governor. No one appeared to be concerned about these interminable delaying actions nor did the state legislature attempt to abolish capital punishment. No one seemed concerned enough about the situation to do either.

Consistent with this indifference is the fact that Vermont has seldom used this penalty. Between 1630 and 1970, only twenty-six people were executed in the state, including only one black.[17] Vermont residents displayed more than mere indifference to executions; prior to the 1905 hanging of convicted murderer Mary Rogers, Governor Charles Bell received in excess of forty thousand appeals to spare her life, with eighteen hundred from Burlington.[18] Even the four law enforcement officials charged with carrying out the execution appealed to the governor for mercy. The hanging itself was botched, with the rope cut too long, leaving the condemned woman's toes barely touching the ground, requiring fourteen minutes for her to die. The 1912 execution of Elroy Kent also went very badly and did nothing to convince Vermonters of the value of capital punishment. The trap door of the gallows opened on cue but as the prisoner dropped, the rope broke. He fell to the concrete floor below, "writhing about in agony," while the executioner fashioned another noose that was used ultimately to kill him.[19] If capital punishment has been used as a vehicle of minority oppression in other states, this is clearly not the case in Vermont. In addition, since 1900, only eight prisoners have been put to death.

Thus, the pattern of delay found in Rhode Island is similarly found in Vermont. Vermont became an abolition state through legislative inaction. As of this writing, the state assembly has not passed a new death penalty statute since 1972, when its existing law was rendered constitutionally questionable by the United States Supreme Court.[20] This inattention is undoubtedly facilitated by Vermont's very low murder rates, and as in Rhode Island, its small, homogeneous population and small geographic territory. Additionally, since 1987, Vermont law has allowed those convicted of first-degree murder to be sentenced to life in prison without the possibility of parole,[21] as does Rhode Island. The population homogeneity of Rhode Island and Vermont mirrors many of the states whose legislatures have abolished capital punishment.

Summary

Throughout the New England states there has always been significant opposition to capital punishment, and executions have been less common in this region than elsewhere in the United States.[22] We

. . . .

noted in Chapter 11 that when abolitionist states abolished capital punishment, the states' populations were quite homogeneous. The homogeneity of the populations of Massachusetts, Rhode Island, and Vermont also helps in understanding the traditions in these three states.[23] Even if legislatures refrain from taking decisive action, the courts feel free to step into the breach—as they did in Rhode Island and as they have repeatedly done in Massachusetts. In addition, the prominence of the Roman Catholic population in most of these states[24] undoubtedly makes capital punishment less normative and judicial support for abolition more acceptable. By comparison, similar court action would be unthinkable in the Deep South.

Data Collection Methods

Michigan

Leading death penalty supporters and opponents were identified for interviews through news reports. Those interviewed were asked to identify additional knowledgeable respondents. Those eventually interviewed included state legislators, journalists, prosecutors, former directors of the Michigan Department of Corrections, and college professors. We also consulted house and senate journals for records of legislation, and records of the Michigan Department of Corrections. In addition, we reviewed records of the United Auto Workers' recommendations on death penalty bills, newspaper clippings from the state library's death penalty file, and all relevant articles appearing in the *Detroit News* between January 1975 and March 1985. We reviewed reports of the Michigan Legislative Service Bureau, which is responsible for writing bills and conducting background research on proposed legislation. Finally, we consulted the *Michigan Report*, a publication of the Gongwer News Service, available from 1962 to July 1985, indicating the progress of legislation.

Wisconsin

To analyze cultural dispositions, structural foundations, and triggering events specific to Wisconsin's anti–death penalty tradition, the following categories of archival data were analyzed: legislative histories, newspaper editorials and articles, narratives from state histories, homicide rates, unemployment rates, ethnic diversity, mobility, and economic characteristics of the population. Official records include: the 1992–1994 *Wisconsin Blue Book*, which describes the structure, rules, and functions of legislative committee records, house and senate journals, and senate and house bills and referenda; crime rate data from the FBI's *Uniform Crime Reports* covering 1991 to 1995; and demographic data from the Census Bureau as reported in the 1995, 1996, and 1997 volumes of the *Statistical Abstract of the United States*. For the period from 1991 to 1995, the following Wisconsin newspapers were reviewed for articles addressing death penalty politics in Wisconsin: *Capital Times*, the *Wisconsin State Journal*, the *Milwaukee Journal Sentinel,* the *Madison Newspapers, Inc.,* and the *New York Times.* The *Madison Newspapers, Inc.,* is the archiving agency for both the *Capital Times* and the *Wisconsin State Journal.* An Internet electronic resource, www.madison.com, provides access to copies of dated articles from the above-noted newspapers, but does not consistently show which paper published a given article. Except for the *New York Times,* the above-noted commercial media outlets were selected because they are published in the state capital of Madison or in Milwaukee, Wisconsin's two major urban centers. We selected the time frame of 1991 to 1995 because this period provides a temporal context when a major death penalty triggering event occurred.

Minnesota

An article in the 1992 *Session Weekly* listed the three major efforts to reinstate capital punishment in Minnesota since abolition in 1911: the legislative sessions of 1913, 1921, and 1923. The legislative records for these years verify their significance. Since 1923, no death penalty bill has been reported out of committee. Legislative records also served as guides in the review of newspaper articles, which in turn helped fill in the gaps left by official records. In addition, the 1923 report of the Minnesota Crime Commission was reviewed for its recommendations regarding capital punishment. Homicide data for these time periods are not available for the state and were only available for Minneapolis (1916 to 1925) in several files in the Minneapolis police department. The data included a binder that contains statistics on homicides from 1916 through 1989, files on individual cases from 1916 through 1989, and handwritten notes on local deaths. In Minnesota, the centrality of the press in the abolitionist process is another reason for our focus on newspaper accounts of these reinstatement efforts. Given the importance of the press, every issue of the largest newspaper in the state, the *Minneapolis Morning Tribune,* was reviewed for articles on crime, violence, and relevant legislative action during these periods. Through this review, we gathered data that allowed us to describe the context in which the debate over capital punishment was taking place. It should be noted that earlier in this century, the Minnesota legislature did not keep detailed legislative records. Thus, the newspapers provided the most comprehensive source of information regarding legislative action as well as information on conflict and controversy in the community. In addition, the editorial position of the newspaper was recorded.

The following time frames were used for newspaper analysis.

1. For 1912 through 1913, all newspapers were read for a ten-month stretch, June 1912 through March 1913; that is, nine months prior to, during, and immediately after the legislature had finished its consideration of capital punishment. These deliberations were from February 8, 1913, to March 7, 1913. This review provided considerable detail on events during the initial

abolitionist experience in Minnesota, prior to the actual introduction of the first reinstatement bill in February 1913.

2. For 1920 through 1921, a fourteen-month span was used, April 1920 through June 1921. This included the 1921 legislative death penalty deliberations from February 24, 1921, to April 20, 1921, as well as the much-publicized lynchings in Duluth in the spring of 1920.

3. Finally, for 1923, only January and February were used to determine what public events developed during the legislative session's death penalty deliberations from January 8 through February 28. Here data from a relatively short time span were deemed adequate.

North Dakota

Content analysis of archival data was conducted in order to extract information to characterize the social context in which North Dakota retains its abolition of the death penalty. Newspaper articles found in the *Bismarck Tribune* provide the primary archival data for this study. These newspaper articles represent traces of the social context within which North Dakota retains its abolition of capital punishment. The *Tribune*, published in the state's capital, is important because of its proximity to the state legislature. Data were collected for the three different time periods when initiatives were attempted to reinstate the death penalty in North Dakota. Articles were selected if they reported news about local reaction or legislative efforts to reinstate the death penalty. The data consist of 470 news articles located by reviewing each issue of the newspaper during the following periods:

1. **January 1, 1926 through December 31, 1927.** This period of time was selected because a death penalty reinstatement bill was introduced in the North Dakota legislature in January 1927.

2. **August 1, 1938 through December 31, 1939.** This time period was chosen because North Dakota's neighbor to the south was, at this time, in the heat of a death penalty reinstatement initiative. South Dakota reinstated the death penalty in late January 1939. Articles were selected if they reported on South Dakota's efforts to reinstate the death penalty. There was initial reason to expect that noteworthy developments in South Dakota might have an impact in its sister state to the north.

3. **January 1, 1975 through February 7, 1979.** Information received from the North Dakota Historical Society noted two legislative efforts to reinstate the death penalty during this time period in North Dakota. We selected articles if they reported on efforts to reinstate capital punishment in either 1977 or 1979.

. . . .

Alaska

Three sources of data were utilized in studying death penalty abolition in Alaska: personal interviews, legislative records, and press accounts. Snowball sampling was used, in which those interviewed nominate additional contacts to be interviewed. Persons interviewed included proponents and opponents of capital punishment in the state legislature, community activists working to retain abolition, along with others seeking reinstatement.

Legislative records dating from 1956, one year preceding abolition, to August 1994 were searched for information on capital punishment. Legislative records retrieved included committee notes, minutes and voice recordings of legislative debates, minutes and voice recordings of committee meetings and public hearings, and legislative reports. Press accounts included articles, editorials, and reader commentary concerning capital punishment published in the *Anchorage Daily News*, currently Alaska's most influential newspaper. For the period January 1989 to August 1994, all editions of the *Daily News* were searched for articles on capital punishment. For the period 1957 through 1988, only those editions of the *Daily News* were searched that were published the month during and the month preceding serious legislative death penalty debate.

Iowa

Interviews were conducted with Harold Hughes, who was governor in 1965, and Terry Branstad, who was governor in 1995. Political reporters George Mills and David Yepsen were also contacted in order to verify information regarding the actions of the state legislature. Jim Ryan, of the Iowa Ecumenical Ministries, served to confirm the role of organized religion in recent legislative activities. An emotional interview was conducted by telephone with Tony and Peggy Emry, the parents of nine-year-old Anna Marie, a 1994 murder victim. A detailed content analysis of the *Des Moines Register* was conducted for the six months prior to, the month during, and the six months following the 1965 and 1995 actions of the Iowa legislature on capital punishment. In this content analysis, special attention was given to murders in Iowa. Topics such as crime rates, domestic homicides, and the gubernatorial elections of 1964 and 1994 were also reviewed. The time frames established for the *Register* review were centered on the dates of the final vote on capital punishment legislation, February 18, 1965, and March 2, 1995. Thus, the time periods for the review were the thirteen months of August 1964 through August 1965 and September 1994 through September 1995. The *Register* is Iowa's largest daily newspaper. The importance of this newspaper in Iowa's abolition efforts in 1965 and 1995 is reflected in the regional dominance of the newspaper as seen in its circulation figures as well as its longevity. The *Register* is much more than a daily newspaper in the state capital; it has in truth been a statewide newspaper for over one hundred years. In order to determine the reported numbers of homicides and crime rates during these thirteen-month periods, August 1964 through August 1965, and September 1994 through September 1995, FBI *Uniform Crime Reports* were examined, as well as the more detailed state version, the *Iowa Uniform Crime Report*, published by the Iowa Department of Public Safety. Legislative records were consulted for proceedings and the vote on death penalty bills. Proceedings from the Iowa senate and Iowa house were published in the 1965 and 1995 House and Senate Journals.

West Virginia

Findings presented here draw on several data sources. During the approximately thirty years of death penalty abolition in West Virginia, there have been frequent house and senate hearings on the merits of reinstatement bills (1971, 1972, 1978–81, and 1985–87). Thus, there exist many government documents concerning this issue. We reviewed the two major daily newspapers in the state capital (Charleston), which gave intensive coverage to legislative activity. We reviewed each edition of these papers for the three months immediately prior to abolition, as well as every edition from 1970 to 1988. We also conducted interviews with those involved on both sides of the abolition debate. This group included legislators, civil servants, and local journalists.

Notes

Chapter 1

1. George Kannar, "Federalizing Death," *Buffalo Law Review* 44 (1996): 325–37.
2. James M. Galliher and John F. Galliher, "Déjà Vu All Over Again: The Recurring Life and Death of Capital Punishment in Kansas," *Social Problems* 44 (August 1997): 369–85.
3. Pub. L. No. 100-690 (1988).
4. Pub. L. No. 103-322 (1994).
5. *Furman v. Georgia*, 408 U.S. 238, 92, 2726 (1972); *Coker v. Georgia*, 433 U.S. 584, 97, 2861 (1977).
6. "History of the Death Penalty," Death Penalty Information Center (2000). Available at http://www.deathpenaltyinfo.org/dpicrecinnoc.html.
7. "Death Takes a Holiday," *Nation*, 6 March 2000.
8. Pub. L. No. 104-133 (1996).
9. Robert M. Bohm, *Deathquest: An Introduction to the Theory and Practice of Capital Punishment in the United States* (Cincinnati: Anderson Publishing, 1999); W. Schabas, *The Abolition of the Death Penalty in International Law*, 2d ed. (Cambridge: Cambridge University Press, 1997).
10. Ibid.
11. Leon Radzinowicz, *A History of English Criminal Law* (New York: Macmillan, 1996).
12. David Greenberg, *Crime and Capitalism* (Philadelphia: Temple University Press, 1993), 517.
13. David Garland, *Punishment and Modern Society* (Chicago: University of Chicago Press, 1990), 226.
14. Ibid.
15. Ibid.
16. Ibid.
17. Roger Hood, *The Death Penalty: A Worldwide Perspective* (New York: Oxford University Press, 1989).
18. "Madame Falls Silent," *Economist*, 20 August–4 September 1981.
19. Franklin E. Zimring and Gordon Hawkins, *Capital Punishment and the American Agenda* (New York: Cambridge University Press, 1986), 5.
20. Bohm, *Deathquest*; Schabas, *The Abolition*.
21. 408 U.S. 238, 92, 2726 (1972).
22. 428 U.S. 153, 96, 2909 (1977).
23. American Friends Service Committee, *The Death Penalty: The Religious Community Calls for Abolition* (Philadelphia: AFSC, 2000).
24. United Nations, *United Nations Commission on Human Rights, Resolutions and Statements* (26 April 1999). Available at http://www.deathpenaltyinfo.org/UN-Statements.html.
25. Amnesty International, *Death Sentences and Executions in 2000* (26 April 2001). Available at http://www.web.amnesty.org/rmp/dplibrary.nsf.
26. Hugo Adam Bedau, *The Death Penalty in America*, 3d ed. (New York: Oxford University Press, 1982), 24.
27. Gideon Sjoberg and Roger Nett, *A Methodology for Social Science* (Prospect Heights, Ill.: Waveland Press, 1997), 22.

28. Robert K. Merton, *Social Theory and Social Structure* (New York: Free Press, 1968), 158.

29. Franklin E. Zimring and Gordon Hawkins, *Capital Punishment and the American Agenda* (New York: Cambridge University Press, 1986), 149.

30. Ibid., 144.

31. Georg Rusche and Otto Kirchheimer, *Punishment and Social Structure* (New York: Columbia University Press, 1939).

32. James Alan Fox, Michael L. Radelet, and Julie L. Bonsteel, "Death Penalty Opinion in the Post-*Furman* Years," *New York University Review of Law and Social Change* 18 (1990–1991): 499–528.

33. Robert M. Bohm, "American Death Penalty Opinion, 1936–1986: A Critical Examination of the Gallup Polls," in *The Death Penalty in America: Current Research* (Cincinnati: Anderson Publishing, 1991).

34. John Hagan, "The Legislation of Crime and Delinquency: A Review of Theory, Method, and Research," *Law and Society Review* 14 (1980): 623.

35. Richard A. Berk, Harold Brackman, and Selma L. Lesser, *A Measure of Justice: An Empirical Study of Changes in the California Penal Code, 1955–1971* (New York: Academic Press, 1977).

36. Marvin Wolfgang and Marc Riedel, "Race, Judicial Discretion, and the Death Penalty," *Annals of the American Academy of Political and Social Science* 407 (1973): 119–33; Michael Hindelang, "Equality Under the Law," in Charles Reasons and Jack Kuykendall, eds., *Race, Crime, and Justice* (Pacific Palisades, Calif.: Goodyear, 1972); David Baldus, Charles Pulaski, and George Woodworth, "Comparative Review of Death Sentences: An Empirical Study of the Georgia Experience," *Journal of Criminal Law and Criminology* 74 (1983): 661–763; David Cole, *No Equal Justice: Race and Class in the American Criminal Justice System* (New York: New Press, 1999); Barry Nakell and Kenneth A. Hardy, *The Arbitrariness of the Death Penalty* (Philadelphia: Temple University Press, 1987).

37. Bijou Yang and David Lister, "Which States Have the Death Penalty: Data from 1980," *Psychological Reports* 65 (1989): 185–86.

38. Anthony M. Orum, Joe R. Feagin, and Gideon Sjoberg, eds., "Introduction: The Nature of the Case Study," in *A Case for the Case Study* (Chapel Hill: University of North Carolina Press, 1991), 1–26.

39. Jacques Hamel with Stephanie Dufour and Dominic Fortin, *Case Study Methods*, Qualitative Research Methods, vol. 32 (London: Sage Publications, 1993), 34.

40. Bruce L. Berg, *Qualitative Research Methods for the Social Sciences* (Boston: Allyn and Bacon, 1989), 85.

Chapter 2

1. Hugo Adam Bedau, *The Death Penalty in America*, 3d ed. (New York: Oxford University Press, 1982), 21A.

2. Louis H. Burbey, "History of Execution in What Is Now the State of Michigan," *Michigan History Magazine* 22 (1938): 443–57.

3. Edward W. Bennett, "The Reasons for Michigan's Abolition of Capital Punishment," *Michigan History Magazine* 62 (1978): 42–55.

4. "The Age-Old Question—Tooth for a Tooth?" *Detroit Free Press*, 20 March 1960, 1D, 6D.

5. Ibid.; "State Has Led Anti-Death Penalty Forces," *Lansing State Journal*, 3 February 1972.

6. "Detroit Bar Owner's Hanging Becomes Death Penalty Symbol," *Lansing State Journal*, 10 March 1977, 10B.

7. "How One Bandit Died," *Detroit News*, 27 January 1959; see also "Tony Chebatoris Failed in All Things—Except Keeping a Date with Hangman," *Detroit Free Press*, 28 December 1958.

8. "How One Bandit Died," *Detroit News*, 27 January 1959.

9. U.S. Department of Commerce, *Statistical Abstracts of the United States*, 68th to 106th ed., 1947–86 (Washington, D.C.: Government Printing Office, 1986).

10. Ibid., 1967–86.

11. Edmund F. McGarrell and Timothy J.

Flanagan, eds., *Sourcebook of Criminal Statistics, 1985* (Albany, N.Y.: Hindelang Criminal Justice Research Center, 1985); U.S. Department of Commerce, *Statistical Abstracts*.

12. U.S. Department of Commerce, *Statistical Abstracts*, 1982.

13. U.S. Department of Commerce, *Historical Statistics of the United States: Colonial Times to 1970, Part 1* (Washington, D.C.: U.S. Government Printing Office, 1975).

14. Dominic Capeci, Jr., *Race Relations in Wartime Detroit* (Philadelphia: Temple University Press, 1984), 9.

15. Alfred McClung Lee and Norman Daymond Humphrey, *Race Riot* (New York: Dryden Press, 1943).

16. Ibid., 92.

17. J. B. Widick, *Detroit: City of Race and Class Violence* (Chicago: Quadrangle Books, 1972), 27.

18. Tony Platt and Paul Takagi, "Intellectuals for Law and Order: A Critique of the New Realists," *Crime and Social Justice* 8 (1977): 1–16.

19. Widick, *Detroit: City of Race*.

20. Capeci, *Race Relations*.

21. Joseph Boskin, *Urban Racial Violence in the Twentieth Century* (Beverly Hills, Calif.: Glencoe Press, 1969).

22. "House OK's Death Bill for Felons," *Lansing State Journal*, 28 May 1952, 1, 2; Michigan Legislature, Michigan House Bill 482, *Journal of the House*, 14 May 1952.

23. "Williams Bars Way for Bill to Provide Death for Slayers," *Detroit News*, 18 June 1950, 1, 24.

24. "Petitions 'Amaze' Legislator: Demands for Death Penalty Mounting," *Detroit News*, 22 June 1950, 1, 2.

25. Barbara Bryant, *Michigan Public Speaks Out on Crime*, eds. 1–5, Market Opinion Research Commissioned by Michigan Executive Office, Detroit, 1974–77.

26. Ibid., 1976, 1977.

27. "Capital Punishment Gets Backing in Detroit Area," *Detroit News*, 24 February 1978, 1A.

28. "Michigan Voters Support Death Penalty, Poll Says," *Detroit Free Press*, 13 August 1982, 1A, 2A.

29. "Two Opinions of Death Penalty," *Detroit News*, 15 July 1985.

30. *Crime in Michigan*, Market Opinion Research Commissioned by Michigan Executive Office, Detroit, 1980, 1982, 1985.

31. Ibid., 1980.

32. Bryant, *Michigan Public Speaks*, 1974–77.

33. *Michigan Revised Statutes* (1846), chs. 152–53: 658, effective 1 January 1847.

34. Austin C. Knapp, ed., *State of Michigan, Constitutional Convention, 1961*, vol. 1 (Lansing, Mich., 1963); *Michigan Constitution* (1963) Article 4, Section 46, Death Penalty.

35. Franklin E. Zimring and Gordon Hawkins, *Capital Punishment and the American Agenda* (New York: Cambridge University Press, 1986), 12.

36. Michigan Legislature, *House Majority Report of the Select Committee on Abolishment of Capital Punishment* (1844), 2.

37. Michigan Legislature, *Senate Report of the Judiciary Committee* (1865), 5.

38. Ibid., 3.

39. Michigan Legislature, *Journal of the Senate* (1929), 639–40.

40. Michigan Legislature, *Journal of the House* (1929), 117.

41. "Death Penalty Won't Cut Crime Rate, Expert Says," *Flint Journal*, 23 June 1955.

42. "Hanging Never Popular in State," *Lansing State Journal*, 14 January 1974, 4B.

43. Michigan Legislature, *House Hearings of the Committee on Constitutional Revision and Women's Rights*, 15 March 1973.

44. "Foes Insist Death Penalty No Crime Cure," *Detroit Free Press*, 11 December 1976.

45. "Michigan and the Death Penalty," *Flint Journal*, 6 January 1980, 5B.

46. "Executive Report: Should Michigan Bring Back the Death Penalty?" Michigan Chamber of Commerce, 7 April 1980, 6, 7.

47. Lt. Governor James H. Brickley, Press Release, 2 February 1980.

48. United Auto Workers, Legislative Program (1977), 9.

49. "Capital Punishment Gnaws at Humanity's Innards," *Detroit News*, 5 June 1979, 21A.

50. Austin C. Knapp, ed., *State of Michigan, Constitutional Convention, 1961*, vol. 1 (Lansing, Mich., 1963).

51. *Capital Punishment* (unpublished legislative pamphlet, Michigan State Library, n.d.), 3.

52. Ibid.

53. Michigan Legislature, *Journal of the Senate* (1929), 1142–43.

54. *Capital Punishment*, 2.

55. "Capital Punishment Banned in Michigan 100 Years Ago," *Lansing State Journal*, 11 July 1946.

56. "State Bar Says No to Death Penalty," *Lansing State Journal*, 12 May 1985.

57. "Death Penalty Bill Defeated," *Grand Rapids Press*, 7 March 1945.

58. "Let's Keep Michigan Civilized," *Saginaw News*, 17 February 1980.

59. "Michigan Report," *Gongwer News Service*, no. 85, 1 May 1984.

60. See also James H. Lincoln, "The Everlasting Controversy: Michigan and the Death Penalty," *Wayne State Law Review* 33 (1987): 1765–90.

61. "Senate Panel May Call for a Return of Death Row," *Detroit Free Press*, 27 May 1985, 3A, 10A.

62. Michigan Legislature, *Journal of the House* (1929).

63. Michigan Legislature, *Journal of the House* (1931), 249.

64. "Death Bill Defeated in House," *Lansing State Journal*, 12 March 1953, 1, 16.

65. "Foe of Death Penalty Drives Home a Point," *Detroit News*, 8 June 1985.

66. Thomas Kohler, unpublished manuscript, 1980, Cooley Law School, Lansing, Mich.

67. Question Box, *Catholic Weekly*, 7 June 1959.

68. Michigan Legislature, Senate Judiciary Committee, *Hearing on Capital Punishment*, 23 May 1985.

69. Ibid.

70. "States Deadly Serious Death Penalty Returns," *Detroit News*, 16 September 1981, 1A, 8A, 9A.

71. "Murder Is Murder: Punishment, Yes—Execution, No," *Detroit News*, 16 March 1981, 11A.

72. "U.S. Death Row Population up 20% in a Year," *Detroit Free Press*, 8 March 1981, 14A.

73. "Death Row Population Sets Record," *Detroit News*, 5 July 1983, 6B.

74. "Dad Wants Tammi's Killers Dead," *Detroit News*, 21 August 1979.

75. "Angry Senator Stalks Out in Death Penalty Hassle," *Lansing State Journal*, 6 February 1970.

76. "T-Shirt Backs Death Penalty," *Detroit News*, 18 March 1982.

77. "Slain Trooper's Widow Wears 'Fry em' Shirt," *Detroit Free Press*, 18 March 1982.

78. "Death Penalty Bill Fails to Clear House Unit," *Detroit News*, 6 April 1973.

79. "Comment During Rap Session: Two of Five Lifers Favor Death Penalty," *Lansing State Journal*, 10 April 1973, 6B.

80. "Senate Panel Oks Death Penalty," *Detroit Free Press*, 29 May 1985, 1A, 15A.

81. "Legislators, Police Join in Campaign for Death Penalty," *Detroit Free Press*, 15 December 1976.

82. "Death Penalty Pushed," *Lansing State Journal*, 4 January 1974, 1B, 4B.

83. "Capital Punishment and Capital Ambitions," *Detroit Free Press*, 21 October 1984, 7, 10, 12.

84. "Ex-Death Row Inmate Fights Death Sentence," *Lansing State Journal*, 15 June 1980, 1A.

85. "States Deadly Serious Death Penalty Returns," *Detroit News*, 16 September 1981, 1A.

86. Political cartoon, *Detroit News*, 12 July 1982, 8A.

87. "Capital Punishment and Capital Ambitions," *Detroit Free Press*, 21 October 1984, 7, 10, 12.

88. "Great Material for a Nightmare: Viewing 189 Executions Solidifies Opposition to Capital Punishment," *Lansing State Journal*, 13 August 1972, 1C.

89. "States Deadly Serious Death Penalty Returns," *Detroit News*, 16 September 1981, 1A.

90. Michigan Legislature, Senate Judiciary Committee, *Hearing* (1985).

91. "States Deadly Serious Death Penalty Re-

turns," *Detroit News*, 16 September 1981, 1A.

92. "Rough Sketches," *Detroit News*, 15 August 1982, 19A.

93. "Friendship with Killer Broke Every Stereotype," *Detroit Free Press*, 27 June 1985, 1A, 7A.

94. "High Court Leaves Door Open—Slightly: New Capital Punishment Laws?" *Detroit News*, 30 June 1972.

95. "Death Penalty Bill Doomed," *Detroit News*, 23 February 1951.

96. Knapp, ed., *State of Michigan*.

97. "Police Join Drive for State Vote on Death Penalty," *Detroit Free Press*, 1 February 1978.

98. "A Hedge on Death Penalty," *Detroit News*, 28 April 1976.

99. "Ex-Death Row Inmate Fights Death Sentence," *Lansing State Journal*, 15 June 1980, 1A.

100. "Death Amendment Killed: Patterson," *Lansing State Journal*, 30 September, 1982, 6B.

101. "State Republican Delegates Vote to Back Death Penalty, 1, 274–310," *Lansing State Journal*, 17 February 1985, 1A.

102. Michigan Legislature, Senate Judiciary Committee, *Hearings* (1985).

103. "Capital Punishment Banned in Michigan 100 Years Ago," *Lansing State Journal*, 11 July 1946.

104. "Precedent Set by Michigan Against Death Penalty Gains Prestige," *Lansing State Journal*, 10 April 1957, 34, 38.

105. "Capital Punishment-State Keeps Eye on Its Slow Death," *Detroit News*, 27 December 1964, 14C.

106. Michigan Legislature, *House Hearings* (1973).

107. "Death Penalty Pushed," *Lansing State Journal*, 14 January 1974, 1B, 4B.

108. Michigan Legislature, Senate Judiciary Committee, *Hearing* (1985).

109. Michigan Legislature, *Journal of the Senate* (1985), 1129.

110. "Michigan's Latest Attempt: Capital Punishment Again Asked," *Lansing State Journal*, 1 May 1967, 4A; "Hanging Never Popular in State," *Lansing State Journal*,

14 January 1974, 4B; "Death Penalty Gaining Favor," *Lansing State Journal*, 29 March 1975; "Gallows Noose Swung Only Twice in Michigan," *Detroit News*, 6 December 1976, 3A, 4A; "Reaction to Hanging Sent Death Penalty to Gallows," *Detroit News*, 9 September 1984, 15.

111. Michigan Legislature, *Journal of the Senate* (1929), 1142–43.

112. "Senate Committee Revamps Foster Death Penalty Bill," *Lansing State Journal*, 11 February 1931, 1.

113. Michigan Legislature, *Journal of the Senate* (1931), 1278.

114. Michigan Legislature, *Journal of the House* (1943).

115. "Death Penalty Up to Senate," *Detroit News*, 7 May 1947.

116. "House OK's Death Bill for Felons," *Lansing State Journal*, 28 May 1952, 1, 2.

117. "Petition Drive Underway: Death Penalty Sought in State," *Detroit News*, 2 August 1973.

118. "Capital Punishment Bill Dead," *Detroit News*, 19 June 1974.

119. "New Death Penalty Petition Drive Is Getting Organized," *Lansing State Journal*, 5 November 1979.

120. "Dad Wants."

121. "Board Bars Vote on Death Penalty," *Detroit News*, 27 August 1982, 1A, 4A.

122. Michigan Public Act 112, 19 August, *Michigan Laws* (1973); Michigan Interoffice Memo, 11 September, Michigan Department of State (1986).

123. Michigan Legislature, *House Hearings* (1973).

124. Zimring and Hawkins, *Capital Punishment*.

125. R. J. Bruxton, "Criminal Law Reform: England," *American Journal of Comparative Law* 21 (1973): 230–44.

126. Gaye Tuchman, *Making News: A Study in the Construction of Reality* (New York: Free Press, 1978), 4.

127. John W. Kingdon, *Agendas, Alternatives, and Public Policies* (Boston: Little, Brown, 1984), 63.

128. John Hagan, Edward T. Silva, and John

H. Simpson, "Conflict and Consensus in the Designation of Deviance," *Social Forces* 56 (1977): 321–22.

129. Zimring and Hawkins, *Capital Punishment*, 155.

130. Hugo Adam Bedau, *Death Is Different: Studies in the Morality, Law, and Politics of Capital Punishment* (Boston: Northeastern University Press, 1987), 137.

131. Harold M. Helfman, "A Forgotten Aftermath to Michigan's Abolition of Capital Punishment," *Michigan History Magazine* 40 (1956): 203–14.

132. James Austin and Marci Brown, "Ranking the Nation's Most Punitive and Costly States," *Focus* (National Council on Crime and Delinquency, July 1989).

133. John Barlow Martin, *Break Down the Walls* (New York: Ballantine, 1954); John J. Dilulio, Jr., *Governing Prisons: A Comparative Study of Correctional Management* (New York: Free Press, 1987).

134. Murray Edelman, *The Symbolic Uses of Politics* (Urbana: University of Illinois Press, 1964).

135. Michel Foucault, *Discipline and Punish: The Birth of the Prison* (New York: Vintage, 1977), 9.

136. Michael Ignatieff, *A Just Measure of Pain: The Penitentiary in the Industrial Revolution, 1750–1850* (New York: Pantheon, 1978), 23.

137. U.S. Department of Justice, Bureau of Justice Statistics, *Capital Punishment 1999* (Washington, D.C.: U.S. Government Printing Office, 2000).

138. "States with No Death Penalty Share Lower Homicide Rates," *New York Times*, 22 September 2000, A1.

139. Ibid., A19.

Chapter 3

1. John W. Kingdon, *Agendas, Alternatives, and Public Policies* (Boston: Little, Brown, 1984).

2. Hugo Adam Bedau, *The Death Penalty in America*, 3d ed. (New York: Oxford University Press, 1982), 24.

3. U.S. Department of Justice, *FBI Uniform Crime Reports*, 1989–1997 (Washington, D.C.).

4. *Statistical Abstract of the United States*, 116–18 eds. (Washington, D.C.: U.S. Department of Commerce, 1995–97).

5. John F. Galliher, Gregory Ray, and Brent Cook, "Abolition and Reinstatement of Capital Punishment During the Progressive Era and Early 20th Century," *The Journal of Criminal Law and Criminology*, 83, no. 3 (1992): 538–76.

6. *Statistical Abstract of the United States*.

7. Carrie Cropley, "The Case of John McCaffary," *Wisconsin Magazine of History* 35 (Madison, Wis.: State Historical Society, 1951): 288.

8. William Francis Raney, *Wisconsin: A Story of Progress* (New York: Prentice-Hall, 1940).

9. Ibid.

10. Robert C. Nesbit, *Wisconsin: A History* (Madison, Wis.: University Press, 1973), 151.

11. Justus F. Paul and Barbara Dotts Paul, *The Badger State: A Documentary History of Wisconsin* (Grand Rapids, Mich.: Wm. B. Eerdmans Publishing, 1979).

12. E. Michael McCann, "Opposing Capital Punishment: A Prosecutor's Perspective," *Marquette Law Review*, 79 (1996): 649–706.

13. "Stop Senators' Death Penalty Ploy," *Capital Times*, 8 February 1994, 7A.

14. *Wisconsin Blue Book, The Legislative Process in Wisconsin* (Wisconsin Legislative Reference Bureau, 1994), 135.

15. Ibid., 137–38.

16. Ibid., 114.

17. Hugo Adam Bedau, *Death Is Different: Studies in the Morality, Law, and Politics of Capital Punishment* (Boston: Northeastern University Press, 1987).

18. *Wisconsin Blue Book*, 112.

19. State of Wisconsin, Legislative Reference Bureau, *Information Bulletin, 95–1*, April 1995, 8.

20. Ibid., 7.

21. M. W. Espy and J. O. Smykla, *Executions in the United States, 1608–1987: The Espy File* (Tuscaloosa, Ala.: J. O. Smykla,

Producer; Ann Arbor, Mich.: Inter-University Consortium for Political and Social Research, Distributor, 1987).

22. Cropley, "The Case."

23. State of Wisconsin, Legislative Reference Bureau, 8.

24. Alexander T. Pendleton and Blaine R. Renfert, "A Brief History of Wisconsin's Death Penalty," *Wisconsin Lawyer* 66, no. 8 (1993): 28.

25. Don Jensen, "Hangman's Work Here Changed Law," *Kenosha News* (2001). Available at http://www.kusd.edu/city/history/lawchange.html.

26. Ibid.

27. Cropley, "The Case," 282.

28. Ibid., 286.

29. Pendleton and Renfert, "A Brief History," 26–30.

30. Cropley, "The Case," 287.

31. Ibid., 288.

32. Pendleton and Renfert, "A Brief History," 26–30.

33. Ibid.

34. State of Wisconsin, Legislative Reference Bureau.

35. Pendleton and Renfert, "A Brief History," 29; Peter Cannon, *Capital Punishment in Wisconsin and the Nation* (Madison, Wis.: Legislative Reference Bureau, 1995).

36. Cannon, *Capital Punishment in Wisconsin.*

37. Ibid., 10.

38. "11 Confirmed Dead in Milwaukee: Man Reportedly Admits Cannibalism," *Madison Newspapers, Inc.*, 24 July 1991. Available at http://www.madison.com.

39. "Dahmer Confesses to 16th, 17th Murder," *Madison Newspapers, Inc.*, 31 July 1991.

40. "11 Confirmed Dead in Milwaukee: Man Reportedly Admits Cannibalism," *Madison Newspapers, Inc.*, 24 July 1991.

41. "Milwaukee Is Sued by Victim's Kin," *Madison Newspapers, Inc.*, 6 August 1991.

42. "Brand Names Bring Familiarity to Dahmer Jurors," *Madison Newspapers, Inc.*, 14 February 1992.

43. Edmund F. McGarrell and Thomas C. Castellano, "Social Structure, Crime, and Politics: A Conflict Model of the Crimi-

nal Law Formation Process," ch. 13 in William J. Chambliss and Marjorie S. Zatz, eds., *Making Law: The State, the Law, and Structural Contradictions* (Bloomington: Indiana University Press, 1993), 354.

44. "Dahmer Fuels Death Penalty Call," *Madison Newspapers, Inc.*, 18 February 1992.

45. "It's Time to Push for Capital Punishment, Sen. Joanne Huelsman," *Madison Newspapers, Inc.*, 11 August 1991.

46. "Dahmer Judge Seeks Court Security Shield," *Chicago Tribune*, 3 November 1991, 3M.

47. "Dahmer Jury Selection Proves No Easy Task," *Wisconsin State Journal*, 28 January 1992.

48. Ibid.

49. "Dahmer Gets Life, No Parole," *Madison Newspapers, Inc.*, 17 February 1992.

50. "15 Life Terms and No Parole for Dahmer," *New York Times*, 18 February 1992, 14A.

51. "Jeffrey Dahmer, Multiple Killer, Is Bludgeoned to Death in Prison," *New York Times*, 29 November 1992, A1.

52. Ibid.

53. "City Sees Decrease in Murder, Rape, Robbery," *Milwaukee Journal Sentinel*, 25 October 1995, 1.

54. "State's Murder Total Lowest Since '89," *Milwaukee Journal Sentinel*, 5 January 1997.

55. "Stop Senators' Death Penalty Ploy," *Capital Times*, 5 February 1994, 7A.

56. "Death Penalty Erodes Struggle for Humanity," *Madison Newspapers, Inc.*, 4 August 1991.

57. Ibid.

58. "GOP Leaders Seek Death for 5 Crimes," *Madison Newspapers, Inc.*, 25 November 1991.

59. "Lawmaker Vows to Kill Death Penalty Bill; Legislative Hearing Thursday," *Madison Newspapers, Inc.*, 10 December 1991.

60. Ibid.

61. "Death Penalty Merits Debated," *Capital Times*, 12 December 1991.

62. "Death Penalty Debate Rages," *Madison Newspapers, Inc.*, 13 December 1991.

63. "Death Penalty Backers Testify," *Wisconsin State Journal*, 17 June 1993, 22.
64. *Bulletin of the Proceedings of the Wisconsin Legislature, 1991–1995* (State of Wisconsin, Legislative Reference Bureau), 9.
65. "Clergy Oppose Death Penalty," *Capital Times*, 11 October 1993.
66. Ibid.
67. Ibid.
68. Ibid.
69. "First Vote on Death Penalty Since 1859 Likely in Senate," *Wisconsin State Journal*, 5 October 1993.
70. "Death Penalty Debate Emotional in Senate," *Wisconsin State Journal*, 20 October 1993, 3C.
71. "Death Penalty Bill Proceeds," *Wisconsin State Journal*, 7 October 1993, 1B.
72. "Senate Says No to Death Penalty," *Wisconsin State Journal*, 20 October 1993, 1A.
73. "Death Penalty Debate Emotional."
74. Ibid.
75. Tim Kelley, "Senate Says No to Death Penalty," *Wisconsin State Journal*, 20 October 1993, 1A.
76. *Bulletin of the Proceedings, 1994.*
77. "Death Penalty Passage Doubted," *Wisconsin State Journal*, 8 October 1993.
78. "State's Murder Total Lowest Since '89," *Milwaukee Journal Sentinel*, 5 January 1997.
79. *Bulletin of the Proceedings, 1993*, 219.
80. "Doyle Opposes Death Penalty," *Wisconsin State Journal*, 3 October 1993, 12A.
81. Ibid.
82. "Death Penalty Debate Swirls at Center of AG Race," *Capital Times*, 22 October 1994.
83. Ibid.
84. "Murdered Girl's Father Makes Political Ad for Wagner, Death Penalty," *Capital Times*, 24 October 1994.
85. Ibid.
86. "Death Penalty Backed in Poll," *Capital Times*, 10 November 1994, 3A.
87. "Death Penalty Debate Swirls at Center of AG Race," *Capital Times*, 22 October 1994.
88. Ibid.
89. Ibid.
90. "Death Penalty Backed in Poll," *Capital Times*, 10 November 1994, 3A.
91. James M. Galliher and John F. Galliher, "Déjà Vu All Over Again: The Recurring Life and Death of Capital Punishment in Kansas," *Social Problems* 44 (1997): 369–85.
92. "State Has Executed 1 Criminal—in 1848," *Wisconsin State Journal*, 18 October 1993, 2A.
93. "Kunicki Betrays Democratic Values—Death of Faith in Democrats," *Madison Newspapers, Inc.*, 29 September 1994.
94. Ibid.
95. "Playing into GOP Hands," *Madison Newspapers, Inc.*, 21 September 1994.
96. Ibid.
97. Ibid.
98. "Support Builds for Death Penalty Wisconsin Banned 140 Years Ago," *New York Times*, 9 October 1994, 18.
99. Ibid.
100. "Republicans Wrestle with Their Tax Relief Dilemma: Pain vs. Gain," *Wisconsin State Journal*, 19 November 1995, 1E.
101. "Legislature Prepares to Wrap It Up; After That Lawmakers Will Hit Campaign Trail," *Wisconsin State Journal*, 3 March 1996, 1A.
102. "Wisconsin Death Penalty Debate in Senate," Prison Activist Resource Center, 20 May 1995. Available at parcer@igc.apc.org.
103. "History of 1995 Senate Joint Resolution 51." Available at http://www.legis.state.wi.us./1999/data/SJR51hst.html.
104. "Restoration of Death Penalty Foreseen," *Wisconsin State Journal*, 4 January 1995, 2B.
105. "Wisconsin Tries Again with Death Penalty with a Narrow Bill," *New York Times*, 19 March 1995, 36.
106. "Thompson Sees Death Penalty Passage," *Milwaukee Journal Sentinel*, 21 April 1995.
107. "Death Penalty Gains 1995 Support," *Green Bay Press-Gazette*, 21 April 1995.
108. "Prosecutors Speak against Death Penalty," *Wisconsin State Journal*, 28 January 1995, 3D.
109. Ibid.

110. Ibid.
111. Ibid.
112. Ibid.
113. "Most Prosecutors Oppose Death Penalty," *Capital Times*, 5 May 1995, 3A.
114. "Dahmer Prosecutor Opposes Death Penalty," *Wisconsin State Journal*, 18 May 1995, 3B.
115. "Churches Fight Death Penalty," *Wisconsin State Journal*, 18 February 1995, 3B.
116. "Lawmakers See Greater Interest in Death Penalty," *Appleton Post*, 30 April 1995.
117. "Death Penalty Support Mounts," *Wisconsin State Journal*, 1 May 1995, 1B; "Lawmaker Leads Crusade to Amend Constitution," *Wisconsin State Journal*, 1 May 1995.
118. "History of 1995 Senate Joint Resolution 51."
119. "History of 1995 Senate Bill 1." Available at http://www.legis.state.wi.us./1999/data/SB1hst.html.
120. State of Wisconsin, Legislative Reference Bureau, *Information Bulletin, 95–1*, April 1995.
121. Zimring and Hawkins, *Capital Punishment*.
122. "States with No Death Penalty Share Lower Homicide Rates," *New York Times*, 22 September 2000, A1, A19.
123. University of Missouri–Columbia, Peace Studies Program, Death Penalty Abolition Conference, 13–14 November 1998.

Chapter 4

1. "State Pondered Long and Hard in Early Days Before Abolishing Death Penalty," *Bangor Daily News*, 4 April 1960.
2. "Capital Punishment in Maine," Legislative Pamphlet, 1 December 1901; Edward Schriver, "Reluctant Hangman: The State of Maine and Capital Punishment, 1820–1887," *The New England Quarterly* 63 (1990): 271–87.
3. "Capital Punishment in Maine," Legislative Pamphlet, 1 December 1901.
4. Schriver, "Reluctant Hangman," 271–87.
5. M. W. Espy and J. O. Smykla, *Executions in the United States, 1608–1987: The Espy File, Codebook* (Tuscaloosa, Ala.: J. O. Smykla, Producer; Ann Arbor, Mich.: Inter-University Consortium for Political and Social Research, Distributor, 1987).
6. Joseph Williamson, "Capital Trials in Maine: Before the Separation," *Maine Historical Society*, 25 May 1883, 59–172.
7. "State Pondered Long and Hard in Early Days before Abolishing Death Penalty," *Bangor Daily News*, 4 April 1960.
8. Schriver, "Reluctant Hangman," 271–87.
9. "Address of Governor Chamberlain to the Legislature of the State of Maine," *Legislative Record* (Augusta: Owen and Nash, Printers to the State, 1869).
10. "State Pondered."
11. Untitled article discusses the executions of Wagner and Hauptmann, *Portland Evening Express*, 9 January 1936, 2A.
12. "Two Hangings," *Portland Press Herald*, 28 July 1972.
13. "Carroll Case Stresses Advantages of State Capital Punishment Ban: Outlawing of Noose Saved Innocent Pair in 1878," *Portland Sunday Telegram*, 24 September 1950.
14. "Capital Punishment Debate an Old One," *Kennebec Journal*, 8 May 1975.
15. Schriver, "Reluctant Hangman," 271–87.
16. "Two Hangings," *Portland Press Herald*, 28 July 1972.
17. Waldo E. Pray, "Chessman Case Recalls: Maine, Too, Had Its Furor Over the Death Penalty," *Portland Sunday Telegram*, n.d.
18. "Capital Punishment," *Portland Sunday Telegram*, 2 November 1958.
19. "Carroll Case."
20. Maine Legislative Archives.
21. Holly Hannon Davis, "Capital Punishment: A Review of Arguments For and Against Its Use and an Overview of Its History in Maine, in the Nation and in Other Countries" (State of Maine: Department of Corrections, 1985).
22. "Report of the Committee to Whom Was Referred the Several Memorials and Petitions for the Abolition of Capital Punish-

ment," *Fifteenth Legislature: House* (Augusta, Maine: Wm. J. Condon, Printer to the State, 1835).

23. Ibid.

24. "Report of the Committee on Capital Punishment," *Sixteenth Legislature: Senate* (Augusta, Maine: Wm. J. Condon, Printer to the State, 1836).

25. Ibid.

26. "Address of Governor Chamberlaine to the Legislature of the State of Maine," *Legislative Record* (Augusta, Maine: Owen and Nash, Printers to the State, 1868).

27. "Remarks of John L. Stevens, in the Senate of Maine, February 11 and 12, 1869 on an Order Instructing the Judiciary Committee to Report a Bill Abolishing Capital Punishment," *Legislative Record* (1869).

28. Ibid.

29. Schriver, "Reluctant Hangman," 271–87.

30. Leonard D. Carver, "Capital Punishment in Maine" (Office of the Secretary of State, 1901), 2.

31. Schriver, "Reluctant Hangman," 271–87.

32. "Murder in Maine," *Portland Evening Express*, 22 May 1930; "Capital Punishment," *Portland Evening Express*, 21 October 1937; Waldo E. Pray, "Chessman Case Recalls: Maine, Too, Had Its Furor Over the Death Penalty," *Portland Sunday Telegram*, n.d.

33. "Report of the Attorney General of the State of Maine," *Legislative Report* (1897–98).

34. Schriver, "Reluctant Hangman," 271–87.

35. The clipping files at the Maine State Library, the *Bangor Daily News*, and the *Blethen, Maine, Newspaper* were compiled by various employees of these organizations over the years. Each file—in theory—contained death penalty articles published in Maine's larger newspapers. While numerous articles were located in all three files, a substantial number of death penalty articles and editorials were located in only one or two of the data sources. Nevertheless, similarities in the three clipping files indicate that newspaper data discussed here are representative of death penalty–related articles and editorials published in Maine over much of the twentieth century. Given the characteristics of clipping files, page numbers were not available for many articles and editorials.

36. "Report of the Attorney General of the State of Maine," *Legislative Report* (1897–98); Leonard D. Carver, "Capital Punishment in Maine" (Office of the Secretary of State, 1901).

37. "Agitation for Capital Punishment," *Portland Evening Express*, 17 July 1930.

38. "A Maine Notebook: The Death Penalty," *Portland Press Herald*, 7 July 1972; "Cruel and Unusual," *Portland Evening Express*, 21 October 1971.

39. "Regarding the Seven Executions," *Courier-Gazette*, 26 September 1927; "Queer Reasoning," *Portland Evening Express*, 5 May 1930; "Use for Criminals," *Portland Evening Express*, 30 June 1930.

40. "State Pondered."

41. "Carroll Case." See also "Regarding the Seven Executions," *Courier-Gazette*, 26 September 1927.

42. "Carroll Case"; "Two Hangings," *Portland Press Herald*, 28 July 1972; untitled article, *Portland Evening Express*, 9 January 1936, 2A; "A Trial of Strength," *Portland Evening Express*, 16 August 1938, 3A.

43. "Carroll Case"; "Capital Punishment," *Portland Sunday Telegram*, 2 November 1958; "Bloody Hanging Stirred Populace," *Portland Sunday Telegram*, 8 December 1968; "A Maine Notebook: The Death Penalty," *Portland Press Herald*, 7 July 1972; "Two Hangings."

44. "Capital Punishment," *Portland Evening Express*, 21 October 1937.

45. "Murder in Maine," *Portland Evening Express*, 22 May 1930.

46. "Capital Punishment," *Portland Press Herald*, 21 October 1937; "No Deterrent," *Portland Press Herald*, 5 July 1971; "Capital Punishment," *Portland Evening Express*.

47. "Push to Reinstate Death Penalty Apparent in Legislatures' Bills," *Portland Press Herald*, 28 February 1973.

48. Legislative Record—House (1973), 3521–22.
49. Ibid., 3533.
50. Legislative Record—Senate (1973), 3732–33; Legislative Record—House (1973), 3534.
51. "Students Debate Death Penalty before Legislators," *Portland Press Herald*, 5 May 1973.
52. "State Death Penalty Move Dies," *Bangor Daily News*, 15 March 1974.
53. "Up Against the Wall," *Kennebec Journal*, 20 March 1974.
54. "Capital Punishment: 'The People of Maine Want It,'" *Kennebec Journal*, 20 January 1977.
55. "The Ultimate Punishment," *Kennebec Journal*, 28 November 1979.
56. "Maine House Defeats Death Penalty Bill," *Bangor Daily News*, 25 January 1979.
57. "The Laffin Bill: Death Penalty Is Not a Good Idea," *Portland Press Herald*, 3 April 1975.
58. Legislative Record—House (1975), B400.
59. Ibid., B1425; "Death Term Called Way to Halt Crime," *Portland Press Herald*, 8 May 1975; "The Laffin Bill," *Portland Press Herald*, 9 May 1975.
60. "House Defeats Death Penalty," *Bangor Daily News*, 6 May 1977.
61. Legislative Record—House (1978), 159.
62. "Death Term Called Way to Halt Crime," *Portland Press Herald*, 8 May 1975; "Beaten Again," *Portland Press Herald*, 8 February 1978.
63. "Laffin Urges Vote on Death Penalty," *Portland Press Herald*, 28 November 1978.
64. Legislative Record—House (1978), 160; "House Defeats Death Penalty," *Bangor Daily News*, 6 May 1977.
65. Legislative Record—House (1977), 875; "House Defeats Death Penalty," *Bangor Daily News*, 6 May 1977.
66. Legislative Record—House (1979), 80; "Dispute on Death Penalty Continues," *Portland Press Herald*, 6 September 1983.
67. "The Laffin Bill," *Portland Press Herald*, 9 May 1975.
68. "The Death Penalty," *Portland Press Herald*, 16 September 1975.
69. Ibid.
70. "Killing the Death Penalty," *Portland Evening Express*, 2 June 1975; "Republicans Should Reject Death Penalty," *Portland Evening Express*, 29 April 1976.
71. "Bill to Reinstate Death Penalty," *Portland Press Herald*, 25 January 1979.
72. "Revival of Maine's Death Penalty Urged," *Kennebec Journal*, 24 January 1979.
73. Legislative Record—House (1975), 1425.
74. Ibid., 1430.
75. Legislative Record—House (1977), 873.
76. Ibid., 877.
77. Ibid., 907.
78. Legislative Record—House (1979), 79.
79. Ibid., 85.
80. Legislative Record—Senate (1979), 98.
81. "Capital Punishment: 'The People of Maine Want It,'" *Kennebec Journal*, 20 January 1977.
82. "Referendum Provision Keeps Death Penalty Alive," *Maine Sunday Telegram*, 21 January 1979.
83. Legislative Report—House (1975), 399–400.
84. Legislative Report—House (1977), 873–77.
85. Legislative Report—House (1979), 79–85.
86. Legislative Record—Senate (1975; 1979).
87. Legislative Record—Senate (1977), 905–7.
88. "Death: Not That Chestnut Again," *Portland Evening Express*, 2 February 1978.
89. "Gartley Favors Death Penalty," *Bangor Daily News*, 27 April 1977.
90. "Referendum Provision Keeps Death Penalty Alive," *Maine Sunday Telegram*, 21 January 1979.
91. A. Henderson, interview of the representative who was among the most vocal critics of capital punishment during the 1970s, June 1994.
92. Legislative Record—House (1975), B1427.
93. "Gilmore Execution Points Up Tense Issue in Maine," *Portland Press Herald*, 18 January 1977.
94. "Laffin Plans Petition Drive on Death Penalty," *Bangor Daily News*, 31 January 1979.

95. "Capital Punishment: 'The People of Maine Want It,'" *Kennebec Journal*, 20 January 1977; "Maine House Defeats Death Penalty Bill," *Bangor Daily News*, 25 January 1979; "Death, The Maximum Penalty," *Portland Evening Express*, 30 May 1979.

96. "Laffin Plans Petition Drive on Death Penalty," *Bangor Daily News*, 31 January 1979.

97. Ibid.

98. Stanley (Tuffy) Laffin, interview with the representative who sponsored the majority of the death penalty bills during the 1970s, June 1994.

99. Linda C. Brawn, interview, 1994.

100. "Mainers Split on Returning Death Penalty," *Portland Press Herald*, 14 March 1979.

101. "Death Cruel and Barbaric," *Portland Press Herald*, 7 January 1984; "Death Too Great a Penalty," *Portland Press Herald*, 25 February 1984; "Death, An Irreversible Penalty," *Portland Evening Express*, 11 April 1981; "Death/Always the Chance for a Mistake," *Portland Press Herald*, 8 December 1982.

102. "Death Penalty Debate Revived: Bill's Foes Outnumber Supporters at Hearing," *Bangor Daily News*, 30 April 1991.

103. "Death Penalty Proposed, Not Supported by Senator," *Courier-Gazette*, 25 February 1993.

104. Committee on Judiciary, Records of Debates, Testimony, and Votes on L.D. 1236, H.P. 924 (1987).

105. Committee on Judiciary, Records of Debates, Testimony, and Votes on L.D. 1238, S.P. 462 (1991).

106. Committee on Judiciary, Records of Debates, Testimony, and Votes on L.D. 42, S.P. 36 (1993).

107. "Death Penalty Voted Down by Judiciary Panel," *Bangor Daily News*, 3 May 1991.

108. Catherine Lebowitz, interview with the cosponsor of 1982–92 house death bills, June 1994.

109. "GOP Balks Backing State Death Penalty," *Portland Press Herald*, 18 January 1985.

110. "State Opinion Not Checked in Poll," *Portland Press Herald*, 12 January 1987.

111. Charles Bagley, personal interview with the senator who sponsored the 1993 capital punishment bill, June 1994.

112. "Getting to Be Routine," *Portland Evening Express*, 28 August 1985.

113. Ibid.

114. "Death: Punishment Beyond Reprieve," *Portland Evening Express*, 28 June 1986.

115. "Sentence: Too Young to Die," *Portland Evening Express*, 25 February 1987.

116. "Death: Here We Go Again," *Portland Evening Express*, 14 April 1987.

117. "Death: The Ultimate Penalty," *Portland Evening Express*, 19 May 1987.

118. Ibid.

119. "Crime: Child on Death Row," *Portland Evening Express*, 14 January 1989.

120. "Death: Botched Executions," *Portland Evening Express*, 21 May 1990.

121. "The Count Goes On," *Portland Evening Express*, 25 June 1990.

122. "Death: Barbarism in America," *Portland Evening Express*, 16 November 1990.

123. Larry Koch and John F. Galliher, "Michigan's Continuing Abolition of the Death Penalty: A Long-term Symbolic Crusade," *Law and Legal Studies* 2 (1993): 323–46; Larry Koch and John F. Galliher, "The History of Death Penalty Abolition in Alaska," unpublished paper, n.d.

124. A. Henderson, personal interview with the representative who was among Maine's most vocal critics of capital punishment during the 1970s, June 1994.

125. Charles Bagley, interview.

126. "Mainers Like No Death Penalty," *Central Maine Morning Sentinel*, 23 April 1992.

127. Koch and Galliher, "Michigan's Continuing Abolition of the Death Penalty," 323–46.

128. "Homicides in Maine," *Legislative Record*, n.d.

129. Koch and Galliher, "Michigan's Continuing Abolition of the Death Penalty," 323–34.

130. A. Henderson, interview.

131. Stanley (Tuffy) Laffin, interview.

132. Paul Gauvreau, interview with the senate chair of judiciary during the late 1980s and early 1990s, June 1994.
133. Charles Bagley, interview.
134. Ibid.

Chapter 5

1. John F. Galliher, Gregory Ray, and Brent Cook, "Abolition and Reinstatement of Capital Punishment During the Progressive Era and Early 20th Century," *The Journal of Criminal Law and Criminology* 83 (1992): 538–76.
2. Dee Brown, *Bury My Heart at Wounded Knee* (New York: Henry Holt, 1970).
3. Ibid., 54.
4. Ibid.
5. Espy and Smykla, *Executions in the United States*.
6. John D. Bessler, "The 'Midnight Assassination Law' and Minnesota's Anti–Death Penalty Movement, 1849–1911," *William Mitchell Law Review* 22 (1996): 577–730.
7. Brown, *Bury My Heart*, 60–61.
8. Ibid.
9. Ibid., 59–60.
10. Bessler, "The 'Midnight Assassination Law.'"
11. Brown, *Bury My Heart*, 64.
12. *Session Weekly* (Minnesota House Public Information Office, 1992). Available at http://www.house.leg.state.mn.us/hinfo.swkly/1995-96/select/death.txt.
13. Bessler, "The 'Midnight Assassination Law.'"
14. Ibid.
15. Galliher, Ray, and Cook, "Abolition and Reinstatement."
16. Bessler, "The 'Midnight Assassination Law.'"
17. *Session Weekly*.
18. Ibid.
19. Ibid.
20. "Professor Kills Man; Says 'Unwritten Law,'" *Minneapolis Morning Tribune*, 6 March 1913, 1.
21. "Olsen Not Worrying over Darling Murder," *Minneapolis Morning Tribune*, 7 March 1913, 8.
22. "Jealous Man Kills Woman and Escapes," *Minneapolis Morning Tribune*, 5 February 1913, 1.
23. "Crazed Man Shoots Two and Ends His Own Life," *Minneapolis Morning Tribune*, 13 July 1912, 7.
24. "Negro Burned at Stake After Confessing Crime," *Minneapolis Morning Tribune*, 9 February 1913, 7.
25. "Capital Punishment Wanted," *Minneapolis Morning Tribune*, 2 February 1913, 9.
26. "Capital Punishment Favored," *Minneapolis Morning Tribune*, 6 March 1913, 7.
27. "Electrocution Proposed in Senator Fossen's Bill," *Minneapolis Morning Tribune*, 11 February 1913, 6.
28. *Minnesota Journal of the House of Representatives*, HF 416, 8 March 1913, 791; "House Kills Death Bill," *Minneapolis Morning Tribune*, 9 March 1913, 7.
29. "Mother of Boy Slain in Store Holdup to Scan Bandit Suspects for Slayer," *Minneapolis Morning Tribune*, 27 June 1920, 1–2.
30. "St. Paul Prepares to Cope with Wave of Organized Crime," *Minneapolis Morning Tribune*, 27 June 1920, 1.
31. "St. Paul Crime Wave Arouses Citizens' Ire; Drastic Steps Asked," *Minneapolis Morning Tribune*, 4 September 1920, 22.
32. Ibid.
33. Ibid.
34. "Kerchief Bandits Hold Up 6 in Night," *Minneapolis Morning Tribune*, 10 November 1920, 1, 10.
35. Ibid.; "Police Take Kerchief Bandit Suspect," *Minneapolis Morning Tribune*, 11 November 1920, 1; "Kerchief Bandits Raid Drug Store, Hold Up Proprietor and 4 Patrons," *Minneapolis Morning Tribune*, 12 November 1920, 1–2.
36. "Study Is Urged of Capital Punishment," *Minneapolis Morning Tribune*, 23 October 1920, 18.
37. Ibid.
38. "Ramsey Delegates Will Meet Today, Plan Drive to Halt Wave of Crime," *Minneapolis Morning Tribune*, 25 October 1920, 8.
39. Ibid.
40. "Grand Jury Recommendations on Crime Wave Investigation," *Minneapolis Morning Tribune*, 21 December 1920, 9.

41. "Grand Jury Report Is Said to Contain Crime Analysis," *Minneapolis Morning Tribune*, 17 December 1920, 8.

42. "Grand Jury Recommendations on Crime Wave Investigation," *Minneapolis Morning Tribune*, 21 December 1920, 9.

43. "Mayor Meyers Endorses Capital Punishment," *Minneapolis Morning Tribune*, 14 January 1921, 7.

44. "Prosecutors Urge Capital Punishment," *Minneapolis Morning Tribune*, 22 January 1921, 2.

45. "Minnesota Mayors Favor Return of Death Penalty," *Minneapolis Morning Tribune*, 8 February 1921, 14.

46. "Duluth Mob Hangs 3 Negroes to Avenge Young Girl; 3 Freed by Lynch Law Court Held in Battered Jail," *Minneapolis Morning Tribune*, 16 June 1920, 1–2.

47. Michael Fedo, *The Lynching in Duluth* (St. Paul: Minnesota Historical Society, 2000).

48. Ibid.

49. Ibid., 114.

50. "Duluth Mob Hangs 3 Negroes to Avenge Young Girl," 1–2.

51. "Duluth Judges Lead Inquiry to Find Chiefs of Lynch Mob," *Minneapolis Morning Tribune*, 17 June 1920, 1–2.

52. "Duluth Judge Declares Lynching Mob Broke Laws of God and Man," *Minneapolis Morning Tribune*, 18 June 1920, 1–2; Fedo, *Lynching in Duluth*.

53. "Duluth Judges Lead Inquiry," 1–2.

54. Ibid., 2.

55. Ibid.

56. Ibid.

57. "The Duluth Mob" (editorial), *Minneapolis Morning Tribune*, 18 June 1920, 16.

58. Fedo, *Lynching in Duluth*, 117–18.

59. Ibid., vii.

60. "Duluth Judge Declares Lynching Mob Broke Laws of God and Man," *Minneapolis Morning Tribune*, 18 June 1920, 1.

61. Ibid., 2.

62. Ibid.

63. Ibid., 2.

64. "Duluth Fears New Lynching: Troops Called," *Minneapolis Morning Tribune*, 19 June 1920.

65. "Trio Indicted in Duluth as Negro Slayers," *Minneapolis Morning Tribune*, 30 June 1920, 1.

66. "Duluth Judge Declares Lynching Mob Broke Laws."

67. "Duluth Fears New Lynchings: Troops Called," 1, 14.

68. "Duluth Crowd Inspects Guns, Forgets Riot," *Minneapolis Morning Tribune*, 20 June 1920, 1.

69. "Duluth Fears New Lynchings: Troops Called."

70. "Duluth Crowd Inspects Guns, Forgets Riot."

71. "Duluth Mob Leader Believed in Custody," *Minneapolis Morning Tribune*, 26 June 1920, 1.

72. "Trio Indicted in Duluth as Negro Slayers"; "Duluth Lyncher Convicted: First of 19 Alleged Mob Leaders Guilty of Rioting," *Minneapolis Morning Tribune*, 2 September 1920, 1, 3.

73. "Duluth Lyncher Convicted."

74. Ibid., 1.

75. Ibid.

76. "The Bill That Tulsa Must Pay" (editorial), *Minneapolis Morning Tribune*, 4 June 1921, 20.

77. "The Georgia Peonage Murder" (editorial), *Minneapolis Morning Tribune*, 15 April 1921, 16.

78. "A Significant Day's Grist" (editorial), *Minneapolis Morning Tribune*, 13 November 1920, 22.

79. "Dealing with the Crime of Murder" (editorial), *Minneapolis Morning Tribune*, 16 October 1920, 22.

80. "Forcing the Death Penalty" (editorial), *Minneapolis Morning Tribune*, 3 December 1920, 20.

81. "Capital Punishment or No Pardons," *Minneapolis Morning Tribune*, 1 March 1921, 8.

82. "Speakers War on Merits of Death Penalty," *Minneapolis Morning Tribune*, 1 March 1921, 7.

83. Ibid.

84. "Capital Punishment Bill Likely to Die in Committee, Is Outlook," *Minneapolis Morning Tribune*, 1 March 1921, 7.

85. "Minnesota Death Penalty Bill Killed," *Minneapolis Morning Tribune*, 4 March

1921, 1; *Minnesota Journal of the House of Representatives*, 1498 HF 473, 20 April 1921.

86. "Crime Wave Taxes State Reformatory," *Minneapolis Morning Tribune*, 21 March 1921, 9.

87. "Bandit Suspect to Face Women Holdup Victims," *Minneapolis Morning Tribune*, 3 January 1923, 6.

88. "Bandits Raid Stores, Home," *Minneapolis Morning Tribune*, 14 January 1923, 1.

89. "Trio Arrested Here Believed St. Paul Bandits," *Minneapolis Morning Tribune*, 21 January 1923, 1, 11.

90. "Bandit Suspect in St. Paul Raid Identified," *Minneapolis Morning Tribune*, 22 January 1923, 1.

91. "Bandits Slay War Veteran," *Minneapolis Morning Tribune*, 10 February 1923, 1–2.

92. "Pellatt Slayers Face Charge of Murder in First Degree," *Minneapolis Morning Tribune*, 14 February 1923, 2.

93. "Capital Punishment" (editorial), *Minneapolis Morning Tribune*, 6 January 1923, 14.

94. Ibid.

95. "Capital Punishment in This Country," *Minneapolis Morning Tribune*, 13 January 1923, 14.

96. Ibid.

97. "Banditry and the Law" (editorial), *Minneapolis Morning Tribune*, 22 January 1923, 6.

98. Ibid.

99. "What's the Matter with Us Americans?" *Minneapolis Morning Tribune*, 26 January 1923, 10.

100. "Punishment of Criminals" (letter to the editor), *Minneapolis Morning Tribune*, 15 January 1923, 6.

101. "Council to Call City Employees in Klan Inquiry," *Minneapolis Morning Tribune*, 15 January 1923, 7.

102. "What We Must Answer For" (editorial), *Minneapolis Morning Tribune*, 2 January 1923, 8.

103. Ibid.

104. Ibid.

105. "Lynchings and Other Crimes" (editorial), *Minneapolis Morning Tribune*, 8 January 1923, 6.

106. "Second District Editors Urge Death Penalty," *Minneapolis Morning Tribune*, 3 February 1923, 23.

107. "Minnesota Sheriffs Favor Return of Death Penalty," *Minneapolis Morning Tribune*, 19 January 1923, 16.

108. "Capital Penalty Urged by County Attorney Group," *Minneapolis Morning Tribune*, 20 January 1923, 18.

109. "Fight Promised on Bills Asking Death Penalty," *Minneapolis Morning Tribune*, 10 January 1923, 15.

110. "Death Penalty Is Debate Topic at Calhoun Club," *Minneapolis Morning Tribune*, 20 February 1923, 15.

111. "Women Urge Criminal Insane Be Segregated," *Minneapolis Morning Tribune*, 9 February 1923, 5.

112. "Sheriff Brown Urges Death Penalty for Murders," *Minneapolis Morning Tribune*, 3 January 1923, 13.

113. "Softness Toward Murderers" (letter to the editor), *Minneapolis Morning Tribune*, 3 February 1923, 14.

114. "Death Penalty Bills Debated at Public Hearing," *Minneapolis Morning Tribune*, 25 January 1923, 1.

115. "Bill for Capital Punishment to Be Introduced," *Minneapolis Morning Tribune*, 6 January 1923, 18.

116. Minnesota Crime Commission: Final Report (State of Minnesota, January 1923), 20.

117. "Death Penalty Bill Submitted to State Senate," *Minneapolis Morning Tribune*, 9 January 1923, 7.

118. Ibid.

119. "Fight Promised on Bills Asking Death Penalty," *Minneapolis Morning Tribune*, 10 January 1923, 15.

120. "New Capital Punishment Bill Is Designed to Quiet Critics," *Minneapolis Morning Tribune*, 4 February 1923, 9.

121. "Death Penalty Hearing Starts Intense Fight," *Minneapolis Morning Tribune*, 7 February 1923, 1.

122. Ibid.

123. "Death Penalty Bill Reported Out for Passage," *Minneapolis Morning Tribune*, 15 February 1923, 1.

124. Ibid.

125. "Pre-Primary Law, Capital Punishment

Bill Up Today," *Minneapolis Morning Tribune*, 27 February 1923, 12.

126. *Journal of the Senate*, SF 20, February 28, 1923, 422.

127. Brown, *Bury My Heart*, 65.

128. *Census of Population* (Washington, D.C.: U.S. Bureau of the Census, 1900–1990, U.S. Government Printing Office).

129. Fedo, *Lynching in Duluth*, 30.

130. Galliher, Ray, and Cook, "Abolition and Reinstatement."

131. Joseph R. Gusfield, *Symbolic Crusade: Status Politics and the American Temperance Movement* (Urbana: University of Illinois Press, 1963).

132. Richard M. Valelly, *Radicalism in the States: The Minnesota Farmer-Labor Party and the American Political Economy* (Chicago: University of Chicago Press, 1989); Theodore Mitau, *Politics in Minnesota* (Minneapolis: University of Minnesota Press, 1960).

133. Fedo, *Lynching in Duluth*, 31.

134. Ibid., 30.

135. Ibid.

136. C. Van Woodward, *The Strange Career of Jim Crow*, 2d rev. ed. (New York: Oxford University Press, 1966).

137. Rep. Dee Long, University of Missouri–Columbia, Peace Program, Columbia, Mo. (14 November 1998).

138. *Session Weekly*, Minnesota House Public Information Office, 1992. Available at http://www.house.leg.state.mn.us/hinfo.swkly/1995-96/select/death.tst.

139. "Ventura Gets Personal in Tell-All Book," *Minneapolis Star Tribune*, 13 May 1999, 1A.

Chapter 6

1. Frank Vyzralek, "Capital Crimes and Criminals Executed in Northern Dakota Territory and North Dakota, 1885–1905," North Dakota Supreme Court News, 2000. Available at http://www.court.state.nd.us/court/news/ExecuteND.htm.

2. John F. Galliher, Gregory Ray, and Brent Cook, "Abolition and Reinstatement of Capital Punishment During the Progressive Era and Early 20th Century," *The Journal of Criminal Law and Criminology* 83 (1992): 539–76.

3. Ibid.

4. North Dakota Century Code (1960).

5. John A. Graham, "Memorandum to Lt. Governor Wayne Sanstead" (on file with the North Dakota State Historical Society, 1976).

6. Lynching, n.d. Available at http://www.triadntr.net/~rdavis/lynching.htm.

7. M. W. Espy and J. O. Smykla, *Executions in the United States, 1608–1987: The Espy File, Codebook* (Tuscaloosa, Ala.: J. O. Smykla, Producer; Ann Arbor, Mich.: Inter-University Consortium for Political and Social Research, Distributor, 1987).

8. Larry Remele, "North Dakota History: Overview and Summary," *North Dakota BlueBook* (1989). Available at http://www.state.nd.us/ndhist.htm.

9. State, MSA, and County Population Source (2000). Available at http://www.state.nd.us/isnd.

10. "N.D. Good Place for Buffalo: *Tribune* Has Covered Western Part of State for a Century," *Bismarck Tribune*, 11 February 2001, 1–3.

11. "Farmers the Lifeblood of North Dakota," *Bismarck Tribune*, 11 February 2001, 1, 2.

12. *Statistical Abstract of the United States, 1931–1992* (Washington, D.C.: U.S. Department of Commerce, 1992).

13. Neal R. Peirce and Jerry Hagstrom, *The Book of America: Inside 50 States Today* (New York: W. W. Norton, 1983), 560.

14. "Farmers the Lifeblood of North Dakota," *Bismarck Tribune*, 11 February 2001, 2.

15. Remele, *North Dakota BlueBook*, 5.

16. Ibid.

17. Ibid.

18. "State Gains $2.75 Billion, Wealth in '74," *Bismarck Tribune*, 7 February 1975, 1.

19. "Gross Product, Up $2.7 Billion in 13 Years," *Bismarck Tribune*, 6 December 1975, 3.

20. "N.D., A Good Place to Live," *Bismarck Tribune*, 16 November 1976, 4.

21. "Farmers the Lifeblood of North Dakota," *Bismarck Tribune*, 11 February 2001, 2.

22. "N.D. Good Place for Buffalo: Tribune Has Covered Western Part of State for a Century," *Bismarck Tribune*, 11 February 2001, 1–3.

23. Remele, *North Dakota BlueBook*, 1.

24. *Uniform Crime Reports: For the United States and Its Possessions—1938–1939, 1977–1978, 1999* (Washington, D.C.: Federal Bureau of Justice, 1938–1999).

25. "Serious Crime Decreases in Bismarck," *Bismarck Tribune*, 4 September 1976, 1.

26. *Bismarck Tribune*, 4 January 1978, 39; *Bismarck Tribune*, 20 February 1978, 39.

27. *Bismarck Tribune*, 22 December 1975, 18.

28. "District Attorney Bill Is Detailed for Senate Panel," *Bismarck Tribune*, 30 January 1975, 15.

29. "Legal Aid System to End," *Bismarck Tribune*, 4 December 1975, 1.

30. "State Drops Criminal Records Plan," *Bismarck Tribune*, 13 April 1976, 1.

31. "Crime Records Plan Draws Fire," *Bismarck Tribune*, 28 February 1976, 22.

32. "State Has Lowest Inmate Count," *Bismarck Tribune*, 21 November 1975, 17.

33. John A. Davis, letter to John F. Galliher, 6 January 1994.

34. Peirce and Hagstrom, *The Book of America*.

35. *Bismarck Tribune*, 3 February 1927, 1.

36. *Bismarck Tribune*, 8 February 1927, 1.

37. "Enactment of Death Penalty Will Be Sought," *Bismarck Tribune*, 14 December 1926, 1.

38. "Attorneys Committee Favors Death Penalty Bill," *Bismarck Tribune*, 30 December 1926, 1.

39. "Senate Votes Against Death Penalty 30–19," *Bismarck Tribune*, 26 January 1927, 1.

40. Ibid.

41. "Capital Punishment Bill Is Killed in North Dakota House," *Bismarck Tribune*, 22 February 1927, 1.

42. *Bismarck Tribune*, 26 January 1927, 1.

43. Ibid.

44. Ibid.

45. "Sheriffs' Meeting Votes in Favor of Capital Punishment," *Bismarck Tribune*, 29 January 1927, 1.

46. "Capital Punishment Bill Is Killed."

47. "South Dakota Girl Slugged, Second Disappears," *Bismarck Tribune*, 29 July 1938, 3.

48. "Corpse Found Near Lake," *Bismarck Tribune*, 2 August 1938, 1; "Charged as Killer of Betty Schnaidt," *Bismarck Tribune*, 4 August 1938, 1.

49. "Man Identified as Fugitive Fatally Wounded in Hotel," *Bismarck Tribune*, 5 August 1938, 1.

50. "Young Identified as Girl's Slayer," *Bismarck Tribune*, 6 August 1938, 1.

51. Galliher, Ray, and Cook, "Abolition and Reinstatement."

52. "Effective Treatment" (editorial), *Bismarck Tribune*, 8 August 1938, 4.

53. "Residents of Zeeland Shocked," *Bismarck Tribune*, 12 July 1976, 1; "Authorities Seeking 3 Suspects in Case," *Bismarck Tribune*, 12 July 1976, 1.

54. "Authorities Seeking 3 Suspects."

55. "Mourners Attend Funeral in Zeeland for Murdered Pair," *Bismarck Tribune*, 15 July 1976, 2.

56. "Huber, Sebastian Feist Both Sentenced to Life," *Bismarck Tribune*, 10 October 1976, 24.

57. House Concurrent Resolution 3074.

58. "Mandatory Jail Sentences Favored," *Bismarck Tribune*, 21 March 1977, 11.

59. "Capital Punishment Remains Issue Despite Vote of Panel," *Bismarck Tribune*, 16 February 1977, 23.

60. "Progress," *Bismarck Tribune*, 9 January 1979, 16.

61. Ibid.; Hearing on Senate Bill 2169, Senate Judiciary Committee Hearings (1979).

62. "Executions Not New," *Bismarck Tribune*, 13 January 1979, 1.

63. "Solon: Death Penalty Would Reduce Crime," *Bismarck Tribune*, 22 January 1979, 18.

64. Ibid.

65. "Many Questions Surround Death Penalty," *Bismarck Tribune*, 5 February 1979, 36.

66. "Senate Votes Down Death Penalty Bill," *Bismarck Tribune*, 8 February 1979, 11.

67. "Death Penalty Fight Vowed by Democrats," *Bismarck Tribune*, 6 February 1979, 15.

68. "Senate Votes Down."

69. "N.D. Death Penalty?" *Grand Forks Herald*, 22 April 1992.

70. Senate Bill 2097.
71. "Lawmaker Wants Death Penalty Restored," *Bismarck Tribune*, 18 January 1994, 5B.
72. Ibid.
73. Hearing on Senate Bill 2097, January 14 and 17, Senate Judiciary Committee Hearings (1995).
74. Ibid.
75. Ibid.
76. Ibid.
77. Ibid.
78. Ibid.
79. Ibid.
80. Ibid.
81. Ibid.
82. North Dakota SB 2097, 30 January, *Journal of the Senate* (1995), 167.
83. "Capital Punishment Debate Continues," *Minot Daily News*, 25 November 1985.
84. Ibid.
85. Peirce and Hagstrom, *Book of America*.
86. Galliher, Ray, and Cook, "Abolition and Reinstatement."

Chapter 7

1. Kermit Kynell, *A Different Frontier, 1935–1965* (Lanham, Md.: University Press of America, 1991).
2. R. G. Liapunova, "Relations with the Natives of Russian America," in S. F. Starr, ed., *Russia's American Colony* (Durham: Duke University Press, 1987).
3. Mari Sardy, "Early Contact between Aleuts and Russians, 1741–1780," *Alaska History* 1 (1985): 52.
4. Henry Aaron Coppock, "Interaction Between Russians and Native Americans in Alaska: 1741–1840" (Master's thesis, Michigan State University, 1971); Sardy, "Early Contact."
5. Sardy, "Early Contact," 45.
6. Ibid., 50.
7. Ibid., 52.
8. Antoinette Skalkop, "The Russian Orthodox Church in Alaska," in S. F. Starr, ed., *Russia's American Colony* (Durham: Duke University Press, 1987).
9. Kynell, *A Different Frontier*.
10. "The General Population Characteristics" (Washington, D.C.: U.S. Department of Commerce, Bureau of the Census, Government Printing Office, 1990).
11. Ernest Gruening, *The State of Alaska*, 2d ed. (New York: Random House, 1968); Kynell, *A Different Frontier*, 27–32.
12. Stephen W. Haycox, "William Paul, Sr., and the Alaska Voters' Literacy Act of 1925," *Alaska History* 2 (Winter 1986/87): 30.
13. Terrence M. Cole, "Jim Crow in Alaska: The Passage of the Alaska Equal Rights Act of 1945," *Western Historical Quarterly* 23 (1992): 431–32.
14. Trefon Angasan, interview with Vice President of Corporate Affairs of the Bristol Bay Native Corporation, 11 June 1996; Cole, "Jim Crow in Alaska."
15. Averil Lerman, "The Trial and Hanging of Nelson Charles," *Alaska Justice Forum* (Anchorage: Justice Center: University of Alaska–Anchorage, 1996), 8.
16. Cole, "Jim Crow in Alaska."
17. John Tetpon, interview with author of "Between Two Worlds: Growing up Native in Alaska," *Sunday Magazine: Anchorage Daily News*, 23 May 1987, 9; Roger Poppe, interview with Democratic legislative assistant, June 1996.
18. Joseph Sullivan, "Sourdough Radicalism: Labor and Socialism in Alaska, 1905–1920," *Alaska History* 7 (1992): 2.
19. Ibid., 6.
20. Kynell, *A Different Frontier*, 44–45.
21. Claus M. Naske and Herman E. Slotnick, *Alaska: A History of the 49th State* (Grand Rapids: Wm. B. Eerdmans Publishing Company, 1979).
22. John Whitehead, "The Governor Who Opposed Statehood: The Legacy of Jay Hammond," *Alaska History* 7 (1992): 19–22.
23. Ibid., 15.
24. Ibid., 22.
25. Diana R. Gordon, *The Return of the Dangerous Classes: Drug Prohibition and Policy Politics* (New York: W. W. Norton, 1994).
26. "The General Population Characteristics" (Washington, D.C.: U.S. Department of Commerce, Bureau of the Census, Government Printing Office, 1990).
27. Kynell, *A Different Frontier*, 40.

28. Ibid., 106.
29. Ibid., 42.
30. Ibid., 70.
31. Ibid., 165.
32. M. W. Espy and J. O. Smykla, *Executions in the United States, 1608–1987: The Espy File, Codebook* (Tuscaloosa, Ala.: J. O. Smykla, Producer; Ann Arbor, Mich.: Inter-University Consortium for Political and Social Research, Distributor, 1987); Kynell, *A Different Frontier.*
33. Lerman, "Hanging of Nelson Charles."
34. Territory of Alaska: Session Laws, Resolutions and Memorials, *Laws of Alaska* (30 March 1957), ch. 132 at 263.
35. Victor Fischer, interview with junior sponsor of the 1957 death penalty abolition bill, 10 June 1996.
36. "House Votes End to Death Penalty," *Anchorage Daily News*, 23 February 1957.
37. Victor Fischer, interview.
38. Legislative File on Capital Punishment, one-page review of the 1957 house of representatives discussion preceding vote on abolition of capital punishment, House Judiciary Committee (1983–84).
39. "House Votes End to Death Penalty," *Anchorage Daily News*, 23 February 1957.
40. Legislative File on Capital Punishment.
41. Fischer, personal interview.
42. Lerman, "Hanging of Nelson Charles."
43. "Death Penalty," *Juneau Empire*, 6 February 1985, A8–A9.
44. *Senate Journal* (Juneau, Alaska: Territorial Legislature, Twenty-Third Session, 1957).
45. Minutes of Committee Debate on HB 675, House Judiciary Committee (26 February 1974).
46. *House Journal* (Juneau, Alaska: Alaska State Legislature, Eighth Legislature, 1973–74), 441.
47. Legislative Files on Capital Punishment, Senate Judiciary Committee (Alaska State Library, 1981–82).
48. "Pestinger Files Death Penalty Bill," *Anchorage Times*, 28 January 1983.
49. *House Journal* (Juneau, Alaska: Alaska State Legislature, Thirteenth Legislature, 1983–84), 401.
50. Full House Debate on HB 235, House Debate, Alaska State Library (5 May 1983).
51. Ibid.
52. Ibid.
53. *House Journal* (Juneau, Alaska: Alaska State Legislature, Eighth Legislature, 1973–74), 1198.
54. Public Hearing on SB 121, Senate Judiciary Committee, Alaska State Library (18 March 1983).
55. Ibid.
56. Ibid.
57. Ibid.
58. "Debate Heats Up Over Capital Punishment Bill: Moral Majority For, Catholics Against It," *Anchorage Times*, 19 March 1983.
59. "Death Penalty Debated," *Anchorage Daily News*, 19 March 1983.
60. *House Journal* (Juneau, Alaska: Alaska State Legislature, Thirteenth Legislature, 1983–84), 401.
61. "Governor Backs Off Death Penalty," *Anchorage Daily News*, 7 July 1983.
62. Susan E. Knighton, Position Paper on Capital Punishment (Juneau, Alaska: Adult Correctional Agency, 1984).
63. "Firing Squad, Lethal Injections Debated Next," *Anchorage Times* 19 March 1984.
64. "Death Penalty Debate" (editorial), *Anchorage Daily News*, 15 February 1983.
65. "Public Reassurance in a Civilized Way" (editorial), *Anchorage Daily News*, 27 February 1983.
66. "We Favor the Death Penalty" (editorial), *Juneau Empire*, 7 March 1983.
67. *House Journal* (Juneau, Alaska: Alaska State Legislature, Fourteenth Legislature, 1985–86), 75; *Senate Journal* (Juneau, Alaska: Alaska State Legislature, Fourteenth Legislature, 1985–86), 50.
68. "Death Penalty," *Juneau Empire*, 6 February 1985, A8–A9.
69. "Death Penalty No Deterrent, City Lawyers Say," *Anchorage Times*, 23 February 1985.
70. "Death Penalty Petition Filed," *Anchorage Daily News*, 9 October 1986.
71. Minutes of Committee Meeting on SB 7 and SB 31, Senate HESS Committee (3 April 1987).
72. Public Hearing on CSSB 7, Senate HESS Committee (13 April 1987).

73. Ibid.
74. Minutes of Committee Meeting on CSSB 7, Senate HESS Committee (22 April 1987).
75. Public Hearing on SB 7, Senate Judiciary Committee (23 October 1987).
76. Minutes of Committee Discussion of SB 17, Senate Judiciary Committee (2 February 1989).
77. "Death Penalty Gains Support, Bill Would Allow Executions," *Anchorage Daily News*, 21 January 1989, C1.
78. Ibid.
79. "Compass, Some Killers Deserve Death," *Anchorage Daily News*, 2 March 1989, E9.
80. "Death Penalty Only Breeds More Death," *Anchorage Daily News*, 29 January 1989.
81. "Some Senators Won't Drop."
82. Public Hearing on SB 17, Senate Judiciary Committee (24 January 1989).
83. Ibid.
84. "Committee Hears Testimony on Death Penalty Bill," *Anchorage Daily News*, 25 January 1989, B2.
85. Public Hearing on SB 17, Senate Judiciary Committee (31 January 1989).
86. "Senators Hear the Arguments," *Anchorage Daily News*, 1 February 1989, A1.
87. Public Hearing on SB 17, Senate Judiciary Committee (16 February 1989).
88. Minutes of the Committee Discussion of SB 17, Senate Judiciary Committee (23 February 1989).
89. Ibid.
90. Public Hearing on SB 17, Senate Finance Committee (8 March 1989).
91. Minutes of Committee Discussion of SB 17, Senate Finance Committee (8 March 1989).
92. Ibid.
93. Minutes of Committee Discussion of CSSB 17, Senate Finance Committee (7 March 1990).
94. "Some Senators Won't Drop Death Penalty Bill," *Anchorage Daily News*, 8 March 1990, B2.
95. Minutes of Committee Discussion of CSSB 17, Senate Finance Committee (13 March 1990).

96. Full Senate Debate of CSSB 17 (Audiotape, 30 April 1990).
97. Ibid.
98. "Capital Punishment in Death Throes," *Anchorage Daily News*, 1 May 1990, B4.
99. "Vote on Death Penalty May Only Be Temporary Reprieve. Soldotna Senator's Capital Punishment Bill Headed Toward the Senate Floor, But Might Lack Support to Pass," *Anchorage Daily News*, 15 April 1990, B5.
100. "Bill Would Put Death Penalty to Vote," *Anchorage Daily News*, 14 March 1991, D5.
101. "Prosecutors Weigh Use of Death Penalty," *Anchorage Daily News*, 19 June 1991, B1; "Jury May Hear Bomb Confession: Judge Rejects Claim That Was Coerced," *Anchorage Daily News*, 25 November 1992, B1; "Prosecutors Seek Death Penalty for Fautenberry," *Anchorage Daily News*, 16 September 1992, B2.
102. "U.S. Seeks Death for Only 2 in Bombing," *Anchorage Daily News*, 27 June 1992, A1; "Prosecutors Weigh Use of Death Penalty," *Anchorage Daily News*, 19 June 1991, B1.
103. "Reviving a Death Penalty, Aide Looks to Next Session," *Anchorage Daily News*, 3 December 1991, A1; "Opinion," *Anchorage Daily News*, 11 December 1991, B6.
104. "Sponsors: Death Penalty's Time Now," *Anchorage Daily News*, 17 November 1993, D1.
105. Ibid.
106. Public Hearing on SB 127, Senate Judiciary Committee (6 April 1994).
107. Minutes of Committee Discussion of SB 127, Senate Judiciary Committee (6 April 1994).
108. "Alaska Legislature '94 House Panel Kills Death Penalty Bill," *Anchorage Daily News*, 1 February 1994, B1.
109. Committee Discussion of HB 162, House Judiciary Committee (31 January 1993).
110. Committee Discussion of HB 162, House Judiciary Committee (1 March 1994).

111. "Judiciary Panel Revives Death Penalty Measure Bill's Expense: Makes Prospects for Passage Uncertain," *Anchorage Daily News*, 1 March 1994, B2.

112. "Death Penalty in Doubt, Backer Says," *Anchorage Daily News*, 12 March 1994, E2.

113. Public Hearing on HB 162 and SB 127, Joint House/Senate Judiciary Committee (16 November 1993).

114. "Alaska Legislature '94."

115. Minutes of Committee Discussion on SB 127, Senate Judiciary Committee (7 February 1994); Committee Discussion of HB 162, House Finance Committee (11 March 1994).

116. "Alaska Legislature '94."

117. Committee Discussion of HB 162, House Finance Committee (11 March 1994).

118. James McComas, interview with past president of Alaskans Against the Death Penalty, 4 June 1996.

119. "Death Penalty in Doubt"; Committee Discussion of HB 162, House Finance Committee (11 March 1994).

120. Minutes of Committee Discussion of SB 127, Senate Judiciary Committee (31 January 1994).

121. Minutes of Committee Discussion of SB 127, Senate Judiciary Committee (7 February 1994).

122. Committee Discussion of HB 162, House Finance Committee (11 March 1994).

123. "Death Penalty Bills Meet Their Ends," *Juneau Empire*, 23 April 1996.

124. John F. Galliher and John R. Cross, *Morals Legislation without Morality: The Case of Nevada* (New Brunswick, N.J.: Rutgers University Press, 1983).

125. "Easy Death Double Standard: Territorial Alaska's Experience with Capital Punishment Showed Race and Money Mattered," *Anchorage Daily News*, 1 May 1994, H5.

126. Public Hearing on HB 162 and SB 127.

127. Joe R. Feagin and Hernan Vera, *White Racism* (New York: Routledge, 1995), 175; Tiffany L. Hogan and Julie K. Netzer, "Knowing the Other: White Women, Gender, and Racism" (unpublished paper delivered at the annual meeting of the American Sociological Association, August 1993).

128. Larry W. Koch, John F. Galliher, and David Keys, "The Life and Death of the Death Penalty in West Virginia" (unpublished paper delivered at the annual meeting of the American Society of Criminology, November 1990).

129. Harold E. Pepinsky, "Norwegian and Polish Lessons for Keeping Down Prison Populations," *Humanity and Society* 17 (1993): 70–89.

130. Trefon Angasan, interview with vice president of Corporate Affairs of the Bristol Bay Native Corporation, 11 June 1996.

131. Ibid.

132. Ibid.

133. Kimberly Martus, interview with vice president of Alaskans Against the Death Penalty, 4 June 1996.

134. Fritz Pettyjohn, interview with long-term advocate of capital punishment and senate sponsor of capital punishment legislation, 8 June 1996.

135. University of Missouri–Columbia, Peace Studies Program, Death Penalty Abolition Conference, 14 November 1998.

Chapter 8

1. HB 706, Act 282, Sec. 1–14, Legislature of the Territory of Hawaii, 4 June 1957; "Death Sentence Commutations Made," *Honolulu Star Bulletin*, 10 October 1957.

2. Helen G. Chapin, *Shaping History: The Role of Newspapers in Hawaii* (Honolulu: University of Hawaii, 1996), 25; Joseph Theroux, "A Short History of Hawaiian Executions, 1826–1947," *Hawaiian Journal of History* 25 (1991): 147–59; M. W. Espy and J. O. Smykla, *Executions in the United States, 1608–1987: The Espy File, Codebook* (Tuscaloosa, Ala.: J. O. Smykla, Producer; Ann Arbor, Mich.: Inter-University Consortium for Political and Social Research, Distributor, 1987); Lawrence Koseki, *Capital Punishment in Hawaii: An Ethnic Per-*

spective, SIR Series no. 7 (Chicago: Asian American Mental Health Research Center, 1978).

3. Hilary Conroy, *The Japanese Frontier in Hawaii, 1868–1898* (Berkeley: University of California Press, 1953), 48–49.

4. William P. McGowan, "Industrializing the Land of Lono: Sugar Plantation Managers and Workers in Hawaii, 1900–1920," *Agricultural History* 69 (1995): 175–201; Ronald Takaki, *Pau Hana: Plantation Life and Labor in Hawaii, 1835–1920* (Honolulu: University of Hawaii Press, 1983).

5. Chapin, *Shaping History*.

6. Herbert Blumer and Troy Duster, "Theories of Race and Social Action," in *Sociological Theories: Race and Colonialism* (Paris: UNESCO, 1980), 211–38; Michael Hechter, *Internal Colonialism: The Celtic Fringe in British National Development, 1536–1966* (Berkeley: University of California Press, 1975); Robert Blauner, "Internal Colonialism," *Social Problems* 16 (1967): 393–408; Eldridge Cleaver, *Soul on Ice* (New York: Dell Publishing, 1968); Harold Cruse, *The Crisis of the Negro Intellectual* (New York: Morrow, 1967); Albert Memi, *The Colonizer and the Colonized* (Boston: Beacon Press, 1967); Frantz Fanon, *A Dying Colonialism* (New York: Grove Press, 1967).

7. Blumer and Duster, "Theories of Race," 219.

8. University of Missouri–Columbia, Peace Studies Program, Death Penalty Abolition Conference, 14 November 1998.

9. Norman Meller and Anne Feder Lee, "Hawaiian Sovereignty," *Publius* 27 (1997): 167–86.

10. Susantha Goonatilake, *Crippled Minds: An Exploration in Colonial Culture* (New Delhi: Vikas, 1982).

11. Espy and Smykla, *Executions in the United States*.

12. Romanzo Colfax Adams, *The Peoples of Hawaii* (Honolulu: Institute of Pacific Relations, 1933).

13. Gavan Daws, *Shoal of Time: A History of the Hawaiian Islands* (New York: Macmillan, 1968), 251.

14. Ibid., 252.

15. Wayne Patterson, *The Korean Frontier in America: Immigration to Hawaii, 1896–1910* (Honolulu: University of Hawaii Press, 1988); Takaki, *Pau Hana*, 4.

16. Roland Kotani, *The Japanese in Hawaii: A Century of Struggle* (Honolulu: Hochi, 1985).

17. Eugene D. Genovese, *Roll, Jordan, Roll: The World the Slaves Made* (New York: Vintage, 1977).

18. Robert C. Lydecker, *Roster Legislatures of Hawaii, 1841–1918* (Honolulu: Hawaiian Gazette, 1918), 27.

19. Andrew W. Lind, *Hawaii's People* (Honolulu: University of Hawaii Press, 1955), 48.

20. Edward Lydon, *The Anti-Chinese Movement in the Hawaiian Kingdom* (San Francisco: R & E Research, 1975), 25–26.

21. Ibid., 26–27; "Chinese," *Pacific Commercial Advertiser*, 29 December 1866, 1.

22. Lydon, *The Anti-Chinese Movement*, 29; Espy and Smykla, *Executions in the United States*; Theroux, "Short History of Hawaiian Executions," 156.

23. Adams, *The Peoples of Hawaii*, 8; Lind, *Hawaii's People*, 27.

24. "Chinese Expelled in California," *Pacific Commercial Advertiser*, 22 April 1876, 1.

25. "Chinatown Fire," *Pacific Commercial Advertiser*, 23 April 1886, 1.

26. McGowan, "Industrializing the Land," 178–79.

27. Board of Immigration, 1st Report, Territory of Hawaii (1907); Francis Hilary Conroy, "The Japanese Expansion into Hawaii, 1868–1898" (unpublished Ph.D. diss., University of California–Berkeley, 1949); Conroy, *The Japanese Frontier*.

28. John Mei Liu, "Cultivating Cane: Asian Labor and the Hawaiian Sugar Plantation Within the World Capitalist Economy" (unpublished Ph.D. diss., University of California–Los Angeles, 1985), 205, 212.

29. Takaki, *Pau Hana*.

30. Rogers M. Smith, *Civic Ideals: Conflicting Visions of Citizenship in U.S. History* (New Haven: Yale University Press, 1997); Glenn A. May, "Why the United States Won the Philippine-American War," *Pa-*

cific Historical Review 52 (1983): 353–77; Reynaldo C. Ileto, *Payson and Revolution: Popular Movements in the Philippines, 1840–1910* (Quezon City: Ateneo de Manila University Press, 1979); F. X. O'Neill, *Re-Union Booklet, Original Company 'F' 30th U.S. Infantry of 1901–1904: History, Letters, and Stories Depicting Army Days in the Philippines*, ed. J. M. Morton (Springfield, Mo.: Morton, 1933); Richard E. Welch, Jr., "American Atrocities in the Philippines: The Indictment and the Response," *Pacific Historical Review* 43 (1974).

31. Howard K. Beale, *Theodore Roosevelt and the Rise of America to World Power* (Baltimore: Johns Hopkins University Press, 1956), 72.

32. Frederick Funston, "Letter to Theodore Roosevelt," 1 September 1901, Theodore Roosevelt Papers, vol. 46 of *Letters to Theodore Roosevelt*, Library of Congress.

33. Ileto, *Payson and Revolution*.

34. Smith, *Civic Ideals*, 430.

35. Welch, "American Atrocities," 241.

36. Emory S. Bogardus, "Native Hawaiians and Their Problems," *Sociology and Social Research* 19 (1929): 477.

37. Smith, *Civic Ideals*, 429.

38. "Marines Land in Honolulu," *New York Times*, 21 March 1893, 1, 2.

39. Beth Bailey and David Farber, "The 'Double-V' Campaign in World War II Hawaii: African-Americans, Racial Ideology, and Federal Power," *Journal of Social History* 26 (1993): 817–43.

40. Lt. John A. Harmon, U.S.N., "Political Importance of Hawaii," *North American Review* 160 (1894): 74–75.

41. Kotani, *The Japanese in Hawaii*.

42. *Duncan v. Kahanamoku*, 327 U.S. 304 (1946).

43. Ibid.

44. Harry N. Scheiber and Jane L. Scheiber, "Bayonets in Paradise: A Half-Century Retrospect on Martial Law in Hawaii, 1941–1946," *University of Hawaii Law Review* 19 (1997): 477–648.

45. "General Order No. 4," *Honolulu Star-Bulletin*, 9 December 1941, 3.

46. Kotani, *The Japanese in Hawaii*, 60.

47. Lockwood Myrick, "Open Letter to Governor Farrington on Fukunaga's Insanity," 5 November 1928, reprinted in Kotani, *The Japanese in Hawaii*, 64.

48. "Taxi Murderer Convicted," *Honolulu Star-Bulletin*, 31 May 1918, 1.

49. Theroux, "Short History of Hawaiian Executions"; "Killer Leaves Prison," *Honolulu Star-Bulletin*, 11 April 1923, 1.

50. Masaji Marumoto, "The Ala Moana Case and the Massie-Fortescue Case Revisited," *University of Hawaii Law Review* 5 (1983): 271–87.

51. "Gang Assaults Young Wife Kidnapped in Automobile, Maltreated by Fiends," *Pacific Commercial Advertiser*, 14 September 1931, 1; "Navy Wife Assaulted," *Hilo Tribune-Herald*, 14 September 1931, 1.

52. *Pacific Commercial Advertiser*, 1931; Kotani, *The Japanese in Hawaii*, 67.

53. "Lust in Paradise," *Time Magazine*, 28 December 1931, 11.

54. "Attacks on Women and Murder of Native Assailant," *New York Times*, 10 January 1932, 30.

55. Ibid.

56. Peter J. Nelligan, "Social Change and Rape Law in Hawaii" (Ph.D. diss., University of Hawaii, 1983); Bernhard Horman, "The Majors-Palakiko Case: What People in Hawaii Are Saying and Doing," Report no. 20 (Honolulu: University of Hawaii Social Research Laboratory, 1952); Bernhard Horman, "The Significance of the Wilder or Majors-Palakiko Case: A Study in Public Opinion," *Social Process in Hawaii* 17 (1953): 1–13.

57. "Local Woman Found Dead," *Honolulu Star-Bulletin*, 16 March 1948, 1, 2; "Prominent Widow Murdered," *Pacific Commercial Advertiser*, 17 March 1948, 1.

58. Nelligan, "Social Change."

59. "Community Aroused," *Pacific Commercial Advertiser*, 18 March 1948, 1.

60. "Hawaii's Last Execution Was 28 Years Ago," *Honolulu Star-Bulletin*, 29 June 1972.

61. Paul R. Spickard, "The Nisei Assume Power: The Japanese Citizens League, 1941–1942," *Pacific Historical Review* 52 (1983): 142–74.

62. Donald Rowland, "Orientals and the Suf-

frage in Hawaii," *Pacific Historical Review* 12 (1943): 11–12.

63. Adams, *Peoples of Hawaii*, 17–18.

64. Michael Haas, "Comparing Paradigms of Ethnic Politics in the United States: The Case of Hawaii," *Western Political Quarterly* 40 (1987): 668.

65. Ibid.

66. Elizabeth Wittermans, *Inter-Ethnic Relations in a Plural Society* (Groningen: J. B. Wolters, 1964); Anthony Didrick Castberg, "The Ethnic Factor in Criminal Sentencing" (Master's thesis, University of Hawaii, 1966).

67. Gene Kassebaum, "Ethnicity and the Disposition of Arrest for Violent Crime in Hawaii," *Social Process in Hawaii* 28 (1981): 33–57.

68. "Fasi: Death for Drug Traffickers," *Honolulu Advertiser*, 3 August 1990, A3.

69. "Death Penalty Decision by Voters Urged," *Honolulu Star-Bulletin*, 29 August 1968.

70. "Storm Clouds Over Paradise," *Time Magazine*, 15 December 1980, 67.

71. "Death Penalty Asked for Officer Slayings," *Honolulu Advertiser*, 1 May 1970, B2.

72. "GOP Senators Ask Study: Republicans Eye Death Penalty," *Honolulu Star-Bulletin*, 2 February 1971.

73. "Kidnap-Death Bill Move by Senator Yee," *Honolulu Advertiser*, 27 February 1974, A1.

74. "Revive the Death Penalty," *Honolulu Advertiser*, 2 March 1976, A3.

75. "Bring Back the Death Penalty, Bills in Both Houses Advocate," *Honolulu Advertiser*, 31 January 1979, A8.

76. "Dealing with Crime in Hawaii," *Honolulu Advertiser*, 13 March 1981, A20.

77. "Moon Calls for Death Penalty for Murder-for-Hire Killers," *Honolulu Advertiser*, 26 October 1984, A6.

78. "Hee Is Drumming Up Death Penalty Support," *Honolulu Advertiser*, 27 February 1988, A3.

79. "Fasi: Death for Drug Traffickers."

80. "Hawaii's Tourism Slump: Short or Long Term?" *Pacific Commercial Advertiser*, 11 October 1998.

81. *Uniform Crime Report* (Washington, D.C.: Federal Bureau of Investigation, Government Printing Office, 1957–1972).

82. *Uniform Crime Reports*, Table 3.

83. Attorney General of Hawaii, "Crime Prevention and Justice Assistance Division: Report of Research and Statistics" (Honolulu: State of Hawaii, 1998).

84. Fanon, *A Dying Colonialism*, 36.

85. Hechter, *Internal Colonialism*; Robert Blauner, "Internal Colonialism."

86. J. Edgar Hoover, "Letter to All Law Enforcement Officials," *FBI Law Enforcement Bulletin*, 1 June 1960.

87. University of Missouri–Columbia, Peace Studies Program, Death Penalty Abolition Conference, 14 November 1998.

88. "States with No Death Penalty Share Lower Homicide Rates," *New York Times*, 22 September 2000, A19.

Chapter 9

1. Richard Acton, "The Magic of Undiscouraged Effort: The Death Penalty in Early Iowa, 1838–1878," *Annals of Iowa* 50 (Winter 1991): 721–50.

2. Ibid.

3. Ibid.

4. "How Iowa Restored the Death Penalty," *Des Moines Register*, 28 February 1960, 14G.

5. Acton, "The Magic of Undiscouraged Effort."

6. Ibid., 739.

7. "How Iowa Restored."

8. Ibid.

9. Paul W. Black, "Some Sociological Aspects of Lynchings in Iowa," *Iowa Journal of History and Politics* (1911; reprint, April 1912): 21–23.

10. Ibid.

11. Acton, "The Magic of Undiscouraged Effort," 741.

12. Ibid., 748.

13. Ibid., 749.

14. "How Iowa Restored."

15. Acton, "The Magic of Undiscouraged Effort," 721–50.

16. William J. Bowers, *Legal Homicide: Death As Punishment in America, 1864–1982* (Boston: Northeastern University Press, 1984), 440–41.

17. Ibid.

18. Franklin E. Zimring, "Ambivalence in State Capital Punishment Policy: An Empirical Sounding," *New York Review of Law and Social Change* 18 (1991): 729–42.

19. Acton, "The Magic of Undiscouraged Effort," 721–50.

20. Edward P. Morgan, *The '60s Experience: Hard Lessons About Modern America* (Philadelphia: Temple University Press, 1991), 14.

21. U.S. Bureau of the Census (Washington, D.C.: Government Printing Office, 1990).

22. *State Statistical Rankings: A Statistical View of the Fifty United States*, 7th ed. (Lawrence, Kans.: Morgan Quinton Oak, 1996), 441.

23. U.S. Bureau of the Census, *Statistical Abstract of the United States*, 118th ed. (Washington, D.C.: Government Printing Office, 1998), 211; U.S. Department of Justice, *Crime in the United States: Uniform Crime Reports* (Washington, D.C.: Government Printing Office, 1966); U.S. Department of Justice, *Crime in the United States: Uniform Crime Reports* (Washington, D.C.: Government Printing Office, 1996); *Iowa Uniform Crime Reports* (Des Moines, Iowa: Iowa Department of Public Safety, 1996).

24. Harold Hughes, interview by Kate McGonigal, Glendale, Arizona, 23 July 1995.

25. James M. Galliher and John F. Galliher, "Déjà Vu All Over Again: The Recurring Life and Death of Capital Punishment in Kansas," *Social Problems* 44 (August 1997): 369–85.

26. "Steal 2 Topcoats, Suit at Cleaners," *Des Moines Register*, 2 March 1965, 5A.

27. "Widow, 87, Is Bilked Again," *Des Moines Register*, 13 July 1965, 1A.

28. "Arrest Girls at Beer Party," *Des Moines Register*, 7 March 1965, 1A.

29. "Arrest 2 Boys in Prowlings," *Des Moines Register*, 9 April 1965, 1A.

30. "Jail 4 Youths for Annoying," *Des Moines Register*, 10 June 1965, 1A.

31. "700 Riot at Arnold's Park," *Des Moines Register*, 5 July 1965, 1A.

32. Ibid.

33. Ibid.

34. Ibid.

35. "Two Charged in Tot's Death," *Des Moines Register*, 12 August 1964, 7A.

36. "Father Shot; Boy, 14, Held," *Des Moines Register*, 1 September 1964, 3M.

37. "Wife Killed, Mate Shot in Dispute," *Des Moines Register*, 15 July 1965, 1A.

38. "Man Is Slain, Woman Held," *Des Moines Register*, 12 April 1965, 6A.

39. "Trace Girl's Last 50 Hours," *Des Moines Register*, 16 April 1965, 1A, 9A.

40. "Question 50 in Slaying of D.M. Girl," *Des Moines Register*, 17 April 1965, 1A.

41. Martha Coco, *Iowa Field Services Department*, 1997.

42. "Hughes Sets Vote Drive," *Des Moines Register*, 2 August 1964, 3L.

43. "Hughes-Hultman Debate," *Des Moines Register*, 11 September 1964, 8A; "The Governor Debate," *Des Moines Register*, 19 September 1964, 6A; "Hughes-Hultman Views on Right-to-Work Law," *Des Moines Register*, 4 October 1964, 7L; "Hultman and Hughes Split on Hangings," *Des Moines Register*, 15 October 1964, 1A.

44. "Hultman and Hughes."

45. Ibid.

46. "The Johnson Victory: Landslide for Hughes; Democrats Win Statehouse," *Des Moines Register*, 4 November 1964, 1A.

47. Ibid.

48. "Hughes Behind Quick Demo Action," *Des Moines Register*, 16 November 1964, 3A.

49. "The Johnson Victory."

50. "Happy Days Ahead for Iowa Demos," *Des Moines Register*, 28 December 1964, 1A.

51. "Key Battles to Center in Iowa Senate," *Des Moines Register*, 12 January 1965, 1A; *Book of the States, 1966–1967*, vol. 16 (Chicago, Ill.: Council of State Governments, 1964).

52. JuliAnn Hughes, telephone interview by Kate McGonigal, 28 April 1997.

53. "Hughes Says Most G.O.P. State Employees Will Stay," *Des Moines Register*, 6 November 1964, 3A.

. . . .

54. "Gov. Hughes Will Second Nomination," *Des Moines Register*, 23 August 1964, 1A.
55. "Hughes Political Dilemma," *Des Moines Register*, 9 July 1965, 12A.
56. "Hughes-Hultman Views."
57. Ibid.
58. "A Unique Opportunity," *Des Moines Register*, 10 January 1965, 6A.
59. "Death Penalty Lifted," *Des Moines Register*, 12 January 1965, 6A.
60. "Tice Parents Are Elated," *Des Moines Register*, 11 January 1965, 4A.
61. Harold Hughes, 23 July 1995.
62. "Key Battles," 1A, 4A.
63. Ibid., 1A.
64. Ibid.
65. "Would End Death Penalty," *Des Moines Register*, 28 January 1965, 3A.
66. *Iowa Journal of the House of Representatives*, HF 8: 203, 19 January 1965.
67. "Would End."
68. "Exception Urged in Ban on Death Penalty," *Des Moines Register*, 4 February 1965, 1A, 8A.
69. "Loses 2 Votes on Death Ban," *Des Moines Register*, 5 February 1965, 4A.
70. Ibid.
71. "Abolishing the Death Penalty," *Des Moines Register*, 6 February 1965, 6A.
72. "Lauds Vote Banning Death Penalty," *Des Moines Register*, 19 February 1965, 3A; *Iowa Journal of the House of Representatives*, HF 8: 213, 19 January 1965.
73. "Lauds Vote"; *Iowa Journal of the Senate*, HF 8: 309, 8 February 1965.
74. "Lauds Vote"; *Iowa Journal*, 8 February 1965; Iowa Legislative Information Office, 1995, fax on public hearings participants.
75. "Lauds Vote."
76. Ibid.
77. Ibid.
78. "Abolishing."
79. Ibid.
80. "An End to Legal Hangings," *Des Moines Register*, 20 February 1965, 6A.
81. "Dilemma of Mississippi—'Undeveloped Nation,'" *Des Moines Register*, 6 March 1965, 4A.
82. Ibid.
83. "Selma's Sheriff Clark Leads Forced March," *Des Moines Register*, 11 February 1965, 7A.
84. Ibid.
85. "Next to King, Clark Called Most Unpopular in Selma," *Des Moines Register*, 12 February 1965, 1A, 6A.
86. "Court Curbs Sheriff Clark," *Des Moines Register*, 17 April 1965, 1A.
87. Ibid.
88. "The Klan Deserves Study," *Des Moines Register*, 25 February 1965, 6A.
89. "Find 3 Bodies in Mississippi," *Des Moines Register*, 5 August 1964, 1A.
90. "19 Accused in Dixie Go to Jail," *Des Moines Register*, 10 December 1964, 1A; "Judge Frees 6 Klansmen: Faced Rights Charges on Negro Death," *Des Moines Register*, 30 December 1964, 1A; "Legal Problem in Mississippi," *Des Moines Register*, 1 March 1965, 10A.
91. "Death Assures Probe of Klan," *Des Moines Register*, 27 March 1965, 2A.
92. "The Klan Deserves Study," 6A.
93. "Whites Beat 3 Ministers After March," *Des Moines Register*, 10 March 1965, 1A.
94. "'Chased, Hit with Clubs, Negro Says,'" *Des Moines Register*, 12 March 1965, 1A.
95. "Chased, Hit with Clubs," 1A; "Thousands Continue Protests in Alabama," *Des Moines Register*, 14 March 1965, 1A, 4A; "4 White Men Face Charge of Murder," *Des Moines Register*, 12 March 1965, 1A, 8A.
96. "Marching in Alabama," *Des Moines Register*, 11 March 1965, 8A.
97. Ibid.
98. Morgan, *The '60s Experience*, 39.
99. "Punishing Alabama," *Des Moines Register*, 12 March 1965, 10A.
100. "Selma Is Seen as Lurid Phase of Crime in U.S.," *Des Moines Register*, 12 March 1965, 10A.
101. *Iowa Rate Comparisons* (Des Moines, Iowa: Iowa Department of Public Safety, 1996), 4–5, 17.
102. Ibid., 5, 17.
103. Martha Coco, 1997; U.S. Department of Justice, *Crime in the United States: Uniform Crime Reports* (Washington, D.C.: Government Printing Office, 1967).
104. Martha Coco, 1997; U.S. Department of

Justice, *Crime in the United States: Uniform Crime Reports* (Washington, D.C.: Government Printing Office, 1966), 193; *Iowa Uniform Crime Reports*, 17.

105. "Emrys Call for Death Penalty," *Des Moines Register*, 7 September 1994, 1A.

106. "Serious Crime Drops," *Des Moines Register*, 22 May 1995, 3A.

107. "Iowa Cuts Its Violent Crime Rate," *Des Moines Register*, 3 November 1994, 11A.

108. "A Question of Life or Death," *Des Moines Register*, 4 September 1994, 1A.

109. "Can Issue Carry Branstad?" *Des Moines Register*, 5 September 1994, 15A.

110. "For Governor: Bonnie Campbell," *Des Moines Register*, 31 October 1994, 1C.

111. Terry E. Branstad, interview by Kate McGonigal, Des Moines, Iowa, 23 May 1995; Tony and Peggy Emry, telephone interview by Kate McGonigal, 23 April 1995.

112. Tony and Peggy Emry, 23 April 1995.

113. "Branstad Campaign Runs, Yanks Ads, Using Anna Emry's Name," *Des Moines Register*, 9 September 1994, 1A; "Crime Ad Attacks Intensified," *Des Moines Register*, 7 September 1994, 5M.

114. Galliher and Galliher, "Déjà Vu," 369–85.

115. Tony and Peggy Emry, interview by Kate McGonigal, 23 April 1995.

116. "Death Penalty Would Run up High Costs, State's Study Shows," *Des Moines Register*, 24 January 1995, 1A, 10A.

117. "Crime Ad."

118. Ibid.

119. "GOP Victors Map Agenda," *Des Moines Register*, 10 November 1994, 1A.

120. Ibid.

121. Terry E. Branstad, 23 May 1995.

122. Ibid.

123. Ibid.

124. Ibid.

125. "Is Death Penalty Worth It?" *Des Moines Register*, 22 February 1995, 10A.

126. "Last Iowa Governor to Allow Executions Doubts Their Effects," *Des Moines Register*, 4 February 1995, 8A.

127. *Iowa Journal of the House of Representatives*, HF 2: 479–544, 22 February 1995.

128. "How Death Penalty Issue Lost Its

Steam," *Des Moines Register*, 2 March 1995, 1A; "Death Penalty Fails," *Des Moines Register*, 3 March 1995, 1A.

129. "Opponents of the Death Penalty," *Des Moines Register*, 11 February 1995, 7A.

130. "Death Penalty Foes Fear Race Affects Sentencing," *Des Moines Register*, 7 February 1995, 4M.

131. "Death Penalty Bill Expanded," *Des Moines Register*, 3 February 1995, 4M; "Framework for Execution of Criminals," *Des Moines Register*, 2 March 1995, 11A; "How Death Penalty."

132. *Iowa Journal of the Senate*, HF 2: 455, 27 February 1995.

133. Tony and Peggy Emry, 23 April 1995.

134. "Death Penalty Fails."

135. "How Death Penalty."

136. Jim Ryan, telephone interview by Kate McGonigal, 10 May 1995.

137. Ibid.

138. Iowa Legislative Information Office, 1995.

139. "Death Penalty: Morbid Trip Backward," *Des Moines Register*, 2 March 1995, 11A.

140. Ibid.

141. Acton, "The Magic of Undiscouraged Effort," 721–50.

142. "How Iowa Restored."

143. Ibid.

144. *Iowa Rate Comparisons*, 7.

145. Richard A. Berk, Harold Brackman, and Selma Lesser, *A Measure of Justice* (New York: Academic Press, 1977); *Iowa Rate Comparisons*, 17; John Hagan, Edward T. Silva, and John H. Simpson, "Legislation of Crime and Delinquency: A Review of Theory, Method, and Research," *Law and Society Review* 14 (1980): 603–28.

146. Galliher and Galliher, "Déjà Vu," 369–85.

147. Steve Pohlmeyer, "Committing to Conscience" (paper presented at the National Coalition for the Abolition of the Death Penalty, San Francisco, California, 17 November 2000).

148. "Vilsack: Death-Penalty Talk Just Politics," *Omaha World Herald*, Iowa ed., 18 January 1998, 16.

Chapter 10

1. Neal R. Peirce and Jerry Hagstrom, *The Book of America: Inside 50 States Today* (New York: W. W. Norton, 1983).
2. Bert Useem and Peter Kimball, *States of Siege: U.S. Prison Riots, 1971–1986* (New York: Oxford University Press, 1989), 161.
3. Ibid.
4. Georg Rusche and Otto Kirchheimer, *Punishment and Social Structure* (New York: Columbia University Press, 1939).
5. Christopher R. Adamson, "Toward a Marxian Penology: Captive Criminal Populations as Economic Threats and Resources," *Social Problems* 31 (1984): 435–58; John F. Galliher, Gregory Ray, and Brent Cook, "Abolition and Reinstatement of Capital Punishment During the Progressive Era and Early 20th Century," *The Journal of Criminal Law and Criminology* 83 (1992): 538–76.
6. M. W. Espy and J. O. Smykla, *Executions in the United States, 1608–1987: The Espy File* (Tuscaloosa, Ala.: J. O. Smykla, Producer; Ann Arbor, Mich.: Inter-University Consortium for Political and Social Research, Distributor, 1987).
7. Franklin E. Zimring and Gordon Hawkins, *Capital Punishment and the American Agenda* (New York: Cambridge University Press, 1986).
8. *West Virginia Codes* (1931), ch. 1, art. 2.
9. Espy and Smykla, *Executions in the United States.*
10. John H. Culver, "Capital Punishment Politics and Policies in the United States, 1977–1997," *Crime, Law and Social Change* 32 (2000): 287–300.
11. Victoria Schneider and John Oritz Smykla, "A Summary Analysis of Executions in the United States, 1608–1987: The Espy File," in Robert M. Bohm, ed., *The Death Penalty in America* (Cincinnati, Ohio: Anderson Publishing, 1991).
12. U.S. Bureau of the Census, *Census of Population* (Washington, D.C.: Government Printing Office, 1900–1990).
13. Ann L. Page and Donald A. Clelland, "The Kanawha County Textbook Controversy: A Study of the Politics of Life Style Concern," *Social Forces* 57 (1978): 265–81.
14. U.S. Bureau of the Census, *Census* (1990).
15. "State's Lowest Crime Rate Baffles Analysts," *Charleston Gazette*, 19 November 1975, 2A; *Uniform Crime Reports: Crime in the United States* (Washington, D.C.: Federal Bureau of Investigation, 1966, 1975, 1980, 1990).
16. House of Delegates, *Journal of the State of West Virginia*, House Bill 293 (1955), 796.
17. "Death Penalty Bill Faces Senate Test," *Charleston Daily Mail*, 24 February 1965, 1, 4.
18. "Capital or Not: The Notion of Crime without Punishment Yields to Chaos" (editorial), *Charleston Daily Mail*, 23 February 1965, 4.
19. House of Delegates, *Journal*, 384–85; "Teachers to Get Raise: Death Penalty Clears House Hurdle," *Charleston Daily Mail*, 13 February 1965, 2.
20. "Death Penalty Bill Clears Senate Panel," *Charleston Gazette*, 17 February 1965, 34.
21. "Senate Amends, Passes: Death Penalty Bill Returns to House," *Charleston Daily Mail*, 26 February 1965, 1, 10.
22. Ibid.
23. "Base Pay Bill Up for House Amendment Votes," *Charleston Daily Mail*, 27 February 1965.
24. House of Delegates, *Recorded Debate, State of West Virginia*, Floor Debate on HB 517, 23 February 1965.
25. House of Delegates, *Recorded Debate, State of West Virginia*, Floor Debate, 26 February 1965.
26. "Death Penalty Nears End: Parole Agreement," *Charleston Daily Mail*, 5 March 1965; "Death Living: Snag in Bill to Abolish Capital Punishment Rises," *Sunday Gazette-Mail*, 7 March 1965.
27. "Senate Group in Agreement on Death Bill," *Charleston Daily Mail*, 9 March 1965.
28. "House Outlaws Death Penalty," *Charleston Gazette*, 12 March 1965.
29. "Capital Punishment Outlawed by Senate Margin of 18 to 16," *Charleston Gazette*, 12 March 1965.
30. *West Virginia Acts* (1965), ch. 40 at 204; "Smith to Sign Act: State Abolishing Capi-

tal Penalty," *Charleston Gazette*, 13 March 1965, 1.

31. "Getting the Pen" (photograph), *Charleston Gazette*, 19 March 1965; "Governor Signs Bill: Death Penalty at End in State after Total of 94," *Charleston Daily Mail*, 19 March 1965; "Crushing of Death Penalty Good Reflection on State" (editorial), *Charleston Gazette*, 13 March 1965.

32. John A. Canfield, *State Papers and Public Addresses of Hulitt C. Smith: Twenty-Seventh Governor of West Virginia*, 1970.

33. "Capital Punishment Brutal Barbaric Rite" (editorial), *Charleston Gazette*, 2 February 1965, 6.

34. "Death Penalty Cruel, Unworthy" (editorial), *Charleston Gazette*, 22 February 1965.

35. "Ex-Warden Holds Mandatory Life Term Meaningless," *Charleston Gazette*, 18 March 1965.

36. "The Criminals Are Entitled to Justice; The Innocent to Adequate Protection" (editorial), *Charleston Daily Mail*, 13 March 1965, 4; "Capital or Not," 4.

37. Senate, *Journal of the State of West Virginia*, Senate Bill 8 (1971), 276–81.

38. Senate, *Journal*, Senate Bill 100 (1972), 515.

39. "Death Penalty Not a Crime Deterrent," *Charleston Gazette*, 16 February 1979, 7A.

40. "Get Qualified People; State Senator Airs View on Penitentiary Squabble," *Charleston Daily Mail*, 10 April 1970.

41. "Absence of Capital Punishment Not the Trouble at Moundsville" (editorial), *Charleston Daily Mail*, 10 April 1970.

42. "Institution's Chief Changes Mind on Capital Punishment," *Charleston Gazette*, 3 June 1972.

43. "By Prison Guards: Capital Punishment Reinstatement Asked," *Charleston Daily Mail*, 16 October 1972.

44. Senate, *Journal*, Senate Bill 100 (1972), 515.

45. "Death Penalty Gets New Support," *Charleston Daily Mail*, 19 February 1973, 1A, 8A.

46. "Death Penalty Dreadful Step Backward for State" (editorial), *Charleston Gazette*, 26 February 1973, 8A.

47. "Prison Riot, Said Reason for Death Penalty Bill," *Charleston Gazette*, 21 March 1973, 7C; "Prison Guards Renew Support of Death Penalty," *Charleston Daily Mail*, 22 March 1973, 1A, 4A.

48. "Death Penalty Bill Tops Law Maker List," *Charleston Daily Mail*, 19 January 1976, 9A.

49. "Death Penalty Return Gains Momentum," *Charleston Daily Mail*, 31 January 1978, 1A.

50. "Of Capital Interest: Tompkins Opposes Death Penalty," *Charleston Daily Mail*, 13 February 1978, 5A.

51. "Reinstatement of Death Penalty Appears Unlikely," *Sunday Gazette-Mail*, 5 February 1978, 2B.

52. "Death Penalty Return Gains Momentum," 1A.

53. "Death Penalty Proponents Confident: Jay Hints OK," *Charleston Daily Mail*, 1 February 1979, 1A, 2A.

54. Ibid.

55. "58 Percent Favor Death Penalty Return," *Charleston Daily Mail*, 12 February 1979, 1A, 2A.

56. "Death Penalty Leads 19–7 in Senate Poll," *Charleston Daily Mail*, 7 February 1979, 1A.

57. "Breakout Stirs Push to Revive Death Penalty," *Charleston Daily Mail*, 15 November 1979, 1A, 8A; "Mostly Poor Executed, Former Warden Says," *Charleston Gazette*, 8 February 1979, 13A.

58. "Death Penalty Not a Crime Deterrent."

59. "Lawmakers Hear Death Penalty Testimony," *Charleston Gazette*, 2 February 1979.

60. "Death Penalty Leads," 1A; "House Judiciary Panel Details Murders Punishable by Death," *Charleston Gazette*, 7 February 1979, 1A, 3A.

61. House of Delegates, *Journal* (1979), 389, 1413, 1416.

62. "House Votes 62–38 to Reinstate Death Penalty," *Charleston Gazette*, 14 February 1979, 1A, 9A.

63. Ibid.

64. House of Delegates, *Journal* (1979), 389, 1413, 1416.

65. "Death Penalty Bill Passage Possible," *Sunday Gazette-Mail*, 28 January 1979.

66. "House to Vote on Death Penalty," *Charleston Daily Mail*, 10 February 1979, 2A.

67. "House Votes," 1A, 9A.

68. "Death Bill Tactics Surfacing: Hearings, Scrutiny, Amendments Loom," *Charleston Gazette*, 20 February 1979, 1A, 2A.

69. "15 Escape Prison, Kill Cop," *Charleston Daily Mail*, 8 November 1979, 1A, 4A.

70. "Breakout Stirs," 1A, 8A.

71. "State Panel Cripples Death Penalty Move," *Charleston Gazette*, 30 January 1980, 1A, 2A.

72. "Popular Vote Idea Killed: Death Penalty Issue Receives 2nd Blow," *Charleston Gazette*, 1 February 1980, 1A, 4A.

73. "Senate Bypass Difficult: House Taking Lead on Death Bill in Vain," *Charleston Daily Mail*, 4 February 1980, 7B.

74. "King Palumbo" (editorial), *Charleston Daily Mail*, 6 February 1980, 6A.

75. "Committee's Death Penalty Vote Depends on Bill, Survey Shows," *Charleston Daily Mail*, 18 February 1981, 3B.

76. "23 Speak at Death Penalty Hearings," *Charleston Daily Mail*, 26 February 1981, 1D.

77. "Senate Judiciary Doesn't Take Up Death Penalty," *Charleston Daily Mail*, 3 March 1981, 1B.

78. Useem and Kimball, *States of Siege*; Crain v. Bordenkircher, "Memorandum of Opinion, Finding of Fact, Conclusions of Law and Order," Civil Action no. 81-C-320 R, Circuit Court of Marshall County, West Virginia (1982).

79. "Death Penalty to Be Proposed in Legislature," *Charleston Daily Mail*, 28 December 1982, 5A.

80. "Most in Favor of Death Penalty, Raising Legal Drinking Age to 21," *Charleston Daily Mail*, 12 January 1984, 1A, 6A.

81. "Lawmakers Favor the Death Penalty," *Charleston Daily Mail*, 9 February 1985, 1A, 6A.

82. Ibid.

83. Ibid.

84. "Chafin Feels Strong Death Bill Support," *Charleston Daily Mail*, 19 February 1985, 8A.

85. "Judiciary Panel Rejects Death Penalty Measure," *Charleston Daily Mail*, 1 March 1985, 12A.

86. "Death Penalty Bill Dies in Judiciary; Betting Approved," *Charleston Gazette*, 3 March 1985, 1A.

87. "Prison Inmates Riot, Hold 13 Hostages; 1 Inmate Dead after Holiday Violence," *Charleston Daily Mail*, 2 January 1986, 1A, 4A.

88. "Inmates 'Vigorously Assaulted' Before Dying," *Charleston Daily Mail*, 3 January 1986, 1A, 12A.

89. Senate, *Journal*, Senate Bill 100 (1986), 1343–48.

90. "Prosecutors Endorse Death Penalty Measure," *Charleston Gazette*, 2 February 1986, 5C.

91. "Church-backed Group to Fight Death Penalty," *Charleston Gazette*, 9 January 1986, 9A.

92. "Capital Punishment Proponents Face Off at Hearing," *Charleston Gazette*, 2 February 1986, 8A.

93. Ibid.

94. "Death Advocates," *Charleston Gazette*, 6 January 1987.

95. "Moundsville" (editorial), *Charleston Daily Mail*, 9 January 1987, 4A.

96. Adamson, "Toward a Marxian"; Galliher, Ray, and Cook, "Abolition and Reinstatement"; Rusche and Kirchheimer, *Punishment*.

97. David Jacobs, "Inequality and Police Strength: Conflict Theory and Coercive Control in Metropolitan Areas," *American Sociological Review* 44 (1979): 913–25; Allen E. Liska, Joseph J. Lawrence, and Michael Benson, "Perspectives on the Legal Order: The Capacity for Social Control," *American Journal of Sociology* 87 (1981): 413–26; David Jacobs and David Britt, "Inequality and Police Use of Deadly Force: An Empirical Assessment of a Conflict Hypothesis," *Social Problems* 26 (1979): 403–12; Kirk R. Williams and Susan Drake, "Social Structure, Crime and Criminalization: An Empirical Examination of the Conflict Perspective," *The Sociological Quarterly* 21 (1980): 563–75.

98. Joseph R. Feagin and Vera Hernan, *White Racism* (New York: Routledge, 1995).

99. Larry W. Koch and John F. Galliher, "Michigan's Continuing Abolition of the Death Penalty and the Conceptual Components of Symbolic Legislation," *Social and Legal Studies* 2 (1993): 323–46.

100. Peirce and Hagstrom, *Book of America*.

101. Hugo Adam Bedau, *Death Is Different: Studies in the Morality, Law, and Politics of Capital Punishment* (Boston: Northeastern University Press, 1987).

102. Edward A. Shils, *Tradition* (Chicago: University of Chicago Press, 1981), 189.

103. *State ex rel., Pingley v. Coiner*, West Virginia Reports 155 at 591, no. 18127 (25 January 1972).

104. Useem and Kimball, *States of Siege*.

105. West Virginia Department of Corrections (1999). Available at http://www.state.wv.us/wvdoc/MOCCI.htm.

106. James Haught, Death Penalty Abolition Conference, University of Missouri–Columbia, Peace Studies Program (14 November 1998).

Chapter 11

1. Samuel Jordan, "Unsuccessful Efforts to Reinstate the Death Penalty in the District of Columbia" (paper presented at the Symposium on the Abolition of Capital Punishment, University of Missouri–Columbia, 14 November 1998).

2. "D.C. Reinstatement Effort Blocked," *Lifelines*, April/May 1992, 1.

3. "A Death Penalty for the District," *Washington Post*, 22 September 1992.

4. "Voters Defeat Death Penalty Referendum in D.C.," *Lifelines*, July–Sept./Oct–Dec. 1992, 5, 10.

5. M. W. Espy and J. O. Smykla, *Executions in the United States, 1608–1987: The Espy File, Codebook* (Tuscaloosa, Ala.: J. O. Smykla, Producer; Ann Arbor, Mich.: Inter-University Consortium for Political and Social Research, Distributor, 1987).

6. "Churches Join Hands to Urge Defeat of Death Penalty," *Washington Post*, 22 October 1992, 1; "Church Group Battles D.C. Death Penalty," *Washington Post*, 24 October 1992, B7.

7. "Death Penalty Killed by the Unexpected," *Washington Post*, 5 November 1992, C1.

8. "Widow Urges Senators to Back Death Penalty," *Washington Post*, 1 May 1997, D1.

9. "Barry to Urge Death Penalty in Slayings of Police Officers," *Washington Post*, 20 April 1997, B1.

10. "Outcry, Suspicions Greet Barry Death Penalty Plan," *Washington Post*, 22 April 1997, B1.

11. Franklin E. Zimring and Gordon Hawkins, *Capital Punishment and the American Agenda* (New York: Cambridge University Press, 1986).

12. Ibid., 136–37.

13. Larry W. Koch, "Michigan's Continuing Abolition of the Death Penalty" (Ph.D. diss., University of Missouri–Columbia, 1987).

14. Georg Rusche and Otto Kirchheimer, *Punishment and Social Structure* (New York: Columbia University Press, 1939).

15. David Garland, *Punishment and Modern Society: A Study in Social Theory* (Chicago: University of Chicago Press, 1990), 229.

16. Zimring and Hawkins, *Capital Punishment*, 14.

17. Robert Jay Lifton and Greg Mitchell, *Who Owns Death? Capital Punishment, the American Conscience, and the End of Executions* (New York: Harper Collins, 2000), 219.

18. Garland, *Punishment and Modern*, 204.

19. Ibid., 246.

20. Richard A. Berk, Harold Brackman, and Selma L. Lesser, *A Measure of Justice: An Empirical Study of Changes in the California Penal Code, 1955–1971* (New York: Academic Press, 1977).

21. John Hagan, "The Legislation of Crime and Delinquency: A Review of Theory, Method, and Research," *Law and Society Review* 14 (1980): 603–28.

22. Bijou Yang and David Lister, "Which States Have the Death Penalty: Data from 1980," *Psychological Reports* 65 (1989): 185–86.

23. "Wisconsin Then and Now," The State Historical Society of Wisconsin, June 1979, 3, 6.

24. Koch, *Michigan's Continuing.*
25. Carrie Cropley, "The Case of John McCaffary," *Wisconsin Magazine of History* 35 (1951): 282.
26. Garland, *Punishment and Modern*, 247.

Epilogue

1. Alan Rogers, "Under Sentence of Death: The Movement to Abolish Capital Punishment in Massachusetts, 1835–1849," *The New England Quarterly* 66 (1993): 27–46.
2. Robert M. Fogelson, ed., *Capital Punishment: Nineteenth-Century Arguments* (New York: Arno Press, 1974), 17.
3. Ibid., 12.
4. Ibid., 27.
5. Francis X. Busch, *Notable American Trials: Prisoners at the Bar* (Indianapolis: The Bobbs-Merrill Co., 1952).
6. Hugo Bedau, "Death Penalty Abolition in Massachusetts" (paper presented at the National Coalition for the Abolition of Capital Punishment Conference, San Francisco, Calif., 17 November 2000).
7. Robert Jay Lifton and Greg Mitchell, *Who Owns Death? Capital Punishment, the American Conscience, and the End of Executions* (New York: Harper Collins, 2000), 12–14.
8. Ibid., 9.
9. Ibid.
10. Ibid., 14.
11. Philip English Mackey, "The Result May Be Glorious—Anti-Gallows Movement in Rhode Island 1838–1852," *Rhode Island History* 33 (1974): 1930.
12. Charles Hoffmann and Tess Hoffmann, *Brotherly Love: Murder and the Politics of Prejudice in Nineteenth-Century Rhode Island* (Amherst: University of Massachusetts Press, 1993).
13. Patrick T. Conley, "Death Knell for the Death Penalty: The Gordon Murder Trial and Rhode Island's Abolition of Capital Punishment," *Rhode Island Bar Journal* 34 (1986): 11–15.
14. Elizabeth Morancy, Death Penalty Abolition Conference, University of Missouri–Columbia, Peace Studies Program, 14 November 1998.
15. Randolph A. Roth, *The Democratic Dilemma: Religion, Reform, and the Social Order in the Connecticut River Valley of Vermont, 1791–1850* (New York: Cambridge University Press, 1987), 34.
16. David M. Ludlum, *Social Ferment in Vermont, 1791–1850* (New York: Columbia University Press, 1939), 214.
17. Espy and Smykla, *Executions in the United States.*
18. Gene Smith, "In Windsor Prison," *American Heritage*, May/June 1996, 100–109.
19. Daniel Allen Hearn, *Legal Executions in New England, 1623–1960* (Jefferson, N.C.: McFarland and Company, 1999).
20. *Furman v. Georgia*, 408 U.S. 238, 92, 2726 (1972).
21. Vincent Illuzzi, Death Penalty Abolition Conference, University of Missouri–Columbia, Peace Studies Program, 14 November 1998.
22. John F. Galliher, David Patrick Keys, James M. Galliher, and Larry W. Koch, "Toward a Typology of Unsuccessful Death Penalty Abolition Campaigns in the United States, 1800–1970" (paper presented at the Law & Society Association Meetings, Glasgow, Scotland, July 1996).
23. U.S. Census 2000, *Census of Population* (Washington, D.C.: U.S. Government Printing Office).
24. Martin B. Bradley, Norman M. Green, Jr., Dales E. Jones, Mac Lynn, and Lou McNeil, *Churches and Church Membership in the United States: An Enumeration by Region, State and County Based on Data Reported for 133 Church Groupings* (Atlanta, Ga.: Glenmary Research Center, 1992).

Bibliography

Acton, Richard. 1991. The Magic of Undiscouraged Effort: The Death Penalty in Early Iowa, 1838–1878. *Annals of Iowa* 50: 721–50.

Adams, Romanzo Colfax. 1933. *The Peoples of Hawaii*. Honolulu: Institute of Pacific Relations.

Adamson, Christopher R. 1984. Toward a Marxian Penology: Captive Criminal Populations as Economic Threats and Resources. *Social Problems* 31: 435–58.

Alaska Legislature, House. 1983. Debate of HB 235 (audiotape), 5 May.

Alaska Legislature, House Finance Committee. 1994. Committee discussion of HB 162, 11 March.

Alaska Legislature, *House Journal*. 1973–78. 8th–10th Legislature, Juneau, Alaska.

———. 1983–86. 13th–14th Legislature, Juneau, Alaska.

Alaska Legislature, House Judiciary Committee. 1974. Committee discussion of HB 675, 26 February.

———. 1983–84. Legislative File on Capital Punishment.

———. 1984. Public hearing on HB 235, 11 February.

———. 1984. Public hearing on HB 235, 16 March.

———. 1993. Committee discussion of HB 162, 31 January.

———. 1994. Committee discussion of HB 162, 1 March.

Alaska Legislature, Joint House/Senate Judiciary Committee. 1993. Public hearing on HB 162 and SB 127, 16 November.

Alaska Legislature, Senate. 1990. Debate of CSSB 17 (audiotape), 30 April.

Alaska Legislature, Senate Finance Committee. 1989. Public hearing on SB 17, 8 March.

———. 1989. Committee discussion of SB 17, 8 March.

———. 1990. Committee discussion of CSSB 17, 7 March.

———. 1990. Committee discussion of CSSB 17, 13 March.

Alaska Legislature, Senate Health, Education and Social Services (HESS) Committee. 1987. Committee discussion of SB 7 and SB 31, 3 April.

———. 1987. Public hearing on CSSB 7, 13 April.

———. 1987. Committee discussion of CSSB 7, 22 April.

Alaska Legislature, *Senate Journal*. 1957. Territorial Legislature, 23d Session. Juneau, Alaska.

———. 1985–86. 14th Legislature, Juneau, Alaska.

Alaska Legislature, Senate Judiciary Committee. 1981–82. Legislative file on capital punishment.

———. 1983. Public hearing on SB 121, 18 March.

———. 1987. Public hearing on SB 7, 23 October.

———. 1989. Public hearing on SB 17, 24 January.

———. 1989. Public hearing on SB 17, 31 January.

———. 1989. Committee discussion of SB 17, 2 February.

———. 1989. Public hearing on SB 17, 16 February.

———. 1989. Committee discussion of SB 17, 23 February.

———. 1994. Committee discussion of SB 127, 31 January.

———. 1994. Committee discussion of SB 127, 7 February.

———. 1994. Public hearing on SB 127, 7 February.

———. 1994. Committee discussion of SB 127, 6 April.

Alaska Territorial Legislature. 1957. HB 99, 16 February.

Alexander, Charles. 1980. Storm Clouds over Paradise. *New York Times Magazine,* 15 December, 67–68.

American Friends Service Committee. 2000. *The Death Penalty: The Religious Community Calls for Abolition.* Philadelphia: AFSC.

Amnesty International. 2001. *Death Sentences and Executions in 2000.* http://www.web.amnesty.org/rmp/dplibrary.nsf.

Angasan, Trefon. 1996. Personal interview with the Vice President of Corporate Affairs of the Bristol Bay Native Corporation, 11 June.

Attorney General of Hawaii. 1998. *Crime Prevention and Justice Assistance Division: Report of Research and Statistics.* Honolulu: State of Hawaii.

Austin, James, and Marci Brown. 1989. Ranking the Nation's Most Punitive and Costly States. *Focus.* July.

Bagley, Charles. 1994. Personal interview with the Maine senator who sponsored the 1993 capital punishment bill, June.

Bailey, Beth, and David Farber. 1993. The "Double-V" Campaign in World War II Hawaii: African-Americans, Racial Ideology, and Federal Power. *Journal of Social History* 26: 817–43.

Baldus, David, Charles Pulaski, and George Woodworth. 1983. Comparative Review of Death Sentences: An Empirical Study of the Georgia Experience. *Journal of Criminal Law and Criminology* 74: 661–753.

Beale, Howard K. 1956. *Theodore Roosevelt and the Rise of America to World Power.* Baltimore: Johns Hopkins University Press.

Bedau, Hugo Adam. 2000. Death Penalty Abolition in Massachusetts. National Coalition for the Abolition of the Death Penalty Conference, San Francisco, Calif., 17 November.

———. 1987. *Death Is Different: Studies in the Morality, Law, and Politics of Capital Punishment.* Boston: Northeastern University Press.

———. 1982. *The Death Penalty in America,* 3d ed. New York: Oxford University Press.

Bennett, Edward W. 1978. The Reasons for Michigan's Abolition of Capital Punishment. *Michigan History Magazine* 62: 42–55.

Berg, Bruce L. 1989. *Qualitative Research Methods for the Social Sciences.* Boston: Allyn and Bacon.

Berk, Richard A., Harold Brackman, and Selma L. Lesser. 1977. *A Measure of Justice.* New York: Academic Press.

Bessler, John D. 1996. The "Midnight Assassination Law" and Minnesota's Anti–Death Penalty Movement, 1849–1911. *William Mitchell Law Review* 22: 577–730.

Black, Paul W. 1911. Some Sociological Aspects of Lynchings in Iowa. *Iowa Journal of History and Politics.* Reprint, April 1912.

Blalock, Hubert M. 1967. *Toward a Theory of Minority-Group Relations.* New York: Wiley.

Blauner, Robert. 1967. Internal Colonialism. *Social Problems* 16: 393–408.

Blumer, Herbert, and Troy Duster. 1980. Theories of Race and Social Action. In *Sociological Theories: Race and Colonialism.* Paris: UNESCO, 211–38.

Bogardus, Emory S. 1929. Native Hawaiians and Their Problems. *Sociology and Social Research* 19: 259–65.

Bohm, Robert M. 1999. *Deathquest: An Introduction to the Theory and Practice of Capital Punishment in the United States.* Cincinnati: Anderson Publishing.

———. 1991. American Death Penalty Opinion, 1936–1986: A Critical Examination of the Gallup Polls. In *The Death Penalty in America: Current Research.* Cincinnati: Anderson Publishing.

Book of the States, 1966–1967. Vol. 16. Chicago: The Council of State Governments.

Boskin, Joseph. 1969. *Urban Racial Violence in the Twentieth Century*. Beverly Hills, Calif.: Glencoe Press.

Bowers, William J. 1984. *Legal Homicide: Death As Punishment in America, 1864–1982*. Boston: Northeastern University Press.

Bradley, Martin B., Norman M. Green, Jr., Dales E. Jones, Mac Lynn, and Lou McNeil. 1992. *Churches and Church Membership in the United States: An Enumeration by Region, State and County Based on Data Reported for 133 Church Groupings*. Atlanta, Ga.: Glenmary Research Center.

Branstad, Terry E. 1995. Personal interview, Des Moines, Iowa, 23 May.

Brickley, Lt. Governor James H. 1980. Press release, 2 February.

Bristol Bay Native Corporation. 1993. Testimony of Trefon Angasan before the November 16 joint public hearing on HB 162. Anchorage, Alaska.

Brown, Dee. 1970. *Bury My Heart at Wounded Knee*. New York: Henry Holt.

Bruxton, R. J. 1973. Criminal Law Reform: England. *American Journal of Comparative Law* 21: 230–44.

Bryant, Barbara. 1974–77. *Michigan Public Speaks Out on Crime*, eds. 1–5. Market Opinion Research, commissioned by Michigan Executive Office, Detroit.

Burbey, Louis H. 1938. History of Execution in What Is Now the State of Michigan. *Michigan History Magazine* 22: 443–57.

Busch, Francis X. 1952. *Notable American Trials: Prisoners at the Bar*. Indianapolis: The Bobbs–Merrill Co.

Calista Corporation. 1993. Testimony of Matthew Nicolai, senior vice president, before the November 16 joint public hearing on SB 127 and HB 162. Anchorage, Alaska.

Canfield, John A. 1970. State Papers and Public Addresses of Hulitt C. Smith: Twenty-Seventh Governor of West Virginia.

Cannon, Peter. 1995. *Capital Punishment in Wisconsin and the Nation*. Information Bulletin 1, Legislative Reference Bureau, Madison, Wis.

Capeci, Dominic, Jr. 1984. *Race Relations in Wartime Detroit*. Philadelphia: Temple University Press.

Carmichael, Stokley, and Charles Hamilton. 1967. *Black Power*. New York: Vintage Books.

Carver, Leonard D. 1901. *Capital Punishment in Maine*. Office of the Secretary of State, Augusta, Maine.

Castberg, Anthony Didrick. 1966. "The Ethnic Factor in Criminal Sentencing." Master's thesis, University of Hawaii.

Chapin, Helen G. 1996. *Shaping History: The Role of Newspapers in Hawaii*. Honolulu: University of Hawaii.

Cleaver, Eldridge. 1968. *Soul on Ice*. New York: Dell Publishing.

Coco, Martha. 1997. *Iowa Field Services Department*.

Coffman, Tom. 1972. *Catch a Wave: Hawaii's New Politics*. Honolulu: Star–Bulletin Publishing.

Cole, David. 1999. *No Equal Justice: Race and Class in the American Criminal Justice System*. New York: New Press.

Cole, Terrence M. 1992. Jim Crow in Alaska: The Passage of the Alaska Equal Rights Act of 1945. *Western Historical Quarterly* 23: 429–49.

Conley, Patrick T. 1986. Death Knell for the Death Penalty: The Gordon Murder Trial and Rhode Island's Abolition of Capital Punishment. *Rhode Island Bar Journal* 34: 11–15.

Conroy, Francis Hilary. 1949. "The Japanese Expansion into Hawaii, 1868–1898." Ph.D. dissertation, University of California–Berkeley.

———. 1953. *The Japanese Frontier in Hawaii, 1868–1898*. Berkeley: University of California Press.

Coppock, Henry Aaron. 1971. "Interaction between Russians and Native Americans in Alaska, 1741–1840." Master's thesis, Michigan State University.

Cropley, Carrie. 1951–52. The Case of John McCaffary. *Wisconsin Magazine of History*, vol. 35.

Cruse, Harold. 1967. *The Crisis of the Negro Intellectual*. New York: Morrow.

Culver, John H. 2000. Capital Punishment Politics and Policies in the United States, 1977–1997. *Crime, Law and Social Change* 32: 287–300.

Davis, Holly Hannon. 1985. Capital Punishment: A Review of Arguments For and Against Its Use and an Overview of Its History in Maine, in the Nation and in Other Countries. Prepared by the Department of Corrections, State of Maine, 13 February.

Davis, John A. 1994. Letter to John F. Galliher, 6 January.

Daws, Gavan. 1968. *Shoal of Time: A History of the Hawaiian Islands.* New York: Macmillan.

Death Penalty Information Center. 2000. *History of the Death Penalty,* http://www.deathpenaltyinfo.org/dpicrecinnoc.html.

Dilulio, John J., Jr. 1987. *Governing Prisons: A Comparative Study of Correctional Management.* New York: Free Press.

Edelman, Murray. 1964. *The Symbolic Uses of Politics.* Urbana: University of Illinois Press.

Emry, Tony, and Peggy Emry. 1995. Telephone interview, 23 April.

Espy, M. W., and J. O. Smykla. 1987. *Executions in the United States, 1608–1987: The Espy File.* Ann Arbor, Mich.: Inter-University Consortium for Political and Social Research.

Executive Order No. 9066. 1942. Office of the President of the United States. Federal Regulations 1407.

Fairman, Charles. 1942. The Law of Martial Rule and the National Emergency. *Harvard Law Review* 55: 1253–1302.

Fanon, Frantz. 1967. *A Dying Colonialism.* New York: Grove Press.

———. 1968. *The Wretched of the Earth.* New York: Grove Press.

Feagin, Joe R., and Hernan Vera. 1995. *White Racism.* New York: Routledge.

Fedo, Michael. 2000. *The Lynching in Duluth.* St. Paul: Minnesota Historical Society.

Fischer, Victor. 1996. Personal interview with the junior sponsor of the 1957 death penalty abolition bill, 10 June.

Fogelson, Robert M., ed. 1974. *Capital Punishment: Nineteenth-Century Arguments.* New York: Arno Press.

Foucault, Michel. 1977. *Discipline and Punish: The Birth of the Prison.* New York: Vintage.

Fox, James Alan, Michael L. Radelet, and Julie L. Bonsteel. 1990–91. Death Penalty Opinion in the Post–Furman Years. *New York University Review of Law and Social Change* 18: 499–528.

Funston, Frederick. 1901. Letter to Theodore Roosevelt. *Letters to Theodore Roosevelt–Theodore Roosevelt Papers.* Vol. 46. Library of Congress.

Galliher, James M., and John F. Galliher. 1997. Déjà Vu All Over Again: The Recurring Life and Death of Capital Punishment in Kansas. *Social Problems* 44: 369–85.

Galliher, John F., Gregory Ray, and Brent Cook. 1992. Abolition and Reinstatement of Capital Punishment During the Progressive Era and Early 20th Century. *The Journal of Criminal Law and Criminology* 83: 538–76.

Galliher, John F., and John R. Cross. 1983. *Morals Legislation without Morality: The Case of Nevada.* New Brunswick, N.J.: Rutgers University Press.

Galliher, John F., David Patrick Keys, James M. Galliher, and Larry W. Koch. 1996. Toward a Typology of Unsuccessful Death Penalty Abolition Campaigns in the United States, 1800–1970. Paper read at the Law & Society Association Meetings, Glasgow, Scotland, July.

Garland, David. 1990. *Punishment and Modern Society: A Study in Social Theory.* Chicago: University of Chicago Press.

Gauvreau, Paul. 1994. Personal interview with the Maine legislator who was senate chair of Judiciary during the late 1980s and early 1990s, June.

Genovese, Eugene D. 1977. *Roll, Jordan, Roll: The World the Slaves Made.* New York: Vintage.

Goonatilake, Susantha. 1982. *Crippled Minds: An Exploration in Colonial Culture.* New Delhi: Vikas.

Gordon, Diana R. 1994. *The Return of the Dangerous Classes: Drug Prohibition and Policy Politics.* New York: W. W. Norton.

Graham, John A. 1976. Memorandum to Lt. Governor Wayne Sanstead. On file with the North Dakota State Historical Society.

Greenberg, David. 1993. *Crime and Capitalism*. Philadelphia: Temple University Press.

Gruening, Ernest. 1968. *The State of Alaska*, 2d ed. New York: Random House.

Gusfield, Joseph R. 1963. *Symbolic Crusade: Status Politics and the American Temperance Movement.* Urbana: University of Illinois Press.

Haas, Michael. 1987. Comparing Paradigms of Ethnic Politics in the United States: The Case of Hawaii. *Western Political Quarterly* 40: 647–72.

Hagan, John. 1980. The Legislation of Crime and Delinquency: A Review of Theory, Method, and Research. *Law and Society Review* 14: 603–28.

Hagan, John, Edward T. Silva, and John H. Simpson. 1977. Conflict and Consensus in the Designation of Deviance. *Social Forces* 56: 320–40.

Hamel, Jacques, with Stephanie Dufour and Dominic Fortin. 1993. *Case Study Methods*. Vol. 32, *Qualitative Research Methods*. London: Sage Publications.

Harmon, Lt. John A., U.S.N. 1894. Political Importance of Hawaii. *North American Review* 160: 74–75.

Harris, Marwood D. 1993. *History of Death Penalty in Alaska*. Alaska State Legislature: Legislative Research Agency, 25 February.

Hawaii Legislature, HB 706. 1957. Act 282, Sec. 1–14, 4 June.

Hawaii Legislature. *Territory of Hawaii*. 1907. Board of Immigration. 1st Report.

Haycox, Stephen W. 1986/87 (winter). William Paul, Sr., and the Alaska Voters' Literacy Act of 1925. *Alaska History* 2: 17–37.

Hearn, Allen Daniel. 1999. *Legal Executions in New England, 1623–1960*. Jefferson, N.C.: McFarland and Company.

Hechter, Michael. 1975. *Internal Colonialism: The Celtic Fringe in British National Development, 1536–1966.* Berkeley: University of California Press.

Helfman, Harold M. 1956. A Forgotten Aftermath to Michigan's Abolition of Capital Punishment. *Michigan History Magazine* 40: 203–14.

Henderson, A. 1994. Personal interview with the representative who was among Maine's most vocal critics of capital punishment during the 1970s, June.

Hindelang, Michael. 1972. Equality under the Law. In *Race, Crime, and Justice*, ed. Charles Reasons and Jack Kuykendall. Pacific Palisades, Calif.: Goodyear.

Hoffmann, Charles, and Tess Hoffmann. 1993. *Brotherly Love: Murder and the Politics of Prejudice in Nineteenth-Century Rhode Island*. Amherst: University of Massachusetts Press.

Hogan, Tiffany L., and Julie K. Netzer. 1993. Knowing the Other: White Women, Gender, and Racism. Paper read at the annual meeting of the American Sociological Association, August.

Hood, Roger. 1989. *The Death Penalty: A Worldwide Perspective*. New York: Oxford University Press.

Hoover, J. Edgar. 1960. Letter to "All Law Enforcement Officials." *FBI Law Enforcement Bulletin*. June: 1.

Horman, Bernhard. 1952. *The Majors-Palakiko Case: What People in Hawaii Are Saying and Doing.* Report no. 20. Honolulu: University of Hawaii Social Research Laboratory.

———. 1953. The Significance of the Wilder or Majors-Palakiko Case: A Study in Public Opinion. *Social Process in Hawaii* 17: 1–13.

Hughes, Harold. 1995. Personal interview with the former governor of Iowa, Glendale, Ariz., 23 July.

Hughes, Harold, with Dick Schneider. 1979. *The Man from Ida Grove*. Lincoln, Va.: Chosen Books.

Hughes, JuliAnn. 1997. Telephone interview, 28 April.

Ignatieff, Michael. 1978. *A Just Measure of Pain: The Penitentiary in the Industrial Revolution, 1750– 1850*. New York: Pantheon.

Ileto, Reynaldo C. 1979. *Payson and Revolution: Popular Movements in the Philippines, 1840–1910*. Quezon City: Ateneo de Manila University Press.

Iowa Department of Public Safety. *Iowa Uniform Crime Reports, 1996*. Des Moines, Iowa.

Iowa Journal of the House of Representatives. 1965, 1995. Des Moines, Iowa.

Iowa Journal of the Senate. 1965, 1995. Des Moines, Iowa.

Iowa Legislative Information Office. 1995. Fax on public hearing participants.

Jacobs, David. 1979. Inequality and Police Strength: Conflict Theory and Coercive Control in Metropolitan Areas. *American Sociological Review* 44: 913–25.

Jacobs, David, and David Britt. 1979. Inequality and Police Use of Deadly Force: An Empirical Assessment of a Conflict Hypothesis. *Social Problems* 26: 403–12.

Kannar, George. 1996. Federalizing Death. *Buffalo Law Review* 44: 325–37.

Kassebaum, Gene. 1981. Ethnicity and the Disposition of Arrest for Violent Crime in Hawaii. *Social Process in Hawaii* 28: 33–57.

Kingdon, John W. 1984. *Agendas, Alternatives, and Public Policies*. Boston: Little, Brown.

Knapp, Austin C., ed. 1963. *State of Michigan, Constitutional Convention, 1961*. Vol. 1. Lansing: State of Michigan.

Knighton, Susan E. 1984. *Position Paper on Capital Punishment*. Report prepared by the Adult Correctional Agency, Juneau, Alaska.

Koch, Larry W., John F. Galliher, and David Keys. 1990. The Life and Death of the Death Penalty in West Virginia. Paper read at the annual meeting of the American Society of Criminology, November.

Koch, Larry W., and John F. Galliher. 1993. Michigan's Continuing Abolition of the Death Penalty and the Conceptual Components of Symbolic Legislation. *Social and Legal Studies* 2: 323–46.

———. Unpublished paper. The History of Death Penalty Abolition in Alaska.

Kohler, Thomas. Unpublished manuscript. Cooley Law School, Lansing, Mich.

Koseki, Lawrence. 1978. *Capital Punishment in Hawaii: An Ethnic Perspective*. SIR Series no. 7. Chicago: Asian American Mental Health Research Center.

Kotani, Roland. 1985. *The Japanese in Hawaii: A Century of Struggle*. Honolulu: Hochi.

Kynell, Kermit. 1991. *A Different Frontier, 1935–1965*. Lanham, Md.: University Press of America.

Laffin, Stanley (Tuffy). 1994. Personal interview with the representative who sponsored the majority of the death penalty bills in Maine during the 1970s, June.

Lebowitz, Catherine. 1994. Personal interview with the cosponsor of 1982–92 house death bills, June.

Lee, Alfred McClung, and Norman Daymond Humphrey. 1943. *Race Riot*. New York: Dryden Press.

Lerman, Averil. 1996. The Trial and Hanging of Nelson Charles. *Alaska Justice Forum*. Justice Center: University of Alaska–Anchorage.

Liapunova, R. G. 1987. Relations with the Natives of Russian America. In *Russia's American Colony*, ed. S. F. Starr. Durham: Duke University Press.

Lifton, Robert Jay, and Greg Mitchell. 2000. *Who Owns Death? Capital Punishment, the American Conscience, and the End of Executions*. New York: Harper Collins.

Lincoln, James H. 1987. The Everlasting Controversy: Michigan and the Death Penalty. *Wayne State Law Review* 33: 1765–90.

Lind, Andrew W. 1955. *Hawaii's People*. Honolulu: University of Hawaii Press.

Liska, Allen E., Joseph J. Lawrence, and Michael Benson. 1981. Perspectives on the Legal Order: The Capacity for Social Control. *American Journal of Sociology* 87: 413–26.

Liu, John Mei. 1985. "Cultivating Cane: Asian Labor and the Hawaiian Sugar Plantation Within the World Capitalist Economy." Unpublished Ph.D. dissertation, University of California–Los Angeles.

Ludlum, David M. 1939. *Social Ferment in Vermont, 1791–1850.* New York: Columbia University Press.

Lydecker, Robert C. 1918. *Roster Legislatures of Hawaii, 1841–1918.* Honolulu: Hawaiian Gazette.

Lydon, Edward. 1975. *The Anti-Chinese Movement in the Hawaiian Kingdom.* San Francisco: R & E Research.

Lynching. No date. http://www.triadntr.net/~rdavis/lynching.html.

Mackey, Philip English. 1974. The Result May Be Glorious—Anti-Gallows Movement in Rhode Island, 1838–1852. *Rhode Island History* 33: 1930.

Maine Legislature, Committee on Judiciary. 1987. Records of debates, testimony, and votes on LD 1236, HP 924.

———. 1991. Record of debates, testimony, and votes on LD 1238, SP 462.

———. 1993. Record of debates, testimony, and votes on LD 42, SP 36.

Maine Legislature, *Legislative Pamphlet.* 1901. "Capital Punishment in Maine." 1 December.

———. No date. *Homicides in Maine.*

Maine Legislature, *Legislative Record.* 1868. Address of Governor Chamberlain to the Legislature of the State of Maine. Augusta: Owen and Nash, Printers to the State.

———. 1869. Address of Governor Chamberlain to the Legislature of the State of Maine. Augusta: Owen and Nash, Printers to the State.

———. 1869. Remarks of John L. Stevens, in the senate of Maine, February 11 and 12, 1869.

Maine Legislature, *Legislative Record of the House.* 1973–79. 106th–109th Legislature of the State of Maine.

Maine Legislature, *Legislative Record of the Senate.* 1973–79. 106th–109th Legislature of the State of Maine.

Maine Legislature, Legislative Report. 1897–98. *Report of the Attorney General of the State of Maine.*

———. 1835. 15th Legislature: House. Report of the Committee to Whom Was Referred the Several Memorials and Petitions for the Abolition of Capital Punishment. Augusta: Wm. J. Condon, Printer to the State.

———. 1836. 16th Legislature: Senate. *Report of the Committee on Capital Punishment.* Augusta: Wm. J. Condon, Printer to the State.

Market Opinion Research. 1980, 1982, 1985. *Crime in Michigan.* Detroit, Mich.

Martin, John Barlow. 1954. *Break Down the Walls.* New York: Ballantine.

Martus, Kimberly. 1996. Personal interview with the vice president of Alaskans Against the Death Penalty, 4 June.

Marumoto, Masaji. 1983. The Ala Moana Case and the Massie-Fortescue Case Revisited. *University of Hawaii Law Review* 5: 271–87.

May, Glenn A. 1983. Why the United States Won the Philippine-American War. *Pacific Historical Review* 52: 353–77.

McCann, E. Michael. 1996. Opposing Capital Punishment: A Prosecutor's Perspective. *Marquette Law Review* 79: 649–706.

McComas, James. 1996. Personal interview with the past president of Alaskans Against the Death Penalty, 4 June.

McGarrell, Edmund F., and Thomas C. Castellano. 1993. Social Structure, Crime and Politics: A Conflict Model of the Criminal Law Formation Process. In *Making Law: The State, the Law, and Structural Contradictions,* ed. William J. Chambliss and Marjorie S. Zatz. Bloomington: Indiana University Press.

McGarrell, Edmund F., and Timothy J. Flanagan, eds. 1985. *Sourcebook of Criminal Statistics, 1984.* Albany, N.Y.: Hindelang Criminal Justice Research Center.

McGowan, William P. 1995. Industrializing the Land of Lono: Sugar Plantation Managers and Workers in Hawaii, 1900–1920. *Agricultural History* 69: 177–201.

Meller, Norman, and Anne Feder Lee. 1997. Hawaiian Sovereignty. *Publius* 27: 167–86.

Memi, Albert. 1967. *The Colonizer and the Colonized.* Boston: Beacon Press.

Merton, Robert K. 1968. *Social Theory and Social Structure.* New York: Free Press.

Michigan Catholic Conference. 1985. *The Death Penalty: A Discussion Guide.* Lansing: Mich.

Michigan Chamber of Commerce. 1980. Should Michigan Bring Back the Death Penalty? In *Executive Report.* 7 April.

Michigan Department of State. 1986. Michigan Interoffice Memo, 11 September.

Michigan Legislature. 1844. House Majority Report of the Select Committee on Abolishment of Capital Punishment.

———. 1865. Senate Report of the Judiciary Committee.

———. 1973. House Hearings of the Committee on Constitutional Revision and Women's Rights, 15 March.

———. 1985. Senate Judiciary Committee, Hearing on Capital Punishment, 23 May.

Michigan Legislature, *Journal of the House.* 1929, 1931, 1943, 1952. Lansing, Mich.

Michigan Legislature, *Journal of the Senate.* 1929, 1931, 1943, 1985. Lansing, Mich.

Michigan Legislature, Legislative Pamphlet. No date. *Capital Punishment.* Michigan State Library.

Minnesota Crime Commission. 1923. *Final Report.* State of Minn., January.

Minnesota Journal of the House of Representatives. 1913, 1921. Minneapolis, Minn.

Minnesota Journal of the Senate. 1923. Minneapolis, Minn.

Mitau, G. Theodore. 1960. *Politics in Minnesota.* Minneapolis: University of Minnesota Press.

Morgan, Edward P. 1991. *The '60s Experience: Hard Lessons About Modern America.* Philadelphia: Temple University Press.

Myrick, Lockwood. 1928. Open Letter to Governor Farrington on Fukunaga's Insanity. 5 November, reprinted in Kotani (1985: 64).

Nakell, Barry, and Kenneth A. Hardy. 1987. *The Arbitrariness of the Death Penalty.* Philadelphia: Temple University Press.

Naske, Claus M., and Herman E. Slotnick. 1979. *Alaska: A History of the 49th State.* Grand Rapids, Mich.: Wm. B. Eerdmans.

Nelligan, Peter J. 1983. "Social Change and Rape Law in Hawaii." Ph.D. dissertation, University of Hawaii.

Nesbit, Robert C. 1973. *Wisconsin: A History.* Madison, Wis.: University Press.

Nicholia, Irene K. 1994. Letter from Representative Nicholia (a Native Alaskan) to Jerry Sanders (cosponsor of the 1993–94 death bill, HB 162). 1993–94 House Judiciary Capital Punishment File, 10 March.

North Dakota Legislature, *Journal of the Senate.* 1995.

North Dakota Legislature, Senate Judiciary Committee Hearings. 1979. Hearing on SB 2169.

———. 1995. Hearing on SB 2097, 14, 17 January.

O'Neill, F. X. 1933. *Re-Union Booklet, Original Company 'F' 30th U.S. Infantry of 1901–1904: History, Letters, and Stories Depicting Army Days in the Philippines,* ed. J. N. Morton. Springfield, Mo.: Morton.

Orum, Anthony M., Joe R. Feagin, and Gideon Sjoberg, eds. 1991. Introduction: The Nature of the Case Study. In *A Case for the Case Study.* Chapel Hill: University of North Carolina Press, 1–26.

Page, Ann L., and Donald A. Clelland. 1978. The Kanawha County Textbook Controversy: A Study of the Politics of Life Style Concern. *Social Forces* 57: 265–81.

Patterson, Wayne. 1988. *The Korean Frontier in America: Immigration to Hawaii, 1896–1910.* Honolulu: University of Hawaii Press.

Paul, Justus F., and Barbara Dotts Paul. 1979. *The Badger State: A Documentary History of Wisconsin.* Grand Rapids, Mich.: Wm. B. Eerdmans.

Peirce, Neal R., and Jerry Hagstrom. 1983. *The Book of America: Inside 50 States Today.* New York: W. W. Norton.

Pendleton, Alexander T., and Blaine R. Renfert. 1993. A Brief History of Wisconsin's Death Penalty. *Wisconsin Lawyer* 66, no. 8: 26–30.

Pepinsky, Harold E. 1993. Norwegian and Polish Lessons for Keeping Down Prison Populations. *Humanity and Society* 17: 70–89.

Pettyjohn, Fritz. 1996. Personal interview with long-term advocate of capital punishment and senate sponsor of capital punishment legislation in Alaska, 8 June.

Platt, Tony, and Paul Takagi. 1977. Intellectuals for Law and Order: A Critique of the New Realists. *Crime and Social Justice* 8: 1–16.

Pohlmeyer, Steve. 2000. *Committing to Conscience.* Prepared by the National Coalition for the Abolition of the Death Penalty, 17 November, San Francisco, Calif.

Poppe, Roger. 1996. Personal interview with Alaska's Democratic legislative assistant, June.

Pray, Waldo E. No date. "Chessman Case Recalls: Maine, Too, Had Its Furor Over the Death Penalty." *Portland Sunday Telegram.*

Prison Activist Resource Center. 1995. Wisconsin Death Penalty Debate in Senate. 20 May. Source: parcer@igc.apc.org.

Radzinowicz, Leon. 1948. *A History of English Criminal Law.* New York: Macmillan.

Raney, William Francis. 1940. *Wisconsin: A Story of Progress.* New York: Prentice-Hall.

Remele, Larry. 1989. North Dakota History: Overview and Summary. *North Dakota BlueBook.* http://www.state.nd.us/ndhist.htm.

Rogers, Alan. 1993. Under Sentence of Death: The Movement to Abolish Capital Punishment in Massachusetts, 1835–1849. *The New England Quarterly* 66: 27–46.

Roth, Randolph A. 1987. *The Democratic Dilemma: Religion, Reform, and the Social Order in the Connecticut River Valley of Vermont, 1791–1850.* New York: Cambridge University Press.

Rowland, Donald. 1943. Orientals and the Suffrage in Hawaii. *Pacific Historical Review* 12: 11–21.

Rusche, Georg, and Otto Kirchheimer. 1939. *Punishment and Social Structure.* New York: Columbia University Press.

Ryan, Jim. 1995. Telephone interview, 10 May.

Sardy, Mari. 1985. Early Contact between Aleuts and Russians, 1741–1780. *Alaska History* 1: 42–58.

Schabas, W. 1997. *The Abolition of the Death Penalty in International Law,* 2d ed. Cambridge: Cambridge University Press.

Scheb, John M., and John M. Scheb II. 1999. *Criminal Law and Procedure.* Belmont, Calif.: West and Wadsworth.

Scheiber, Harry N., and Jane L. Scheiber. 1997. Bayonets in Paradise: A Half-Century Retrospect on Martial Law in Hawaii, 1941–1946. *University of Hawaii Law Review* 19: 477–648.

Schneider, Victoria, and John Oritz Smykla. 1991. A Summary Analysis of Executions in the United States, 1608–1987: The Espy File. First published in *The Death Penalty in America,* ed. Robert M. Bohm. Cincinnati: Anderson Publishing, 1–19.

Schriver, Edward. 1990. Reluctant Hangman: The State of Maine and Capital Punishment, 1820–1887. *The New England Quarterly* 63: 271–87.

Shils, Edward A. 1981. *Tradition.* Chicago: University of Chicago Press.

Sjoberg, Gideon, and Roger Nett. 1997. *A Methodology for Social Science.* 1997. Prospect Heights, Ill.: Waveland Press.

Skalkop, Antoinette. 1987. The Russian Orthodox Church in Alaska. In *Russia's American Colony,* ed. S. F. Starr. Durham: Duke University Press.

Smith, Gene. 1996. In Windsor Prison. *American Heritage* May/June: 100–109.

Smith, Rogers M. 1997. *Civic Ideals: Conflicting Visions of Citizenship in U.S. History.* New Haven: Yale University Press.

Spickard, Paul R. 1983. The Nisei Assume Power: The Japanese Citizens League, 1941–1942. *Pacific Historical Review* 52: 147–74.

State Statistical Rankings: A Statistical View of the Fifty United States, 7th ed. 1996. Lawrence, Kans.: Morgan Quinton Oak.

Steinhoff, Patricia G., and Milton Diamond. 1977. *Abortion Politics: The Hawaii Experience.* Honolulu: University of Hawaii Press.

. . . .

Sullivan, Joseph. 1992. Sourdough Radicalism: Labor and Socialism in Alaska, 1905–1920. *Alaska History* 7: 1–15.

Takaki, Ronald. 1983. *Pau Hana: Plantation Life and Labor in Hawaii, 1835–1920.* Honolulu: University of Hawaii Press.

Tetpon, John. 1996. Personal interview with the author of "Between Two Worlds: Growing up Native in Alaska." *Sunday Magazine: Anchorage Daily News,* 23 May 1987.

Theroux, Joseph. 1991. A Short History of Hawaiian Executions, 1826–1947. *Hawaiian Journal of History* 25: 147–59.

Tuchman, Gaye. 1978. *Making News: A Study in the Construction of Reality.* New York: Free Press.

United Auto Workers. 1977. *Legislative Program.*

United Nations. 1999. *United Nations Commission on Human Rights, Resolutions and Statements.* 26 April. http://www.deathpenaltyinfo.org/UN–Statements.html.

U.S. Bureau of the Census. 1990. Census of Housing, Summary Tap File 3A. Washington, D.C.: Government Printing Office.

———. 1990–2000. *The General Population Characteristics.* Washington, D.C.: U.S. Government Printing Office.

———. 2000. State, MSA, and County Population Source. http://www.state.nd.us/jsnd.

———. 1999. Population Estimates Division, September.

———. 1900–90. *Census of Population.* Washington, D.C.: U.S. Government Printing Office.

———. 1990. *Census of Population: Social and Economic Characteristics: North Dakota.* Washington, D.C.: U.S. Department of Commerce.

U.S. Department of Commerce. 1975. *Historical Statistics of the United States: Colonial Times to 1970, Part 1.* Washington, D.C.: U.S. Government Printing Office.

———. 1931–98. *Statistical Abstracts of the United States,* 68th–118th editions. Washington, D.C.: U.S. Government Printing Office.

U.S. Department of Justice. 2000. *Capital Punishment 1999.* Bureau of Justice Statistics, Washington, D.C.: U.S. Government Printing Office.

———. 1938–99. *Crime in the United States: Uniform Crime Reports.* Washington, D.C.: U.S. Government Printing Office.

University of Missouri–Columbia, Peace Studies Program, Death Penalty Abolition Conference. 1998. 13–14 November, Columbia, Mo.

———. Chatfield, Sister Joan. 1998. Presentation, 14 November.

———. Haught, James. 1998. Editor of the *Charleston (West Virginia) Gazette,* Presentation, 14 November.

———. Illuzzi, Vincent. 1998. Vermont Republican senator, Presentation, 14 November.

———. Long, Dee. 1998. Minnesota representative, Presentation, 14 November.

———. Morancy, Elizabeth. 1998. Rhode Island representative, Presentation, 14 November.

Useem, Bert, and Peter Kimball. 1989. *States of Siege: U.S. Prison Riots, 1971–1986.* New York: Oxford University Press.

Valelly, Richard M. 1989. *Radicalism in the States: The Minnesota Farmer–Labor Party and the American Political Economy.* Chicago: University of Chicago Press.

Vyzralek, Frank. 2000. Capital Crimes and Criminals Executed in Northern Dakota Territory and North Dakota, 1885–1905. *North Dakota Supreme Court News.* http://www.court.state.nd.us/court/news/ExecuteND.html.

Welch, Richard E., Jr. 1974. American Atrocities in the Philippines: The Indictment and the Response. *Pacific Historical Review* 43: 233–53.

West Virginia Department of Corrections. 1999. http://www.state.wv.us/wvdoc/MOCCI.html.

West Virginia Legislature, House of Delegates, *Journal of the State of West Virginia.* 1955, 1965, 1975, 1979. Charleston, W. Va.

West Virginia Legislature, Senate, *Journal of the State of West Virginia.* 1971, 1972, 1986. Charleston, W. Va.

Whitehead, John. 1992. The Governor Who Opposed Statehood: The Legacy of Jay Hammond. *Alaska History* 7: 15–28.

Widick, J. B. 1972. *Detroit: City of Race and Class Violence*. Chicago: Quadrangle Books.

Williams, Kirk R., and Susan Drake. 1980. Social Structure, Crime and Criminalization: An Empirical Examination of the Conflict Perspective. *The Sociological Quarterly* 21: 563–75.

Williamson, Joseph. 1883. Capital Trials in Maine: Before the Separation. *Maine Historical Society* 25 May, 59–172.

Wisconsin Blue Book. 1994. Madison, Wis.

Wisconsin State Historical Society. 1979. Wisconsin Then and Now.

Wisconsin Legislature. *Bulletin of the Proceedings of the Wisconsin Legislature.* 1991–95. Legislative Reference Bureau, Madison, Wis.

———. History of 1995 Senate Bill 1. http://www.legis.state.wi.us./1995/data/SB1hst.html.

———. History of 1995 Senate Joint Resolution 51. http://www.legis.state.wi.us./1999/data/SJR51hst.html.

———. 1995. *Legislative Reference Bureau: Information Bulletin* 95–1, April.

Wittermans, Elizabeth. 1964. *Inter-Ethnic Relations in a Plural Society.* Groningen: J. B. Wolters.

Wolfgang, Marvin, and Marc Riedel. 1973. Race, Judicial Discretion, and the Death Penalty. *Annals of the American Academy of Political and Social Science* 407: 119–33.

Woodward, C. Van. 1966. *The Strange Career of Jim Crow*, 2d rev. ed. New York: Oxford University Press.

Yang, Bijou, and David Lister. 1989. Which States Have the Death Penalty: Data from 1980. *Psychological Reports* 65: 185–86.

Zimring, Franklin E. 1991. Ambivalence in State Capital Punishment Policy: An Empirical Sounding. *New York Review of Law and Social Change* 18: 729–42.

Zimring, Franklin E., and Gordon Hawkins. 1986. *Capital Punishment and the American Agenda.* New York: Cambridge University Press.

Newspapers and Magazines

Anchorage Daily News. 23 February 1957–1 May 1994.
Anchorage Times. 19 March 1983–23 February 1985.
Appleton Post. 30 April 1995.
Bangor Daily News. 4 April 1960–3 May 1991.
Bismarck Tribune. 14 December 1926–11 February 2001.
Capital Times (Madison, Wis.). 12 December 1991–5 May 1995.
Catholic Weekly. 7 June 1959.
Central Maine Morning Sentinel. 22 April 1992.
Charleston Daily Mail. 13 February 1965–6 January 1987.
Charleston Gazette. 2 February 1965–6 January 1987.
Chicago Tribune. 3 November 1991.
Courier-Gazette (Maine). 26 September 1927, 25 February 1993.
Des Moines Register. 28 February 1960–22 May 1995.
Detroit Free Press. 28 December 1958–27 June 1985.
Detroit News. 7 May 1947–15 July 1985.
Economist. 20 August–4 September 1981.
Flint Journal. 23 June 1955, 6 January 1980.
Gongwer News Service: Michigan Report, no. 85. 1 May 1984.
Grand Forks Herald. 22 April 1992.
Grand Rapids Press. 7 March 1945.
Green Bay Press-Gazette. 21 April 1995.
Hilo Tribune-Herald. 14 September 1931.

Honolulu Advertiser. 10 December 1941–3 August 1990.
Honolulu Star-Bulletin. 31 May 1918–29 August 1968.
Juneau Empire. 7 March 1983, 6 February 1985, 23 April 1996.
Kennebec Journal. 20 March 1974–28 November 1979.
Kenosha News. 2001. "Hangman's Work Here Changed Law." http://www.kusd.edu/city/history/law_change.html.
Lansing State Journal. 11 February 1931–12 May 1985.
Lifelines. April/May–October/December 1992.
Madison Newspapers, Inc. 24 July 1991–29 September 1994, http://www.madison.com.
Maine Sunday Telegram. 21 January 1979.
Milwaukee Journal Sentinel. 21 April 1995, 25 October 1995, 5 January 1997.
Minneapolis Morning Tribune. 13 July 1912–27 February 1923.
Minneapolis Star Tribune. 13 May 1999.
Minot Daily News. 25 November 1985, 5 April 1990.
Nation. 6 March 2000.
New York Times. 21 March 1893, 10 January 1932, 18 February 1992–22 September 2000.
Omaha World Herald. 18 January 1998.
Pacific Commercial Advertiser. 29 December 1866, 1 April 1886, 14 September 1931, 17–18 March 1948, 5 May 1998.
Portland Evening Express. 5 May 1930–16 November 1990.
Portland Press Herald. 21 October 1937–12 January 1987.
Portland Sunday Telegram. 24 September 1950, 2 November 1958, 8 December 1968.
Saginaw News. 17 February 1980.
Session Weekly. 1992. Minnesota House Public Information Office. http://www.house.leg.state.mn.us/hinfo.swkly/1995-96/select/death.txt.
Sunday Gazette-Mail (Charleston, W. Va.). 7 March 1965, 5 February 1978, 28 January 1979.
Time Magazine. 28 December 1931, 15 December 1980.
Washington Post. 22 September 1992–22 April 1997.
Wisconsin State Journal. 28 January 1992–3 March 1996.

Laws

Coker v. Georgia. 1977. 433 U.S. 584, 97, 2861.
Crain v. Bordenkircher. 1982. "Memorandum of Opinion, Finding of Fact, Conclusions of Law and Order." Civil Action No. 81-C-320 R, Circuit Court of Marshall Co., West Virginia, February.
Duncan v. Kahanamoku. 1946. 327 U.S. 304.
Furman v. Georgia. 1972. 408 U.S. 238, 92, 2726.
Laws of Alaska. 1957. Territory of Alaska: Session Laws, Resolutions, and Memorials 1957, ch. 132 at 262–63, 30 March.
Literacy Act of 1925. Compiled Laws of the Territory of Alaska. 1933, 326–27.
Michigan Constitution. 1963. Article 4, Section 46, Death Penalty.
Michigan Laws. 1973. Michigan Public Act 112, 19 August.
Michigan Revised Statutes. 1846. Chs. 152–53: 658, 1 January 1847.
North Dakota Century Code. 1960.
Pingley v. Coiner. 1972. *West Virginia Reports* 155 at 591, no. 18127, 25 January.
United States Congress. *Organic Act of 1884,* 48th Congress, 1st Session, 4180.
United States Congress. *Organic Act of 1900,* 31 Stat. 153 (1900), 48 U.S.C. 532 (1940).
United States Congress. *Organic Act of 1912,* 62d Congress, 2d Session, 11853.
West Virginia Codes. 1931. *Crime and Their Punishment,* Ch. 1, Article 2.
West Virginia Acts. 1965. Ch. 40 at 204, passed 12 March 1965.
Wisconsin Act 48. 16 August 1995. Wisconsin State Legislature, AB 167 (denies parole eligibility for persons serving life sentences).

Index